How to Use a Law Library
An Introduction to Legal Skills

THIRD EDITION

by

PHILIP A. THOMAS
Professor of Socio Legal Studies, Cardiff Law School, University of Wales, Cardiff

CATHERINE COPE
Information Specialist, Centre for Professional Legal Studies, University of Wales, Cardiff

with contributions by:

David Hart
Law Librarian, University of Dundee

Elizabeth Madill
Formerly Sub-Librarian (Law), Queens University, Belfast

Paul Norman
Institute of Advanced Legal Studies, London

Grainne Smith
Formerly Assistant Librarian, Law Library, Dublin

Barbara Zolynski
European Communities Librarian, Law Society, London

LONDON
SWEET & MAXWELL
1996

First Edition 1979
Second Impression 1980
Second Edition 1987
Second Impression 1992
Third Edition 1996

Published in 1996 by
Sweet & Maxwell Limited
South Quay Plaza, 183 Marsh Wall,
London E14 9FT
Typeset by Mendip Communications Limited,
Frome, Somerset
Printed in England by
Clays Ltd, St Ives plc

No natural forests were destroyed to make this product, only farmed
timber was used and replanted

A CIP catalogue record for this book is available from the British
Library

ISBN 0 421 460903

How to Use a Law I

An Introduction to Legal Skills

AUSTRALIA
The Law Book Company
Brisbane : Sydney : Melbourne : Perth

CANADA
Carswell
Ottawa : Toronto : Calgary : Montreal : Vancouver

AGENTS
Steimatzky's Agency Ltd, Tel Aviv
N.M. Tripathi (Private) Ltd, Bombay
Eastern Law House (Private) Ltd, Calcutta
M.P.P. House, Bangalore
Universal Book Traders, Delhi
Aditya Books, Delhi
MacMillan Shuppan KK, Tokyo
Pakistan Law House, Karachi, Lahore

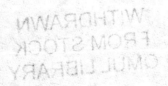

PREFACE

As a new law student you will quickly discover that you are required to spend considerable time in the law library. At secondary education level you may have been prepared carefully for state examinations by teachers who provided you with the essential information for the examination. The responsibility for learning was possibly a shared function: one between you and your teachers with the teachers taking the principal role. The balance within this relationship changes on entering university as an undergraduate. The emphasis of higher education study is on self preparation leading to self learning. You must not rely on your lecturers to "tell you all the law". If you do you will be sadly disappointed. Guidance, ideas, principles and support should come from the staff via lectures and seminars but ultimately the responsibility of coming to terms with legal knowledge belongs with you: the student.

Thus, the law library is your "laboratory" where you will prepare for a seminar, read references provided in lectures, or research an essay topic. Legal studies are essentially a library based exercise. Learn how to use the library wisely and effectively. It is a resource to be used properly. Inefficient use will result in you wasting valuable time and your academic work will suffer. Acquiring a proper working knowledge of the law library is a skill which will carry you through your degree programme and beyond into legal practice. Increasingly, skills training is recognised as an essential and important element of legal education. Skills acquisition is commonly found in the undergraduate syllabus and is also located in the post graduate courses which all potential legal practitioners are obliged to undertake. Remember that lawyers carry only a certain amount of legal knowledge in their heads and even that information might be incomplete, wrong or out of date. A lawyer who relies only on memory is one who is in danger of being subject to a negligence claim from the client! The law is dynamic and fast moving. No person knows it all and a clever lawyer will admit to knowing only a little law. A good lawyer is one who knows where and how to look for the relevant law and is able to understand and apply it in the best interests of the client. The library skills that you learn now will stand you in good stead for the future. Develop proper techniques and good habits about library usage now and the benefits will be both immediate and long term.

The fast and ever changing shape and substance of law means that you must keep up to date, whether as a student, lecturer, or practitioner. There is no escaping the dynamic nature of law. You cannot hope to keep abreast of change through legal gossip, looking at other people's notes, reading a standard text, which by definition is out of date by the time it is printed, hoping the lecturer has got it right and that, in turn, you have written down your notes from lectures correctly and fully. Ultimately the responsibility for learning the law rests with you and the most appropriate and efficient way is through a careful and informed use of the law library. It is there that you will find the latest information on changes to the law.

The principal purpose of this book is to provide you with basic information about how a law collection is organised and how you can access the information that is contained within the library. In a sense, this book is a labour saving device. Use it as a reference book throughout your student days and indeed probably thereafter should you decide to enter legal practice. It is not intended to be treated as a textbook and thereby associated with a particular course. It is a reference aid to be consulted when you have a problem. Consequently, you might use the book selectively, referring to those sections which are useful at a particular point in your studies, or when recommended to look up a case, statute or issue by a member of the teaching staff. This book is essentially a handy tool, it is a practical work which tells you how to use library materials properly. Thus, the obvious place to use it is in the library itself.

The book concentrates on the law in England and Wales. However, Scotland, Northern Ireland and the Republic of Ireland are covered. In addition, chapters are provided on European Union law and public international law. In the first edition of this book, which appeared in 1979, there was nothing on computers but today no book would be complete without covering this fast growing and important issue and, indeed, there is a chapter on this crucial topic.

Your introductory library tour, valuable though it is, usually takes place during the first hectic weeks of your new life as a student. We hope that you will supplement this introduction by regular reference to this book. Some of the most important reference works can be difficult to use. To help you, we have provided summaries of the steps to be taken when consulting them and, in some cases, we have also provided algorithms (flow-charts). Both the summaries and the flow-charts are intended to be used in conjunction with the main text. Remember that the library staff are there to help you. If, after consulting this book, you are still unable to find what you want, do not hestitate to ask for assistance or information.

October, 1995   *Philip A. Thomas*
                                                   Cathie Cope

ACKNOWLEDGMENTS

The authors and publishers would like to thank the following for granting permission to reproduce material included in this book:

Bowker Saur Ltd
Butterworth (Telepublishing) Ltd
Butterworth & Co (Publishers) Ltd
Butterworth Ireland Ltd
Controller, Stationery Office, Dublin
Department of Justice, Dublin
Her Majesty's Stationery Office
Incorporated Council of Law Reporting
Kluwer Academic Publishers
Legal Information Resources Ltd
Oceana Publications Ltd
Professional Books
The Roundhall Press
SLA Publications (NI)
Stevens & Sons Ltd
Sweet & Maxwell Ltd

While every care has been taken to establish and acknowledge copyright, and contact the copyright owners, the publishers tender their apologies for any accidental infringement. They would be pleased to come to a suitable arrangement with the rightful owners in each case.

CONTENTS

3. LEGISLATION

6. HOW TO FIND INFORMATION ON A SUBJECT

7. USING COMPUTERS TO FIND THE LAW

8. SCOTS LAW

11. EUROPEAN COMMUNITY LAW

12. PUBLIC INTERNATIONAL LAW

CHAPTER 1

Using a Library

INTRODUCTION   1–1

Large libraries can at first appear quite confusing to use. Most libraries are, however, arranged on the same basic principles and once these have been mastered you should not experience too much difficulty in finding your way around, even in the largest library. University and college libraries contain two main types of material: journals (often called periodicals or magazines) and books.

BOOKS   1–2

In some institutions, books on different subjects may be housed in separate buildings. For instance, you may find that the law books have been placed in a separate law library. If this has not been done, the law books will be collected together in one area of the library.

Arrangement of Books on the Shelves   1–3

Books are usually grouped on the shelves according to their subject. The subject dealt with in each book is indicated by numbers, or letters and numbers, which are usually written on the spine of the book. These symbols indicate the exact subject matter of each volume. They are known as the classification number or classmark and bring together, in one area of the library, all books dealing with the same subject. The classification number serves

1

two purposes: it indicates the subject of the book and tells you where the book is to be found on the shelves.

There may be a number of separate sequences in the library. Some books, such as dictionaries and encyclopedias, are designed by their nature to be used as reference books, rather than as books to be read from cover to cover; these may be shelved in a separate reference collection. Very large books (folios) and very thin books (pamphlets) may be kept in a separate sequence. Thus, the size of the book may be important in helping you to find it on the shelves. There will normally be some indication on the catalogue entry (para. 1–4) if the book is shelved separately. Parliamentary papers and publications of international bodies, such as the European Communities and the United Nations, are often located in areas of the library set aside for this purpose. Most important from your point of view, there may be a separate reserve, short loan or undergraduate collection of basic textbooks which are in great demand. These are normally available only for reference or for loan for a short time. Such a collection may include photocopies of articles from journals and extracts from books on your reading lists. Copies of examination papers set in previous years will also often be available.

1–4   Using the Library Catalogue

To find out what books are available in the library, you will need to consult the library catalogue. Many catalogues are now computerised and you will find computers in prominent places throughout the library. In some libraries, however, you will still need to search for books using the card catalogue, which consists of drawers containing cards, with a separate card for every book in the library. Alternatively, the catalogue may be on microfiche sheets, with a microfiche reader machine nearby.

Computerised catalogues are usually quite straightforward to use. There will be instructions on the screen and often nearby leaflets, which will help you learn how to search the catalogue. All computerised library catalogues will allow you to search for books by either the author's name or the title of the item, and often by other means, such as by subject area, by classification number or by any word in the title. If the library has the book for which you are searching, the catalogue entry will give you full details about the book (*e.g.* its publisher, the date of publication and the length of the book in pages) and the classification number, which tells you where to find the book on the shelves. Many computerised catalogues will also tell you whether the book is on loan at the moment and, if so, when it is due back.

Even if your library has a computerised catalogue, you may find that you will need to use a back-up microfiche catalogue should the computer system fail. You may also find that the older books in the library have not been entered onto the computer catalogue and can therefore only be found by using the card catalogue.

Using Microfiche and Card Catalogues 1–5

Whatever the physical format of the catalogue, there are usually two main sequences: an author (or name) catalogue and a subject catalogue. The author catalogue contains records, arranged alphabetically by the authors' names, for all books in the library. In some libraries, it may also include entries under the titles of books. The subject catalogue contains the same records, but rearranged in subject order (see para. 6–25).

If you know the author's name, look up the surname in the author (or name) catalogue. The entries are arranged in alphabetical order by the author's surname. If there are several authors with the same surname, *e.g.* Smith, the entries are then filed by the authors' forenames or initials, *e.g.*:

SMITH, A. B.
SMITH, Alan Norman
SMITH, Barbara

We have said that the arrangement of the entries is alphabetical. Unfortunately, this is not as simple as it seems. There are two ways of arranging entries in alphabetical order. One system is to arrange them "letter by letter", that is, as if they all form part of one long word, ignoring any spaces between words. The other arrangement is "word by word". You should find out which arrangement is used in your library, otherwise you can miss entries. This is shown by the change in the order of the following examples, using the two different filing methods. Indexes to books, and lists of the names of cases, may use either method.

Letter by Letter	*Word by Word*
Law Commission	Law Commission
Lawler, J.	*Law Society*
Lawrence, R. J.	Lawler, J.
Law Society	Lawrence, R. J.
Lawson, F. H.	Lawson, F. H.

When you have located the author's name, you will find an entry for every book available in the library by that author. The

entries are arranged alphabetically by the titles of the books
(ignoring words such as "The" or "A" at the beginning of the title).
If a book has run into several editions, they will be arranged in
order, with the latest edition at the back or at the front of the
sequence (libraries vary in their practice on this point).

Suppose that you are looking for a book which continues to be
known by the name of the original author, even though that
person is dead (this is common practice in law publishing). Let us
take, as an example, *Winfield and Jolowicz on Tort*. This is in its
fourteenth edition. Winfield has not been involved with the work
for many years, but it is still referred to by his name. You would,
therefore, find an entry in the author catalogue under Winfield,
but, in addition, there would also be an entry under Rogers, W. V.
H., who is the author of the present edition.

Many other well-known textbooks have been written jointly by
two authors: Megarry and Wade (*The Law of Real Property*), Cross
and Jones (*Introduction to Criminal Law*), Smith and Hogan
(*Criminal Law*), Cheshire and Fifoot (*The Law of Contract*)—these
are standard works with whose names you will soon become
familiar. If you are looking for the book by Cheshire and Fifoot,
you can look in the author catalogue under either Cheshire or
Fifoot; you will find an entry in the catalogue under both names.
Some authors have double barrelled names. Library practice
varies on which part of the name the entry is filed under. For
instance, a book by O. Hood Phillips may be under Phillips or
Hood Phillips in the catalogue. Therefore, you may need to look
under both forms of the name.

Sometimes a book does not appear to have an individual author.
It has been published by an organisation or society and the
organisation is, in effect, the author. In this case, you will find an
entry in the catalogue under the name of the body, *e.g.* Law
Commission, Law Society, Legal Action Group, United Nations.

1–6   Finding and Borrowing Books

The classification number (para. 1–3) will appear prominently on
the catalogue entry. This number will enable you to trace the book
on the shelves. If the library is a large one, there is usually a guide
near the catalogue showing you where books with that
classification number are to be found.

If you have any difficulty in understanding how the books are
arranged on the shelves, or in using the catalogue, ask a member of
the library staff for help.

If the book is not on the shelves it may be:

(a) in use by another reader in the library;
(b) on loan to another reader;
(c) in a separate sequence of books which are larger or smaller than average, or which are in heavy demand (para. 1–3);
(d) mis-shelved or missing;
(e) removed by the library staff for some reason, *e.g.* rebinding.

Most computerised catalogues are able to show whether the book you want is on loan or is missing. If the book is on loan, it may be possible for you to reserve it, in which case the book will be recalled from its present borrower.

Much of the material in your law library will not be available for loan. Law reports, journals and reference materials, for example, are usually only for use within the library. The library staff will explain which materials are available for loan, how many items you can borrow and for how long. You will need to show your library ticket every time you borrow books. The staff will stamp the label on the inside cover of the books with the date by which you need to return them, although you may find that you can renew the books if you require them for longer.

LAW REPORTS AND JOURNALS   1–7

In the course of your studies, you will need to look at the reports of cases which have been heard in courts, both in this country and abroad. These reports are published in a number of publications called law reports. Amongst the best known series of law reports are the *All England Law Reports*, the *Weekly Law Reports* and the *Law Reports*. We shall examine these series in more detail in Chapter 2. There is a standard form of writing references to law reports, and this is explained in para. 2–3. The law reports are usually shelved in a separate sequence in the law library and they will often be grouped together by country, so that all the English law reports are together. You may find that the international law reports are shelved separately.

You will also find that you are referred to articles and case notes in journals (periodicals or magazines). Your reading list should give you the author and title of the article, the year, the volume number, the title of the journal in which the article appeared and the first page number on which the article is printed, *e.g.* Genn, Hazel, "Tribunals and Informal Justice" (1993) 56 M.L.R. 393.

The form in which this information is written varies but it is important that you should learn to distinguish a reference to a journal article from a reference to a chapter or pages in a book. If you are in any doubt as to the nature of the reference (*i.e.* whether it is a book, a journal article or a law report), ask a member of the library staff for advice. The library catalogue will only include the title of journals. You will need to use other indexes (*e.g.* the *Legal Journals Index*—see para. 4–3) to find the location of individual articles within journals.

1–8   Abbreviations

One of the major difficulties facing a new student is the tradition, adopted by lecturers and authors, of referring to journals and law reports only by an abbreviated form of their title. Instead of writing the name of the journal or law report in full, they are invariably shortened to such cryptic abbreviations as: [1993] A.C.; [1994] 2 All E.R.; 136 N.L.J.; 4 L.M.C.L.Q. This may make it very difficult for you to know whether you are looking for a law report or a journal article. Many of the references are confusingly similar, *e.g.* L.R. can be the abbreviation for both "law report" and "law review" (the law reports are shelved together, but separate from law reviews, which are journals). Consequently, you could find yourself looking in the wrong sequence. A common mistake, for instance, is to assume that a reference to a report of a case in "Crim.L.R." means that you must search amongst the law reports for a series entitled the Criminal Law Reports. There is no such series (although there is a series called the *Criminal Appeal Reports*). The reference "Crim.L.R." is to the *Criminal Law Review*, which is a journal, shelved with the other journals. This contains both articles and reports of cases.

There are several publications which list the meaning of abbreviations in common use. These publications are outlined in para. 2–4.

1–9   Tracing Journals and Law Reports

To find out if a journal or law report is available, look in the periodical catalogue. In your library, this may be a card catalogue, a printed list, on microfiche or part of the computerised library catalogue. The entry will indicate which volumes are available in the library and where they are shelved.

One point is especially worthy of note. Suppose that you are looking for a journal which includes the name of an organisation or body in its title, *e.g.* the *Journal of the Law Society of Scotland*, or the *American Bar Association Journal*. If the publication you require is the bulletin, transactions, proceedings, journal, yearbook or annual report of an organisation, you may find in some libraries that the title has been reversed, so that the entry appears under the name of the organisation. For instance, in some libraries, the *Journal of the Law Society of Scotland* would be entered under Law Society of Scotland, whilst in others it appears under Journal.

If the journal or law report you require is not available in your own library, the staff may be able to help you to locate a copy in another library in the area. Alternatively, it may be possible to obtain a photocopy of the article on inter-library loan or through a commercial document supply service, such as Legal Information Resources Ltd, who publish the *Legal Journals Index*.

OTHER LIBRARY SERVICES   1–10

In addition to printed sources such as books, journals and law reports, you will find other useful sources of information in your library. The library, for example, may have some material (such as old editions of *The Times* newspaper) available only in the form of microfiche or microfilm, and there may be collections of audio-visual material (audio cassettes, videotapes, slides, etc.), press cuttings and other materials which do not form part of the normal book collection. You may also find electronic sources such as CD-ROMs and online databases contain the information you need. Chapter 7 deals with these electronic sources in more detail.

Academic libraries often offer a wide range of other resources. Almost all libraries, for example, provide photocopying facilities. You may find that your library also offers graphic design facilities, a bindery (should you need to bind your dissertation) and fax machines. Some academic libraries also provide computers, allowing you to type up your essays using the word processor, access the campus network or undertake any other computer-related work, whilst in the library.

WHICH LIBRARIES CAN I USE?   1–11

If you are studying at a university or college, the majority of the books you require should be available in your own institution's library. Remember that there may be more than one library available. For instance, in addition to the main library collection, there may be a smaller collection of books and reports in your department or faculty building. If you are living in a hall of residence, the hall's library may include some textbooks.

You may join the public library in the area in which you live, work or study. Most large towns will have some legal textbooks and law reports in their central library. If what you want is not available, the library staff may be able to borrow the material you require through inter-library loan. This may take some time, so ask for the material well in advance of your actual need.

When you return home for the vacation, the university nearest your home may allow you to use their library for reference. Your library may offer access to the computerised library catalogues of other libraries through computers in your own library. If so, you may wish to check whether they have the books you require before you go. These catalogues may also give details of the libraries' opening hours and other useful information.

If you are studying for a professional examination, your professional body will have a library, from which you may be able to borrow books (by post, if necessary). The nearest large public library is another possible source of supply, and your employer may have a library to which you can have access.

Students studying for the Bar may use the library of their Inn. Local public libraries, the libraries attached to the courts and the collections available in chambers are other possible sources. Those training to be solicitors can use the facilities of the Law Society's library, and the collections held by local law societies may be made available to students.

The addresses of libraries can be found in the Library Association's *Libraries in the United Kingdom and the Republic of Ireland*, or the information can be obtained, by telephone or in person, from any public library. A more detailed guide is the *Directory of British and Irish Law Libraries* (4th ed.).

1–12   DICTIONARIES

The newcomer to law rapidly discovers that lawyers have a language of their own, which is a mixture of Latin, French and English. There are several small pocket dictionaries of legal terms which are useful for students, *e.g.* P. G. Osborn, *Concise Law Dictionary* and Mozley and Whiteley, *Law Dictionary*. Students should also consult standard English dictionaries, such as the multi-volumed *Oxford English Dictionary* or one of its smaller versions. W. A. Jowitt, *Dictionary of English Law* is a larger legal dictionary. D. M. Walker, *Oxford Companion to Law*, is another source of information on legal terms, institutions, doctrines and general legal matters. It includes lists of judges and law officers.

Latin phrases and maxims may cause difficulties for students who have no classical languages. Latin phrases appear in most legal dictionaries and a collection of legal maxims will be found in H. Broom, *A Selection of Legal Maxims*: see also Appendix II, at the back of this book. If you are carrying out research in legal history, you may need J. H. Baker, *Manual of Law French*.

TRACING PEOPLE AND ADDRESSES   1–13

If you want to trace the address of a solicitor or barrister, or to find the addresses of courts, legal firms, professional bodies, etc., there are a number of reference works available which provide this information. Waterlow's publish a *Solicitors' and Barristers' Directory and Diary*, which gives alphabetical lists of solicitors and barristers, with their addresses. Lists of Q.C.s, judges, Benchers of the Inns, Recorders and members of the Institute of Legal Executives are also included. There are lists of barristers' chambers and solicitors' firms in each geographical area, with their membership. Similar information is to be found in *Butterworths Law Directory and Diary*, in the Law Society's *Directory of Solicitors and Barristers* and in *Hazell's Guide to the Judiciary and the Courts* (which lists barristers, but not solicitors). Law students looking for articles should consult the *Register of Solicitors Employing Trainees*, issued by the Law Society. The annual *Legal Aid Handbook* gives addresses of area legal aid offices, and details of eligibility for legal aid. Biographical details of prominent members of the legal profession can be found in *Who's Who* and *Who's Who in the Law*, whilst *Debrett's Correct Form* provides advice on the correct form of address when writing to, or addressing, members of the judiciary and other eminent people.

The addresses of many organisations and bodies are to be found in the *Directory of British Associations*, and in *Councils, Committees and Boards*. The humble telephone directory should not be overlooked as a source of information. The reference collection in your library will contain many other sources of this type of information: ask the reference librarian for advice if you need help.

ASSISTANCE FROM LIBRARY STAFF   1–14

Remember that the library staff are there to help you. They will be pleased to explain how the books are arranged on the shelves, to decipher abbreviations, help with difficulties with reading lists and suggest possible sources of information. Do not hesitate to ask them for advice, no matter how busy they may appear to be. They can also help you load your microfilm, show you how to use the CD-ROMs, help with computer problems and search online databases on your behalf.

Most libraries produce handouts or library guides. You should make a point of reading those which are relevant. They will explain how the books are arranged on the shelves, how to use the library catalogue, how to borrow books, etc. In academic libraries, tours of the library are often arranged at the beginning of the session. If such a tour is available, you should certainly attend, as it will help you to familiarise yourself with the library. You may also find that the law librarian will lead lectures or seminars to introduce you to important legal sources. Those lessons will reinforce the skills you will learn in the following chapters.

CHAPTER 2

Law Reports

INTRODUCTION

Law reports are one of the basic (or "primary") sources of English law. Traditionally, the common law has developed through the practical reasoning of the judges. This is based on the particular facts of the case in question, social forces and previous judicial reasoning when it has a bearing on the case being heard. Legal principles stated in earlier decisions are given effect in later cases by the operation of the doctrine of precedent, which is described in detail in Glanville Williams, *Learning the Law*, Chap. 6. The successful development of the common law depends largely upon the production of reliable law reports which carry not only the facts, issues and decision but also, most importantly, the legal principles upon which the judgment is made. Increasingly, the judiciary have also been called upon to consider the scope and application of particular Acts of Parliament.

Only a very small proportion of cases decided by the courts are reported. A case is selected for reporting if it raises a point of legal significance. Just because a case is widely reported in the media, it does not follow that it will appear in law reports.

Judges, to a greater or lesser extent, follow or are influenced by their own previous decisions and those of colleagues and predecessors. Throughout your legal training and practice you will make constant use of law reports. Hence, a thorough working knowledge of them is essential. Glanville Williams (*Learning the Law* (11th ed.), p. 32) has offered the following advice to students of law:

"The great disadvantage of confining oneself to textbooks and lecture notes is that it means taking all one's law at second hand. The law of England is contained in statutes and judicial decisions; what the textbook writer thinks is not, in itself, law. He may have misinterpreted the authorities, and the reader who goes to them goes to the fountainhead. Besides familiarising himself with the law reports and statute book, the lawyer-to-be should get to know his way about the library as a whole, together with its apparatus of catalogues and books of reference."

2–2   THE HISTORY OF LAW REPORTS

Law reports have existed, in one form or another, since the reign of Edward I. These very early law reports are known as the *Year Books*. If you wish to see a copy, reprints of a number of these *Year Books* are available in the series of publications published by the Selden Society, in the Rolls Series and in facsimile reprints issued by Professional Books.

After the *Year Books* had ceased, collections of law reports published privately by individuals began to appear. These reports, the first of which were published in 1571, were normally referred to by the name of the reporter or compiler. For this reason, they are collectively referred to as the *Nominate Reports* and they vary considerably in accuracy and reliability (Glanville Williams, *Learning the Law* (11th ed.), p. 35). Few libraries will have a complete collection of these old reports and if you do obtain a copy, you may find that the antiquated print makes it difficult to read. Fortunately, the great majority of these *Nominate Reports* can be found in at least one of the three reprint series, called the *English Reports*, the *Revised Reports* and the *All England Law Reports Reprint*. The most comprehensive of the three series is the *English Reports*, which is examined in detail later in the chapter (para. 2–9).

In 1865, a body called the Incorporated Council of Law Reporting commenced publication of the *Law Reports*, a single series of reports covering all the major courts. These reports were rapidly accepted by the legal profession as the most authoritative version of law reports and, as a result, most of the earlier series published by individuals ceased publication in 1865 or soon after. Judgments in the *Law Reports* have been checked by the relevant judges before publication and are cited in court in preference to any other series. The *Law Reports* series is described in more detail in para. 2–7.

Today, there are over 50 different series of law reports for England and Wales. The *Weekly Law Reports* and the *All England*

Law Reports, like the *Law Reports*, cover a wide range of topics and are aimed at the lawyer in general practice. There are also a large number of law reports which cover a specialised area of the law, such as the *Criminal Appeal Reports* and the *Road Traffic Reports*.

A case may be reported in more than one series of law reports. For example, a short report may appear in *The Times* newspaper (under the heading "Law Report") a day or so after the judgment is heard. A summary or a full report may be published in some of the weekly legal journals, such as the *New Law Journal* and the *Solicitors' Journal*, or a case note may discuss the significance of the new judgment. Several months later, the case may be published in one or both of the two general series of law reports which appear weekly, the *All England Law Reports* and the *Weekly Law Reports*, and in specialist law reports and journals (*e.g. Tax Cases*, the *Criminal Law Review*). Some time later, a final, authoritative version checked by the judges concerned may be published in the *Law Reports*. Thus, if your library does not hold the series of law reports given in the reference you have, it is worth checking whether the case is reported elsewhere (see para. 2–11).

CITATION OF LAW REPORTS   2–3

Lawyers often use abbreviations when referring to the sources where a report of a case can be found. These can appear confusing at first, but constant use will rapidly make you familiar with the meaning of most of the abbreviations used. References to cases (called *citations*) are structured as shown in the following example:

Giles v. *Thompson*[1] [1993][2] 2[3] W.L.R.[4] 908[5]

[1] the names of the parties involved in the case;
[2] the year in which the case is reported. Square brackets indicate that the date is an essential part of the citation. Some series of law reports number the volumes serially from year to year, so the reference is sufficient even if the year is omitted. Round brackets are used if the date is not essential but merely an aid;
[3] the volume number, *i.e.* the second volume published in 1993. Where only one volume is published in a year, the volume number is omitted unless it is essential for finding the correct volume;
[4] the abbreviation for the name of the law report or journal;
[5] the page number on which the case begins.

Thus, in this example, the case of *Giles* v. *Thompson* will be found in the 1993 volumes of the *Weekly Law Reports* (abbreviated to

First Page of a Law Report from the All England Law Reports Series

C.A.   CLEVELAND PETROLEUM *v.* DARTSTONE (LORD DENNING, M.R.)   **201**

A

CLEVELAND PETROLEUM CO., LTD. *v.* DARTSTONE, LTD. AND ANOTHER. ①

[COURT OF APPEAL, CIVIL DIVISION (Lord Denning, M.R., Russell and Salmon, L.JJ.), November 26, 1968.] ②

B

Trade—Restraint of trade—Agreement—Petrol filling station—Solus agreement— Lease by garage owner to petrol supplier—Underlease to company to operate service station—Covenant in underlease for exclusive sale of supplier's products—Assignment of underlease by licence granted by supplier—Interim injunction to restrain breach of covenant. ③

C

S. the owner in fee simple of a garage, leased the premises to the plaintiffs for 25 years from 1st July 1960. The plaintiffs granted an underlease to C.O.S.S., Ltd., by which C.O.S.S., Ltd., covenanted, inter alia, to carry on the business of a petrol filling station at all times and not to sell or distribute motor fuels other than those supplied by the plaintiffs. After several assignments the underlease was assigned to the defendants who undertook to observe and perform the covenants. The defendants thereupon challenged the validity of the ties. The plaintiffs issued a writ claiming an injunction restraining the defendants from breaking this covenant. The plaintiffs obtained an interim injunction against which the defendants appealed. ④

D

Held: the appeal would be dismissed, the tie was valid and not an unreasonable restraint of trade because the defendants, not having been in possession previously, took possession of the premises under a lease and entered into a restrictive covenant knowing about such covenant, and thereby bound themselves to it (see p. 203, letters C, F and G, post).

E

Dicta in *Esso Petroleum Co., Ltd.* v. *Harper's Garage (Stourport), Ltd.* ([1967] 1 All E.R. at pp. 707, 714, and 724, 725) applied.

Appeal dismissed. ⑤

F

[As to agreements in restraint of trade, see 38 HALSBURY'S LAWS (3rd Edn.) 20, para. 13; and for cases on the subject, see 45 DIGEST (Repl.) 443-449, 271-297.] ⑥

Case referred to:

Esso Petroleum Co., Ltd. v. *Harper's Garage (Stourport), Ltd.,* [1967] 1 All E.R. 699; [1968] A.C. 269; [1967] 2 W.L.R. 871; Digest (Repl.) Supp. ⑦

G

Interlocutory Appeal.

This was an appeal by the defendants, Dartstone, Ltd., and James Arthur Gregory, from an order of EVELEIGH, J., dated 1st November 1968, granting an interim injunction restraining the defendants from acting in breach of a covenant contained in an underlease made on 1st July 1960 between the plaintiffs, Cleveland Petroleum Co., Ltd., and County Oak Service Station, Ltd., and assigned to the defendants on 30th August 1968. The facts are set out in the judgment of LORD DENNING, M.R. ⑧

H

Raymond Walton, Q.C., and *M. C. B. Buckley* for the defendants. ⑨

A. P. Leggatt for the plaintiffs. ⑩

I

LORD DENNING, M.R.: This case concerns a garage and petrol station called County Oak service station, at Crawley in Sussex. Mr. Sainsbury was the owner in fee simple. On 1st July 1960, there were three separate transactions: First, Mr. Sainsbury granted a lease of the entire premises to the plaintiffs, Cleveland Petroleum Co., Ltd., for 25 years, from 1st July 1960. The plaintiffs paid him £50,000 premium and agreed also to pay a nominal rent of £10 a year. Secondly, the plaintiffs granted an underlease of the premises to a company called County Oak Service Station, Ltd. That company was one in which Mr. Sainsbury had a predominant interest. The underlease was for 25 years, less three days from

W.L.R.). There are three volumes of the *Weekly Law Reports* containing the cases reported in 1993. The case referred to will be found in the second volume, at page 908.

If you wish to draw attention to a particular phrase or section in the judgment, you should write out the citation for the case, followed by "at" and the page number where the section or phrase is printed, hence:

Giles v. *Thompson* [1993] 2 W.L.R. 908 at 910

HOW TO FIND THE MEANING OF ABBREVIATIONS 2–4

If you are faced with an abbreviation for a law report or journal which you do not recognise, look in any of the following works.

D. Raistrick, *Index to Legal Citations and Abbreviations*;
Sweet & Maxwell's Guide to Law Reports and Statutes;
Current Law;
The Digest (near the front of Vol. 1(1) and the *Cumulative Supplement*);
Halsbury's Laws of England (4th ed., Vol. 1(1) reissue, pp. 15–41);
Osborn's Concise Law Dictionary;
Manual of Legal Citations (Pts. I and II);
Legal Journals Index (near the front of any issue).

The simplest source for the beginner is the list which is printed in each issue of *Current Law*. If you do not find the answer here, look in one of the alternative sources. A list of some of the most commonly used abbreviations will be found in Appendix I of this book.

FORMAT OF LAW REPORTS 2–5

Page 14 gives a typical example of the first page of a law report. The citation is *Cleveland Petroleum Co. Ltd* v. *Dartstone Ltd. and Another* [1969] 1 All E.R. 201. Several key points in the illustration are numbered.

1. The names of the parties. In a civil case, the name of the plaintiff (the person bringing the action) comes first, followed by the name of the defendant. The small letter "v." between the names is an abbreviation of the Latin "versus" but when speaking of a civil case, you say "*and*" not "*versus*". A criminal case, on the other hand, might appear as *R.* v. *Smith*. R. is the abbreviated form for the Latin words

Rex (king) or *Regina* (queen). The charge against Smith, the accused, is brought on behalf of the Crown and this case would be said as *"the Crown against Smith"*.

2. The name of the court in which the case was heard, the names of the judges (M.R.: Master of the Rolls; L.JJ.: Lords Justices) and the date on which the case was heard.
3. A summary of the main legal issues of the case. You are advised not to rely on this, as it is not necessarily complete nor accurate.
4. The headnote, which is a brief statement of the case and the nature of the claim (in a civil case) or the charge (in a criminal case). Again, do not rely on the publisher's précis but instead read the case.
5. The court's ruling is stated, with a summary of reasons.
6. In certain reports, *e.g.* the *All England Law Reports*, the major legal points are cross-referenced to *Halsbury's Laws* and *The Digest*.
7. A list of cases which were referred to during the hearing.
8. A summary of the history of the previous proceedings of the case. The final sentence explains where in the report you can find the details of the facts of the case.
9. The names of the counsel (the barristers) who appeared for the parties. Q.C.s (Queen's Counsel) are senior counsel.
10. The start of the judgment given by Lord Denning M.R.

2–6 RECENT CASES

Because the law is constantly changing, with new cases being reported every week, you will often be asked to consult recent cases. The most up-to-date cases are found in the newspapers. *The Times*, *The Financial Times*, *The Daily Telegraph*, *The Independent* and *The Guardian* all regularly publish law reports. The library you use may keep the daily copies (perhaps bound up into large volumes), or the law librarian may have cut the law reports out of the newspaper and filed them in folders. Older newspapers are often available on microfilm. Your library may also hold newspapers on CD-ROM, or it may be possible to search the newspapers online.

If you are referred to a report of a case in the *All England Law Reports* or the *Weekly Law Reports* (or, indeed, most other series of law reports) which has been published during the last few months, you will not find a bound volume on the shelves but a series of paper covered parts, or issues. However, your reference (citation) will make it appear that you are looking for a bound volume. So how do you find it? Page 17 shows the front cover of a weekly issue of the *All England Law Reports*. You will find, at the top of the front

Front Cover of an Issue of the All England Law Reports: Weekly Part

[1994] 1 All ER 385–480   Part 6   9 February 1994

THE
ALL ENGLAND
LAW REPORTS

CASES REPORTED

Bank of America National Trust and Savings Association v Chrismas	QBD	401
Barretto, Re	CA	447
Hounslow London BC v Pilling	CA	432
M (a minor) (care order: threshold conditions), Re	CA	424
Pan Ocean Shipping Ltd v Creditcorp Ltd	HL	470
R v Secretary of State for Foreign and Commonwealth Affairs, ex p Rees-Mogg	QBD DC	457
Target Home Loans Ltd v Clothier	CA	439
Walpole v Partridge & Wilson (a firm)	CA	385

Editor	Peter Hutchesson *Barrister New Zealand*
Assistant Editor	Brook Watson *of Lincoln's Inn Barrister*
Consulting Editor	Wendy Shockett *of Gray's Inn Barrister*

Butterworths

Front Cover of an issue of the Weekly Law Reports

Part 45

17 December 1993

[1993] 1 W.L.R. 1529–1568
[1993] 3 W.L.R. 1137–1169

Index

NOTICE

This is the last part for 1993. The 45 weekly issues and the index part which you will receive early in January should be sent to the Binding Department at 3 Star Yard, London, WC2A 2JL for binding.

N.B. The Pink Indexes are not required for binding. Part 1 of the Weekly Law Reports for 1994 will be published on 7 January.

Cases in Volume 1 are those not intended to be included in the Law Reports

Annual subscription £175 (U.K.)
£190 (overseas)

The Weekly Law Reports

Consultant Editor
CAROL ELLIS Q.C.

Managing Editor
ROBERT WILLIAMS
Barrister

Deputy Editor
CLIVE SCOWEN
Barrister

THE INCORPORATED COUNCIL OF LAW REPORTING FOR ENGLAND AND WALES

3 Stone Buildings,
Lincoln's Inn,
London, WC2A 3XN

cover, the date of this issue, the part (or issue) number, and the year, volume and page numbers covered by this issue, *i.e.*:

[1994] 1 All E.R. 385–480   Part 6   9 February 1994

This indicates that this issue (Part 6) will eventually form pages 385–480 of the first bound volume of the *All England Law Reports* for 1994. Also on the front cover appears a list of all the cases reported in that part, showing the page number on which each report begins.

Many other law reports are published in a number of parts during the current year. At the end of the year, these are replaced by a bound volume or volumes. Every part will indicate on its cover the volume and pages in the bound volume where it will finally appear.

The *Weekly Law Reports* is a series (which commenced in 1953) that you will consult frequently. The arrangement of its weekly issues is rather confusing. Three bound volumes are produced each year, and each weekly issue contains some cases which will eventually appear in Volume 1 of the bound volumes for that year, and some cases which will subsequently appear in either Volume 2 or Volume 3. The front cover of each issue shows the contents and the volume in which these pages will eventually appear. For example on the front cover shown on page 18, is printed:

Part 45
17 December 1993
[1993] 1 W.L.R. 1529–1568
[1993] 3 W.L.R. 1137–1169

Part 45 therefore contains pages 1529–1568 of what will eventually form Volume 1 of the *Weekly Law Reports* for 1993, and pages 1137–1169 of Volume 3. A sheet of green paper is inserted in the issue to mark the division between the pages destined for Volume 1 and those forming part of Volume 3. A list of all the cases included in the part is printed on the front cover, and the volume and page number for each case is shown. You may wonder why the publishers (the Incorporated Council of Law Reporting, who also publish the *Law Reports*) have chosen this method of publishing the issues. The reason is that the cases in Volumes 2 and 3 will be republished, after being checked by the judges and with a summary of counsel's arguments, in the *Law Reports*. Those cases appearing in Volume 1, however, will not reappear in the *Law Reports*.

You may find that the latest issue of each journal and law reports series will be displayed in a separate area of the library. The remainder of the issues for the current year may also be filed in this area, or they may be in a box on the shelves alongside the bound volumes.

Some series of law reports are, in addition, published in electronic format. The *Weekly Law Reports*, for example, from 1971 volumes onwards, are available on CD-ROM.

2–7   THE LAW REPORTS SERIES

The publication known as the *Law Reports*, which commenced publication in 1865, was originally published in 11 series, each covering a different court. The rationalisation of the court structure since that time has reduced this to four series. These are:

Appeal Cases (abbreviated to A.C.);
Chancery Division (Ch.);
Queen's Bench Division (Q.B.);
Family Division (Fam.).

The *Law Reports* are usually arranged on the shelves in this order. Paper-covered parts are issued monthly and are replaced by bound volumes at the end of the year. The monthly issues of the Chancery Division and Family Division, however, are published within the same paper-covered part, although they are bound as separate series.

The location on the shelves of the various earlier series often reflects their relationship to the present four series, for example, the historical predecessors of the present Queen's Bench Division (called the King's Bench Division when a King is on the throne) were the Court for Crown Cases Reserved, the Court of Common Pleas and the Court of Exchequer. These are therefore usually shelved before the Queen's Bench Division reports (because they are its predecessors) but after the Appeal Cases and Chancery Division reports. The same arrangement is applied with the other three current series (*i.e.* reports of the predecessors of the present courts are filed at the beginning of each series).

The figure on page 21 shows the way in which the *Law Reports* are arranged on the shelves in most libraries. The abbreviations used to denote each series are shown, and also the dates during which each series appeared.

Citations for the *Law Reports* have varied over the years as the system of numbering the reports changed. Until 1891, for example, each volume in the various series had its own individual number, running sequentially through the years. The date in the citation is

Law Reports

TABLE OF THE LAW REPORTS

The mode of citation is given in brackets. In the first, second and third columns, dots (. . .) are put where the number of the volume would appear in the citation. In the fourth column square brackets([ ]) are put where the year would appear in the citation.

1866–1875	1875–1880	1881–1890	1891–present
House of Lords. English and Irish Appeals (L.R. ... H.L.)			
House of Lords. Scotch and Divorce Appeals (L.R. ... H.L.Sc. or L.R. ... H.L.Sc. and Div.) Privy Council Appeals (L.R. ... P.C.)	Appeal Cases (...App.Cas.)	Appeal Cases (...App.Cas.)	Appeal Cases ([ ]) A.C.)
Chancery Appeal Cases (L.R. ... Ch. or Ch. App.) Equity Cases (L.R. ... Eq.)	Chancery Division (...Ch.D.)	Chancery Division (...Ch.D.)	Chancery Division ([ ]) Ch.)
Crown Cases Reserved (L.R. ... C.C. or, ... C.C.R.)	Queen's Bench Division (...Q.B.D.)		
Queen's Bench Cases* (L.R. ... Q.B.)		Queen's Bench Division (...Q.B.D.)	Queen's (or King's) Bench Division ([ ] Q.B. or K.B.)†
Common Pleas Cases (L.R. ... C.P.)	Common Pleas Division (...C.P.D.)		
Exchequer Cases‡ (L.R. ... Ex.)	Exchequer Division (...Ex.D.)		
Admiralty and Ecclesiastical Cases (L.R. ... A. & E.) Probate and Divorce Cases (L.R. ... P. & D.)	Probate Division (...P.D.)	Probate Division (...P.D.)	Probate Division ([ ]P.) Since 1972 Family Division ([ ]Fam.)

* Note that there is also a series called Queen's Bench Reports in the old reports (113–118 E.R.).

† After 1907 this includes cases in the Court of Criminal Appeal, later the Court of Appeal, in place of the previous Court for Crown Cases Reserved.

‡ Note that there is also a series called Exchequer Reports in the old reports (154–156 E.R.).

(Reproduced from G. Williams, *Learning the Law* (11th ed.), p.39.)

therefore in round brackets, to show it is not essential to the reference. For the *Law Reports* after 1891, however, the date is in square brackets, since the year must be quoted in order to locate the correct volume. The other slight complication in the citation of the *Law Reports* is the use of the abbreviation L.R. (for *Law Reports*) which is placed before the volume number in citations of *Law Reports* before 1875, *e.g. Rylands* v. *Fletcher* (1868) L.R. 3 H.L. 330.

The figure on page 21 clarifies the use of abbreviations and brackets for the *Law Reports*. It is worth noting, however, that the abbreviation H.L. stands for *Law Reports: English and Irish Appeal Cases* and not, as you might guess, Law Reports: House of Lords.

2–8 OLDER LAW REPORTS

We have concentrated upon the modern series of law reports because these are the reports which you will be using most frequently. However, from time to time you will need to look at older cases, that is, those reported in the first half of the nineteenth century or even several centuries earlier. Reports of older cases can be found in several series: the *English Reports*, *Revised Reports*, the *Law Journal Reports*, the *Law Times Reports* and the *All England Law Reports Reprint* series. We shall now look at some of these series in more detail.

The reports published privately by individuals (and known as the *Nominate Reports*) ceased publication around 1865, when the *Law Reports* were first published. If the date of the case you want is before 1865, you are most likely to find it in a series known as the *English Reports*.

2–9 How to Use the English Reports

If you know the name of the case, look it up in the alphabetical index of the names of cases, printed in Volumes 177–178 of the *English Reports*. Beside the name of the case is printed the abbreviation for the name of the original nominate reporter, and the volume and page in his reports where the case appeared. The number printed in **bold** type next to this is the volume number in the *English Reports* where the case will be found, and this is followed by the page number in that volume:

> *Daniel* v. *North*[a]   11 East, 372[b]   **103**[c] 1047

[a] name of the case;
[b] volume, name of the original reporter, page number in the original report, *i.e.* the original report of this case appeared in Volume 11 of *East's Reports* p. 372;

Table of Cases in the English Reports

424 DAN (A) (B) INDEX OF CASES		(C)
→ Daniel *v.* North, 11 East, 372		. **103** 1047
—— *v.* Phillips, 4 T. R. 499		. **100** 1141
—— *v.* Pit, Peake Add. Cas. 238		. **170** 257
—— *v.* Pit, 6 Esp. 74		. **170** 834
—— *v.* Purbeck, W. Kel. 97		. **25** 510
—— *v.* Purkis, W. Kel. 97		. **25** 510
—— *v.* Purkurst, 2 Barn. K. B. 214, 220		**94** 457, 461
—— *v.* Russell, 14 Ves. Jun. 393 ; 2 Ves. Jun. Supp. 376 .		. **33** 572 ; **34** 1139
—— *v.* Skipwith, 2 Bro. C. C. 155		. **29** 89
—— *v.* Sterlin, 1 Freeman, 50		. **89** 39
—— *v.* Thompson, 15 East, 78		. **104** 774
—— *v.* Trotman, 1 Moo. N. S. 123		. **15** 649
—— *v.* Turpin, 1 Keble, 124		. **83** 852
—— *v.* Ubley, Jones, W. 137		. **82** 73
—— *v.* Uply, Latch, 9, 39, 134		. **82** 248, 264, 312
—— *v.* Upton, Noy, 80		. **74** 1047
—— *v.* Waddington, Cro. Jac. 377		. **79** 322
—— *v.* Waddington, 3 Bulstrode, 130		. **81** 111
—— *v.* Warren, 2 Y. & C. C. C. 290		. **63** 127
—— *v.* Wilkin, 7 Ex. 429		. **155** 1016
—— *v.* Wilkin, 8 Ex. 156		. **155** 1300
—— *v.* Wilson, 5 T. R. 1		. **101** 1
Daniel's Case, 2 Dy. 133 b		. **73** 291
—— Trust, *In re*, 18 Beav. 309		. **52** 122

^{c} the reprint of the report appears in Volume 103 of the *English Reports* at page 1047.

You will see that Volume 103 of the *English Reports* has the volumes and names of the *Nominate Reports* which are to be found in that volume printed on the spine. Page 1047 appears in its normal position at the top outer corner of the page whilst the volume and page number of the original report are printed at the inner margin.

Sometimes you may only have a citation (reference) to the original nominate report, *e.g.* 3 Car. & P. (Carrington and Payne); 2 Barn. & Ald. (Barnewall and Alderson). This reference is often printed in an abbreviated form. You do not know the name of the case, so you are unable to look it up in the index to the *English Reports*. Let us suppose, for example, that you have come across a reference to (1809) 11 East 372. Because the date is before 1865, you know that it is likely to be found in the *English Reports*; but you do not know the name of the case. How do you find it? If the name of the report has been abbreviated, *e.g.* 3 Car. & P., you will need to look in Raistrick's *Index to Legal Citations and Abbreviations* or one of the similar reference works (see para. 2–4) to find the meaning of the abbreviation. You then turn to the *Chart to the English Reports*. This may be displayed near the *English Reports*, or it may be a slim

24   Law Reports

Sample Page from the English Reports

before; but they could not agree on the person to be substituted, and therefore the original appointment stood as before.

Per Curiam. Rule absolute.

AMBROSE *against* REES. Wednesday, June 14th, 1809. Notice having been given for the trial of a cause at Monmouth, which arose in Glamorganshire, as being in fact the next English county since the st. 27 H. 8, c. 26, s. 4, though Hereford be the common place of trial; the Court refused to set aside the verdict as for a mis-trial, on motion; the question being open on the record.

Marryat opposed a rule for setting aside the verdict obtained in this cause, upon the ground of an irregularity in the trial. The venue was laid in Glamorganshire, and the cause was tried at Monmouth, as the next English county where the King's writ of venire runs(*b*); but it was objected that it ought to have been tried at Hereford, according to the general custom that all causes in which the venue is laid in any county in South Wales should be tried at Hereford. But the rule being that the cause should be tried in the next English county, and Monmouth being in fact the next English county to Glamorganshire, and more conveniently situated for the trial of the cause, there seems no solid ground for impeaching the validity of the trial; though the practice relied on is easily accounted for by the consideration that Monmouthshire was originally a Welch county, and till it became an English county in the 27th year of Hen. 8, Herefordshire was in fact the next English county to Glamorgan. And there is no reason for setting aside this verdict on the ground of surprize; for the defendant had not merely a notice of trial in the next English county, generally, which might have misled him by the notoriety of the **[371]** practice, but a specific notice of trial at Monmouth, to which he made no objection at the time.

Abbott, in support of the rule, relied on the known practice which had always prevailed, as well since as before the Statute 27 H. 8; and referred to *Morgan* v. *Morgan* (*a*), where the question arose in 1656, upon an ejectment for lands in Breknock-shire, which was tried at Monmouth; and afterwards judgment was arrested, on the ground of a mis-trial, as it ought to have been tried in Herefordshire; for that Monmouthshire was but made an English county by statute within time of memory; and that trials in the next English county of issues arising in Wales have been time out of mind and at the common law; so that a place newly made an English county cannot have such a trial. And he observed, that if this trial were good, all the judgments in causes out of Glamorganshire tried at Hereford have been erroneous.

Lord Ellenborough C.J. If the question appear on the record, then the defendant cannot apply in this summary manner. And as he did not object at the time, we shall not relieve him upon motion.

Per Curiam. Rule discharged.

➜ **[372]** DANIEL *against* NORTH. Wednesday, June 14th, 1809. Where lights had been put out and enjoyed without interruption for above 20 years during the occupation of the opposite premises by a tenant; that will not conclude the landlord of such opposite premises, without evidence of his knowledge of the fact, which is the foundation of presuming a grant against him; and consequently will not conclude a succeeding tenant who was in possession under such landlord from building up against such encroaching lights.

[Considered and applied, *Wheaton* v. *Maple* [1893], 3 Ch. 57; *Roberts* v. *James*, 1903, 89 L. T. 286. For *Rugby Charity* v. *Merryweather*, 11 East, 375, n., see *Woodyer* v. *Hadden*, 1813, 5 Taunt. 138; *Wood* v. *Veal*, 1822, 5 B. & Ald. 457; *Vernon* v. *St. James's, Westminster*, 1880, 16 Ch. D. 457; *Bourke* v. *Davis*, 1889, 44 Ch. D. 123.]

The plaintiff declared in case, upon his seisin in fee of a certain messuage or dwelling-house in Stockport, on one side of which there is and was and of right ought to be six windows; and stated that the defendant wrongfully erected a wall 60 feet high and 50 in length near the said house and windows, and obstructed the light and

(b) Vide 1 Term Rep. 313.　　　　　　　　*(a)* Hard. 66.

Algorithm designed to show how to look up a case in the *English Reports*

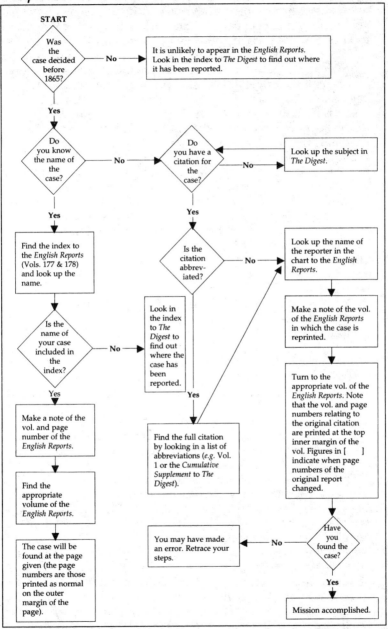

volume shelved with the *English Reports* themselves. The Chart contains an alphabetical list of the names of all the reporters whose work has been reprinted in the *English Reports*, showing which volume their work appears in. The Chart indicates that Volumes 7 to 11 of *East's Reports* are reprinted in Volume 103 of the *English Reports*. If you open Volume 103 at random, you will see that, at the top of each page (at the *inner* margin) the volume and page numbers of the original report are printed. Find the volume and page reference which most nearly corresponds to your reference. There is no entry at the top of the page for Volume 11 of *East's Reports*, page 372, but there is an entry, at the top inner margin, for page 371. If you look at the figure on page 24, you will see the heading "11 East 371" at the top of the page. There are also numbers printed, in square brackets, in the body of the text. These indicate when the page numbers in the original report changed. For instance, in the original Volume 11 of *East's Reports*, page 371 began with the words "practice, but a specific notice of trial at Monmouth ...". Page 372 began with the case of *Daniel* v. *North*.

2–10   Other Older Law Reports

If the *English Reports* are not available in your library, you may find the case you need reprinted in the *Revised Reports*. The *Revised Reports* has similar coverage to the *English Reports* but is not as comprehensive.

The *All England Law Reports Reprint* series is another useful source for old cases between 1558 and 1935. The cases are reprinted from the reports which originally appeared in the *Law Times Reports*, which commenced in 1843, and from earlier reports. The *Reprint* series contains some 5,000 cases selected principally upon the criterion that they have been referred to in the *All England Law Reports* and in *Halsbury's Laws of England*. There is an index volume containing an alphabetical list of cases and a subject index of the cases included in the reprint.

Two other series of nineteenth century cases are also referred to regularly: the *Law Journal Reports* and the *Law Times Reports*. The *Law Journal Reports* cover the period 1822–1949. They can be complicated to use because usually two volumes were published each year, both bearing the same volume number. In one volume were printed the cases heard in common law courts, while in the other were printed equity cases. You will need to check both volumes, unless you know whether the case you want is equity or common law. To add to the difficulty, the volume numbering and the method of citation changed during the course of its publication. The first nine volumes (1822–1831) are known as the

Chart to the English Reports

8			TABLE OF ENGLISH REPORTS		
Old Reports.	Volume in English Reports.	Abbreviation.		Period covered (approximate).	Series.
Dow & Clark, 1 & 2 · · ·	6	Dow & Cl.		1827–1832	H.L.
Dowling & Ryland · · ·	171	Dowl. & Ry. N.P.		1822–1823	N.P.
Drewry, 1–3 · · ·	61	} Drew.		1852–1859	V.C.
„ 4 · · ·	62				
Drewry & Smale, 1 & 2	62	{ Drew & Sm. or Dr. & Sm. }		1860–1865	V.C.
Dyer, 1–3 · · · ·	73	Dy.		1513–1582	K.B.
East, 1–6 · · ·	102	} East.		1801–1812	K.B.
„ 7–11 · · ·	103				
„ 12–16 · · ·	104				
Eden, 1 & 2 · · ·	28	Eden.		1757–1766	Ch.
Edwards · · ·	165	Edw.		1808–1812	{ Ecc. Adm. P. & D.
Ellis & Blackburn, 1–3	118	} El. & Bl.		1851–1858	K.B.
„ „ 4–7 ·	119				
„ „ 8 ·	120				
Ellis, Blackburn & Ellis	120	El. Bl. & El.		1858	K.B.
Ellis & Ellis, 1 · ·	120	} El. & El.		1858–1861	K.B.
„ „ 2 & 3 ·	121				
Eq. Cases Abridged, 1	21	} Eq. Ca. Abr.		1667–1744	Ch.
„ „ 2	22				
Espinasse, 1–6 · ·	170	Esp.		1793–1807	N.P.

Old Series (L.J.O.S.). References to the New Series (1832–1949) omit the letters N.S. Citations give the abbreviation for the court in which the case was heard. It is therefore necessary to decide if the court was a court of common law or equity, so that you consult the correct volume. For example, the reference 16 L.J.Q.B. 274 is a reference to Volume 16 of the *Law Journal (New Series)* in the common law volumes (since Queen's Bench was a court of common law), at page 274 of the reports of Queen's Bench. Volume 16 contains law reports from several different courts. Each court's reports have a separate sequence of page numbers. You are looking for page 274 in the sequence of Queen's Bench reports.

The *Law Times Reports* (L.T.) cover the period 1859–1947. Prior to this, the reports were published as part of the journal entitled *Law Times* and these are cited as the *Law Times, Old Series* (L.T.O.S.) which ran from 1843–1860. You may find this Old Series is shelved with the journals, not with the law reports.

HOW TO FIND A CASE WHEN YOU ONLY KNOW ITS NAME   2–11

We will now turn to some of the problems frequently encountered by students and show how these are solved. Often you know the name of a case but you have no idea where the case was reported;

or else the reference which you have been given has proved to be inaccurate. How can you find out where a report of the case appears?

The easiest way of tracing a case is to look it up in the *Current Law Case Citators*, especially if you think your case was probably decided in or after 1947. *The Digest* (para. 2–13) is the best place to find older cases. In addition, most series of law reports have indexes to cases reported in their publication.

2–12   How to Use the Current Law Case Citators

The *Current Law Case Citator* contains an alphabetical list of the names of cases which have been published or quoted in court between the dates specified on the spine. The *Citator* has been published in a number of parts:

1. *The Current Law Case Citator 1947–1976* is a bound volume covering cases which were reported or cited in court between 1947 and 1976;
2. *The Current Law Case Citator 1977–1988* is a bound volume covering cases which were reported or cited in court between 1977 and 1988;
3. In the spring of each year a paperback issue of the *Current Law Case Citator* is produced. It includes references to cases reported or cited between 1989 and the end of the preceding year;
4. The *Citator* is updated monthly in the *Current Law Monthly Digest*. To find cases reported in the current year, look in the Table of Cases in the most recent issue of the *Monthly Digest*. The December issue of the previous year's *Monthly Digest* can be used to find cases in that year, if the cumulative supplement described in point 3 has not yet been published.

The number of parts to the *Citator* may at first seem confusing. It is best, to look through the *Citators* in chronological order, as above, in order to ensure that you have looked in all the relevant issues.

You may find your library has copies of the *Scottish Current Law Case Citator* for the periods 1948–1976 and 1977–1988. Despite its name, the Scottish version does contain all the English cases but, in addition, it lists Scottish cases in a separate alphabetical sequence at the back of the volume. The two publications have now merged and the *Current Law Case Citator* volumes since 1989 now also include Scottish cases. Part 1 of the *Citator* lists all the English cases, while the Scottish cases are listed in Part 2. Make sure you look for your case in the right section!

In each of the *Citators*, the cases are listed in alphabetical order. Cases which start with a single letter, *e.g. S.* v. *Cox*, are at the beginning of that letter of the alphabet; criminal cases starting with *R.* v. are at the beginning of the letter R section. If the title of the case is *Re Smith*, or *Ex p. Smith*, look under *Smith*. (See Appendix II for the meaning of *Re* and *Ex p*.) When you have traced the case you require, you will find an entry similar to the following:

CASE CITATOR 1947–76   **BIN**

Bigos *v.* Bousted [1951] 1 All E.R. 92; [95 S.J. 180; 211 L.T. 346; 67
    L.Q.R. 156] .... *Digested,* **1751**
—— *v.* J.R.S.S.T. Charitable Trust (Trustees of) (1965) 109 S.J. 273, C.A. *Digested,* 65/2206
Bilainkin *v.* Bilainkin [1959] 1 W.L.R. 139; 103 S.J. 90; [1959] 1 All
    E.R. 161, C.A. .... *Digested,* 59/948
Bilang *v.* Rigg [1972] N.Z.L.R. 954 .... *Digested,* 72/1886
Bilbee *v.* Hasse & Co. (1889) 5 T.L.R. 677 .... *Considered,* 30
Bilbow *v.* Bilbow and Zandos (October 25, 1957), unreported .... *Reported,* 57/1019
Bilcon *v.* Fegmay Investments [1966] 2 Q.B. 221; [1966] 3 W.L.R. 118;
    110 S.J. 618; [1966] 2 All E.R. 513 .... *Digested,* 66/373
Bildt *v.* Foy (1892) 9 T.L.R. 34 .... *Considered,* 67/3093
→ Biles *v.* Caesar [1957] 1 W.L.R. 156; 101 S.J. 108; [1957] 1 All E.R.
    151; [101 S.J. 141; 21 Conv. 169], C.A. ...... *Digested,* 57/1943: *Followed,* 59/1834:
                                                                    Applied, 68/2181; 69/2037
Bilham, *Re* [1901] 2 Ch. 169 .... *Distinguished,* 60/3322
Bill *v.* Short Brothers and Harland [1963] N.I. 1 .... *Digested,* 62/2014
Billage *v.* Southee (1852) 9 Hare 534 .... *Applied,* 52/1485; 70/1145
Billam *v.* Griffith (1941) 23 T.C. 757 .... *Applied,* 4759
Billericay U. D. C., Plot No. 9B, Pitsea Temporary Housing Site, *Re* (1950)
    1 P. & C.R. 239, Lands Tribunal .... *Noted,* 1498

The entry will give you a complete "life history" of the case through the years covered by the *Citator*. It will tell you where and when the case was originally reported, where you can find journal articles explaining the meaning of the case, and perhaps criticising the decision, and in which cases the decision has since been quoted in court, and whether the court to which it was quoted agreed with the decision of the judges in the case.

Let us look at each part of the entry for *Biles* v. *Caesar*, to find out what it means.

(1) After the name of the case (*Biles* v. *Caesar*) you have a list of three places where you can find a full report of the cases:
   (i) [1957] 1 W.L.R. 156—in the first of the three volumes of the *Weekly Law Reports* for 1957 at page 156;
   (ii) 101 S.J. 108—in Volume 101 of the *Solicitors' Journal* at page 108 (this, as its name suggests, is a journal, which you will find shelved with the journals);
   (iii) [1957] 1 All E.R. 151—in the first volume of the *All England Law Reports* for 1957, at page 151.

(2) The entries which are completely enclosed in square brackets—[101 S.J. 141; 21 Conv. 169]—are references to articles or comments in legal journals where the case is discussed in some detail. If you turn to Volume 101 of the *Solicitors' Journal*, or Volume 21 of *The Conveyancer*, you will find articles discussing the case of *Biles* v. *Caesar.*

(3) You will find that all the abbreviations which have been used—S.J., Conv., W.L.R., etc.—are listed at the front of the *Current Law Case Citator*, showing the full title of the journal or law report.

(4) The C.A. after the references to the case tells us that the references report the Court of Appeal decision. If the original decision had also been reported, references to these reports would have been included after the C.A.

(5) The word *Digested* followed by the figures 57/1943 indicates that you will find a digest (a summary) of the case in the 1957 volume of the *Current Law Year Book* (see para. 6–9). Every item in the 1957 volume has its own individual number; you will find that item 1943 is a summary of the facts and decision in the case of *Biles* v. *Caesar.*

(6) You may also wish to know whether the decision given in a particular case has been approved subsequently, *i.e.* whether the case has been quoted with approval by another judge in a later case. By 1976, when the *Citator* was published, the case of *Biles* v. *Caesar* had been quoted in three other cases—in 1959, when the decision was followed, and in 1968 and 1969 when the courts applied the decision in the *Biles'* case to two other cases, following the doctrine of precedent. You can find the names of the cases in which *Biles* was referred to by looking in the 1959 *Current Law Year Book*, at item 1834, and in the 1968 and 1969 *Year Books*, at the item numbers given. The meaning of terms such as *Applied* and *Followed* is given in the front of the *Cumulative Supplement* to *The Digest* (para. 2–13), under the heading "Meaning of terms used in classifying annotating cases".

If, as in the above example, you find a reference to your case in the *Citator* for 1947 to 1976, it is still advisable to check through the more recent *Citators* to find the present status of the judgment. You can find out whether since 1976, for example, the case has been taken to a higher court or the decision has been approved or overruled in other judgments. For more information on how to trace the subsequent judicial history of a case, see para. 6–14.

If you are unable to find the case you require in the *Current Law*

Case Citators, it may be that the case is either very old or from another jurisdiction. The next place to look is in *The Digest*.

How to Trace a Case in The Digest   **2–13**

Older English and Scottish cases can most easily be traced using *The Digest* (formerly known as the *English and Empire Digest*), as can many cases heard in Irish, European and Commonwealth courts. *The Digest* consists of the main work (around 70 volumes), several *Continuation Volumes*, a *Cumulative Supplement*, a *Consolidated Table of Cases* and a *Consolidated Index*. *The Digest* is in its third edition which is called the *Green Band Reissue* because of the green stripe on the spine. Some of the *Green Band Reissue* volumes have now been updated and reprinted. These volumes say *2nd Reissue* on the spine. The date of reissue of any volume is printed on the title page inside the front cover.

To trace a particular case in *The Digest*, go first to the four-volume *Consolidated Table of Cases*. This contains an alphabetical list of the 400,000 cases summarised in *The Digest* and gives a reference to the volume in which the case can be found. Page 32 shows the entry in the *Consolidated Table of Cases* for the case of *Bell v. Twentyman*. This case is included in Volumes 19, 36(1) and 36(2) of *The Digest*, since it is relevant to the law of easements, negligence and nuisance. At the front of each of these volumes, there is another Table of Cases which refers you to the *case* number (or *page* number in older volumes—see the heading at the top of the column) where you can find a summary of the case and a list of citations where the full report can be found. If, for example, you wished to find a summary of the negligence aspects of the case of *Bell v. Twentyman*, you would now look up the name of the case in the Table of Cases at the front of Volume 36(1). Alongside the name of the case is the number 133, which refers you to case number 133 in that volume. The entry is shown on page 33. The case number is given in **bold**, followed by a summary of the case and references to where the full text of the report can be found. The case of *Bell v. Twentyman* was reported in a number of series. To find the meaning of the abbreviations used, look in the list of abbreviations in the *Cumulative Supplement*.

The *Consolidated Table of Cases* is updated and reprinted every two years. To find the latest cases, you will need to look in the annual *Cumulative Supplement*. There is a Table of Cases at the front of the volume, which indicates where in the *Cumulative Supplement* a summary of the case can be found. For more information on *The Digest*, refer to para. 6–10.

Example Page from The Digest Consolidated Table of Cases A–C

Bell v London & North Western Ry Co (1852) **8(2) Chos**
Bell v London & South Western Bank (1874) **7 Bldg Soc**
Bell v Long (CAN) **21 Exon**
Bell v Love (1883) **11 Comns; 34 Mines**
Bell v McKindsey (CAN) **17 Deeds**
Bell v Macklin (1887) (CAN) **40 S Land**
Bell v McLean (1868) (CAN) **42 Shrffs**
Bell v Manning (1865) (CAN) **6 B of Exch**
Bell v Mansfield (1893) (AUS) **42 Ship**
Bell v Marsh (1903) **21 Estpl**
Bell v Marsh (CAN) **19 Easmt**
Bell v Martin (1831) **11 Confl**
Bell v Matthewman (1920) (CAN) **23 Exors**
Bell v McCubbin (1989) **CVH**
Bell v McDougall (1882) (CAN) **5(1) Bkpcy**
Bell v Midland Ry Co (1861) **17 Damgs; 19 Easmt; 36(2) Nuis**
Bell v Miller (1862) (CAN) **3 Arbn**
Bell v Miller (AUS) **29 Insce**
Bell v Milner (1957) (CAN) **9(2) Coys**
Bell v Moffat (1880) (CAN) **6 B of Exch**
Bell v Montreal Trust Co (1956) (CAN) **45 Stats**
Bell v Murray (1833) (SCOT) **27(2) H&W**
Bell v Nangle (IR) **17 Deeds**
Bell v National Forest Products Ltd, Luttin, Porter (CAN) **26 Guar**
Bell v National Provincial Bank of England Ltd (1904) **28(1) Inc T**
Bell v Nevin (1866) **36(2) Prtnrs**
Bell v New Zealand Rugby Football Union (1931) (NZ) **12(1) Contr**
Bell v Nicholls, ex p Richards (CAN) **21 Exon**
Bell v Nixon (1816) **29 Insce**
Bell v North Staffordshire Ry Co (1879) **37(2) Pract**
Bell v Northern Constitution Ltd (1943) (NI) **32 Libel**
Bell v Northwood (1886) (CAN) **45 Sp Pfce**
Bell v Norwich (Bp) (1565) **19 Eccl**
Bell v Oakley (1814) **18 Distr**
Bell v Ogilvie (1863) (SCOT) **44 Solrs**
Bell v Ontario Human Rights Commission & McKay (1971) (CAN) **CVD**
Bell v Ontario Human Rights Commission and McKay (CAN) **16 Cr Pract**
Bell v Ottawa Trust & Deposit Co (1897) (CAN) **5(1) Bkpcy**
Bell v Parent (CAN) **33 Mags**
Bell v Park (1914) (IR) **50. Wills**
Bell v Parke (1860) (IR) **32 Libel**
Bell v Petry (1897) (NZ) **27(1) H&W**
Bell v Phyn (1802) **36(2) Prtnrs; 50 Wills**
Bell v Pitt (AUS) **19 Easmt**
Bell v Plumbly (1900) **46 Stk Ex**
Bell v Port of London Assurance Co (1850) **22(2) Evid**
Bell v Portland Shire (1876) (AUS) **1(1) Admin L**
Bell v Postlethwaite (1855) **3 Arbn**
Bell v Puller (1810) **42 Ship**
Bell v Quebec Corpn (1879) **49 Water**
Bell v R (1973) (CAN) **CVD**
Bell v Raisbeck (1844) **23 Exors**
Bell v Rea (1852) **1(2) Agcy**
Bell v Reid (1813) **2 Aliens**
Bell v Reuben (1946) **31 L&T**
Bell v Riddell (1882) (CAN) **27(1) H&W**
Bell v Riddell (1884) (CAN) **12(1) Contr**
Bell v Robinson (1824) **18 Distr; 25 Fraud Conv**
Bell v Robinson (1909) (CAN) **5(2) Bkpcy**
Bell v Rogers (1914) (CAN) **6 B of Exch**

Bell v Rokeby (1905) (CAN) **1(2) Agcy**
Bell v Ross (1885) (CAN) **5(1) Bkpcy**
Bell v Rowe (1901) (AUS) **12(2) Contr**
Bell v Ry Comr (1861) (AUS) **2 Animals**
Bell v Sarvis (1903) (CAN) **50 Wills**
Bell v Schultz (1912) (CAN) **39(2) S Goods; 46 Tort**
Bell v Scott (1922) (AUS) **40 S Land**
Bell v Searight, Re Searight (1899) **50 Wills**
Bell v Secretary of State for Defence (1985) **CVG**
Bell v Shuttleworth (1841) **6 B of Exch; 12(2) Contr; 26 Guar; 30 Jdgmts**
Bell v Simpson (1857) **4(1) Bkpcy**
Bell v Skelton (1831) **23 Exors**
Bell v Smith (1826) **22(2) Evid**
Bell v Spelliscy (1932) (CAN) **23 Exors**
Bell v Spereman (1726) **39(1) Recrs**
Bell v Stewart (1842) (IR) **6 B of Exch**
Bell v Stocker (1882) **27(1) H&W**
Bell v Stockton, etc Tramway Co (1887) **39(1) R Traf**
Bell v Stone (1798) **32 Libel**
Bell v Sunderland Bldg Soc (1883) **35 Mtge**
Bell v Tainthorp (1834) **30 Juries**
Bell v Tape (1837) (IR) **11 Const L**
Bell v Taxes Comr (NZ) **30 Land Tax**
Bell v Taylor (1836) **44 Solrs**
Bell v Thatcher (1675) **32 Libel**
Bell v Thompson (1934) (AUS) **2 Animals**
Bell v Timiswood (1812) **23 Exors**
Bell v Toronto Transportation Commission (1926) (CAN) **18 Discy**
Bell v Travco Hotels Ltd (1953) **29 Inns**
Bell v Turner (1874) **22(2) Evid**
Bell v Turner (1877) **48 Trusts**
Bell v Twentyman (1841) **19 Easmt; 36(1) Negl; 36(2) Nuis** ←
Bell v Union Bank (1923) (NZ) **3 Bank**
Bell v Walker & Debrett (1785) **13 Coprt**
Bell v Wardell (1740) **17 Custom; 46 Time**
Bell v Welch (1850) **12(1) Contr; 26 Guar**
Bell v Wermore (CAN) **21 Exon**
Bell v Westmount Town (1899) (CAN) **8(2) Comwlth**
Bell v Wetmore (1880) (CAN) **27(1) H&W**
Bell v Wetmore (CAN) **17 Damgs**
Bell v Whitbread & Co Ltd (1970) **25 Gaming**
Bell v White (1857) (CAN) **7 Bounds&F**
Bell v Whitehead (1839) **13 Coprt**
Bell v Wilson (1865) (1866) **17 Deeds**
Bell v Wilson (1866) **34 Mines**
Bell v Wilson (1900) (CAN) **32 Libel**
Bell v Windsor & Annapolis Ry Co (1892) (CAN) **8(1) Carr**
Bell v Witts, Re Mercer (1894) **48 Trusts**
Bell v Wright (1895) (CAN) **44 Solrs**
Bell v Wyndham (1865) **25 Fish**
Bell, exp (1988) **CVH**
Bell, In the Estate of (1908) **23 Exors**
Bell, In the Goods of (1859) **23 Exors**
Bell, In the Goods of (1878) **23 Exors**
Bell, In the Goods of Hunt v Hunt (1866) **50 Wills**
Bell, R v (1731) **14(2) Crim**
Bell, R v (1737) **14(2) Crim**
Bell, R v (1753) **15 Crim**
Bell, R v (1822) **36(2) Nuis**
Bell, R v (1829) **14(2) Crim**
Bell, R v (1841) **15 Crim**
Bell, R v (1857) (CAN) **28(3) Infts**
Bell, R v (1859) (IR) **14(2) Crim; 15 Crim**

Example Page from The Digest, Vol. 36(1), 2nd Reissue

General Principles of the Law of Negligence   Cases 132–139

ii THE DUTY TO TAKE CARE

1 Necessity for

CROSS REFERENCES See ACTION vol 1(1) (reissue) nos 228, 229 (*injuria absque damno*); no 230 et seq (*damnum absque injuria*)

132 No negligence without duty In an action by the consignor of goods against the proprietor of a general booking-office for the transmission of parcels by coach, etc, charging negligence, whereby consignor lost his goods, it is not sufficient to prove that they never reached their destination or were accounted for. The office-keeper's duty is to deliver to a carrier; and some evidence must be given, showing specifically a breach of that duty. A tradesman, having made up goods by order, delivered them at a booking-office, with the customer's address, and booked them, to be forwarded to him, not specifying any particular conveyance, and no particular mode of transmission having been pointed out by the customer.

Quaere: whether the consignor could maintain an action against the office-keeper for a negligent loss of the goods while under his charge.

Gilbart v Dale (1836) 5 Ad & El 543; 2 Har & W 383; 1 Nev & PKB 22; 6 LJKB 3; 111 ER 1270
ANNOTATION **Apld** Mid Ry v Bromley (1856) 17 CB 372

➤ **133** —— In case for an injury to plaintiff's reversionary interest by defendant's obstruction of a watercourse on his land and thereby sending water upon and under the house and land in the occupation of plaintiff's tenant, defendant pleaded, that the obstruction was caused by the neglect of plaintiff's tenant to repair a wall on the demised land, that in consequence it fell into the watercourse, and caused the damage, and that within a reasonable time after defendant had notice he removed it: *Held* to be a bad plea, it not showing any obligation on the tenant to repair the wall merely as terre-tenant. *Quaere*: whether it would have been good if it had.

Bell v Twentyman (1841) 1 QB 766; 1 Gal & Dav 223; 10 LJQ B 278; 6 Jur 366; 113 ER 1324
ANNOTATION **Distd** Taylor v Stendall (1845) 5 LTOS 214

134 —— A declaration in case stated, by way of inducement, that plaintiff was possessed of a dwelling-house as tenant to defendant, and that defendant, at the request of plaintiff, promised to fit up a cellar for a wine cellar, with brick and stone binns; and then charged that it became the duty of defendant to use due care in fitting up the same, but that he did not, and that the slabs gave way, and broke plaintiff's wine bottles. It was proved that defendant did fit up a wine cellar with brick and stone binns; but that plaintiff afterwards required more binns to be made, and defendant consented to have the partitions carried up to the roof of the cellar. The workmen, however, by plaintiff's directions, erected the new partitions upon the centre of the slabs which covered the binns first made, and the slabs then gave way. It was proved that those slabs would have been strong enough to bear the weight of empty bottles; but some of the witnesses thought not that of full bottles: *Held* under these circumstances no breach of duty was shown, defendant having only undertaken to fit up a wine cellar with brick and stone binns, and not one of any particular character.

Richardson v Berkeley (1847) 10 LTOS 203

135 —— The declaration stated that defendants were possessed of a mooring anchor, which was kept by them fixed in a known part of a navigable river, covered by ordinary tides, that the anchor had become removed into, and remained in, another part of the river covered by ordinary tides, not indicated, whereof defendants had notice, and although they had the means and power of refixing and securing the anchor, and indicating it, they neglected so to do, whereby plaintiffs' vessel, whilst sailing in a part of the river ordinarily used by ships, ran foul of and struck against the anchor, and was thereby damaged, etc: *Held* bad, for not showing that defendants were privy to the removal of the anchor, or that it was their duty to refix it and to indicate it.

Hancock v York, Newcastle & Berwick Ry Co (1850) 10 CB 348; 14 LTOS 467; 138 ER 140

136 —— Negligence creates no cause of action unless it expresses a breach of a duty (*Erle, CJ*).
Dutton v Powles (1862) 2 B&S 191; 31 LJQB 191; 6 LT 224; 8 Jur NS 970; 10 WR 408; 1 Mar LC 209; 121 ER 1043, Ex Ch

137 —— Plaintiff, a carman, being sent by his employer to defendants for some goods, was directed by a servant of defendants to go to the counting house. In proceeding along a dark passage of defendants in the direction pointed out, plaintiff fell down a staircase, and was injured: *Held* defendants were not guilty of any negligence; for if the passage was so dark that plaintiff could not see his way, he ought not to have proceeded; and if, on the other hand, there was sufficient light, he ought to have avoided the danger.
Wilkinson v Fairie (1862) 1 H&C 633; 32 LJ Ex 73; 7 LT 599; 9 Jur NS 280; 158 ER 1038
ANNOTATIONS **Apld** Lewis v Ronald (1909) 101 LT 534 **Consd** Campbell v Shelbourne Hotel Ltd [1939] 2 KB 534

138 —— *Skelton v London & North Western Ry Co* (1867) no 485 post

139 —— Plaintiffs, merchants at Valparaiso, received through defendants a telegram purporting to come from London and addressed to them, ordering a large shipment of barley. No such message was ever in

21

2–14   Tracing a Case through the Indexes in Law Reports

In addition to the *Current Law Case Citators* and *The Digest*, there
are a number of indexes to the cases in individual series of law
reports. For instance, the *All England Law Reports* has published a
volume containing a list of all the cases in the *All England Law
Reports Reprint* (see para. 2–10), which covers selected cases
between 1558 and 1935. In addition, there are three volumes
containing the *Consolidated Tables and Index 1936–1992*. Volume 1
contains a list of all the cases included in the *All England Law
Reports* between these dates. The reference given is to the year,
volume and page number. Cases reported since 1992 appear in the
annual cumulative *Tables and Index*, updated quarterly by the
Current Tables and Index.

If you know that the case you are looking for is old, you can turn
to the index in Volumes 177 and 178 of the *English Reports*, and this
will tell you if the case has been printed in the *English Reports* (see
para. 2–9). Several other series of law reports also publish indexes
and these can be useful if you know that a case is reported in a
particular series but you have not got an exact reference. Some
series of law reports (*e.g.* the *Weekly Law Reports*) are now available
on CD-ROM. This provides a very quick way to find the text of a
report and will find not only the original case but any references to
it in other cases reported in the series.

The indexes to the *Law Reports* are very useful. From 1865 to
1949, a series of *Law Reports: Digests* were published. These contain
summaries of the cases reported in the *Law Reports*, in subject
order, and a list of cases is usually included. From 1950 this has
been published as the *Law Reports Consolidated Index* (lettered on
the spine *Law Reports Index*), usually referred to as the *Red Index*.
Four bound volumes, each covering cases in a 10-year period, have
been published for the period 1951–1990. An annual paper-
covered *Red Index* is published, containing cases from 1991 to the
end of the last year. This is supplemented by the *Pink Index*, which
is issued at intervals during the year and lists all the cases
published during the current year. The main arrangement of all
the indexes is by subject, but there are two alphabetical lists. The
list of Cases Reported, at the front of each volume, covers recently
reported cases, whilst the separate list of Cases Judicially
Considered, at the back of the volume, gives information on older
cases which have been mentioned in court during the period
covered by the index. In addition to cases published in the *Law
Reports* and the *Weekly Law Reports*, the indexes also include cases
published in the *All England Law Reports*, the *Criminal Appeal
Reports*, the *Lloyd's Law Reports*, the *Local Government Reports*, the

Industrial Cases Reports, the *Road Traffic Reports* and *Tax Cases*. If the *Current Law Case Citators* are not available in your library, this index to the *Law Reports* will fulfil a similar function.

HOW TO TRACE VERY RECENT CASES   2–15

Many of the indexes already mentioned have regular updates throughout the year. In addition, there are "current awareness" publications that aim to keep their readership as up to date as possible with legal developments. It is in these two types of publication that you will look to find references to very recent cases.

The *Current Law Monthly Digest* includes a Cumulative Table of Cases. Look in the list in the *latest* issue. If the name of your case appears, the reference given is to the monthly issue of the *Current Law Monthly Digest* and to the individual item number within that issue, where you will find a summary of the case and a note of where it has been reported. For example, suppose the Table of Cases gives your case a reference such as: Jan 129. This means that if you look in the January issue of the *Monthly Digest*, item 129 (not page 129) is a summary of the case, with a list of places where the case is reported in full. Scottish cases are included in the Table of Cases, but the reference will lead you to the Scottish law section of the *Monthly Digest*.

The indexes to the *Law Reports* and the *All England Law Reports* can be used to trace recent cases. The *Pink Index* to the *Law Reports* will cover cases reported in several of the major series of law reports; its front cover indicates the exact period it covers. If the case is too recent to be included in here, look inside the latest copy of the *Weekly Law Reports*. The front cover of the *Weekly Law Reports* lists only the contents of that particular issue. The list inside covers all cases reported in the series since the last *Pink Index* was published.

The *All England Law Reports Current Tables and Index* covers all cases published in the *All England Law Reports* in the current year. A list inside the latest issue of the *All England Law Reports* brings the *Current Tables* up to date. There is also a list of cases to be reported in future issues.

There is usually a delay of several months before a case is reported in law report series such as the *All England Law Reports* and the *Weekly Law Reports*. Reports of cases heard in the past few weeks will only be available in newspapers or weekly journals.

Newspaper law reports are the quickest to appear, with most being published within a week and some appearing the day after the end of the case. Since 1988, an index of newspaper law reports has been published every fortnight. The *Daily Law Reports Index* abstracts law reports from *The Times, The Financial Times, The Independent, The Guardian, The Daily Telegraph* and *Lloyd's List*. The entries are ordered by case name and include references to the newspapers which carry the report and a summary of the facts of the case and decision reached. There is also an index listing each party in the cases, should you only know the name of the defendant. The fortnightly loose parts are cumulated into a quarterly bound volume, which includes an additional index listing cases which have been reported by a newspaper and have now been more fully reported in one of the major law report series. An annual bound volume cumulates these quarterly volumes.

Reports of recent cases can also be found in legal journals. Some of the weekly journals, such as the *New Law Journal*, and specialist journals, such as the *Journal of Planning and Environmental Law* and the *Estates Gazette*, produce short reports of relevant cases. References to these reports can be found in the Case Index in the *Legal Journals Index* (see para. 2–16).

Electronic sources such as LEXIS, Lawtel and FT Profile are all helpful in finding references to very recent cases. Chapter 7 gives further information on these sources.

SUMMARY: TRACING WHERE A CASE HAS BEEN REPORTED

1. If the date is unknown, look in the *Current Law Case Citators* or in *The Digest* in the *Consolidated Table of Cases* and in the *Cumulative Supplement*.
2. If the case is thought to be old, look in *The Digest Consolidated Table of Cases*. If this is not available, look in the index to the *English Reports* or the index to the *All England Law Reports Reprint*.
3. If the case is thought to be very recent, look in the *Daily Law Reports Index* and the *Legal Journals Index*. Look also in the latest *Current Law Monthly Digest* and the *Pink Index* to the *Law Reports* and then in the latest issue of the *Weekly Law Reports* or the *All England Law Reports*.
4. If the case is known to have been reported in one of the leading series but the reference you have is incomplete, look in the index to that series, if there is one; otherwise try the *Current Law Case Citators* or *The Digest*.
5. For a Scottish case, look in the separate list of Scottish cases at the back of the *Scottish Current Law Case Citator 1947–1976* and *1977–1988* or in the *Current Law Case Citators* for cases since 1988. If not traced there, look in *The Digest*.
6. For Commonwealth cases, check *The Digest*.

HOW TO TRACE JOURNAL ARTICLES AND COMMENTARIES ON A CASE

2–16

You may want to find out if any journal articles have been written about a case, or to trace comments on a recent court decision. Such articles and comments usually explain the significance of the case and relate it to other decisions on the same aspect of the law. Sometimes writers who disagree with a decision may even argue that the case provides a justification for a change in the law.

Journal articles on a case can be traced by using the *Legal Journals Index* (para. 4–3), the *Current Law Case Citators* or the *Index to Legal Periodicals* (para. 4–5). If you look again at the specimen entry (*Biles v. Caesar*) from the *Current Law Case Citator* (para. 2–12), you will see that the entries which were completely enclosed in square brackets were journal articles on that case. For articles published in the current year, you should look in the Table of Cases in the latest *Current Law Monthly Digest*. If your case appears in *lower* case, it means either that there has been a journal article on the case or that the case has been judicially considered during the year. If you turn to the issue of the *Monthly Digest* indicated and then to the item number, you will either find another case in which your case has been cited or a note of a journal article which has been written about your case.

The easiest and most comprehensive way to find articles on an English case is to use the *Legal Journals Index*, which indexes all the major British legal journals. The Case Index provides details of journal articles and commentaries on the case as well as references to any reports of the case in journals. The printed version of the *Legal Journals Index* is published monthly, with quarterly cumulations and an annual bound cumulative volume. The *Legal Journals Index* is also available, along with the *Daily Law Reports Index* and the *European Legal Journal Index*, on CD-ROM updated three times a year, and on magnetic tape, which your library may load onto a central computer. A new magnetic tape is sent to update the database every fortnight and therefore this method supplies the most current information.

The *Legal Journals Index* was first published in 1986. If your library does not hold the *Legal Journals Index*, or if you require articles prior to 1986, you may trace articles on your case in the *Index to Legal Periodicals* (para. 4–5). Look in the back of the issues under the heading "Table of Cases Commented Upon". Most will be American cases, but important British cases are included, if there has been a fairly lengthy article written about them.

The weekly journals, such as the *New Law Journal* and the *Solicitors' Journal*, and many of the specialist journals, such as *Public Law*, the *Criminal Law Review* and *The Conveyancer*, include notes and comments on recent cases. Since these are relatively short, they often do not appear in the list of journal articles printed in *Current Law* or the *Legal Journals Index*. If you know roughly when the case was decided, you may find helpful material by browsing through the contents pages of relevant journals of the time. A quick glance through recent issues is also often rewarding when searching for comments on a case decided within the last month.

2–17 TRIBUNALS

The establishment of the welfare state led to the creation of a large number of tribunals. They were set up to resolve disputes over entitlement to welfare benefits. Subsequently, other areas, such as problems between landlords and tenants, and between employer and employees because of unfair dismissal, have been subject to resolution through tribunals. Tribunals can be extremely busy, hearing many thousands of cases each year, but only a comparatively small number of cases are eventually reported in the law reports. Some law reports, such as the *Industrial Cases Reports* and *Immigration Appeals*, carry reports of appeals from the tribunal to an appeal court but the vast majority of cases heard by tribunals are not reported.

2–18 Social Welfare Law

The most important decisions taken by the Social Security Commissioners are published individually by HMSO and are subsequently reissued in bound volumes. The form of *citation* for the Commissioners' decisions differs from that used in conventional law reports and references to cases do not include the names of the parties. All cases reported since 1950 bear the prefix R, followed, in brackets, by an abbreviation for the series. For example, the prefix R(U) indicates a Commissioner's decision on unemployment benefit, and R(P) a decision on entitlement to pensions. Within each series, reports are cited by the report number and the year: R(U) 7/62 indicates a reported unemployment benefit decision, case number 7 of 1962.

The following abbreviations are used in the series which are available in the *Reported Decisions of the Social Security Commissioners*, published by HMSO:

R(A)	Attendance allowance
R(F)	Child benefit
R(FIS)	Family income supplements
R(G)	General—miscellaneous (maternity benefit, widow's benefit, death grant, etc.)
R(I)	Industrial injuries benefit
R(IS)	Income support
R(M)	Mobility allowance
R(P)	Retirement pensions
R(S)	Sickness and invalidity benefit
R(SB)	Supplementary benefit
R(SSP)	Statutory sick pay
R(U)	Unemployment benefit

Decisions which are not published by HMSO may be read at the Commissioners' offices. Unpublished reports are prefaced by C instead of R. For example, CP 3/81 is a reference to an unpublished 1981 Commissioner's decision on pensions and CSB 15/82 is an unreported decision on supplementary benefits.

In 1987, there were changes to the way Commissioners made decisions available. Commissioners now "star" decisions which they think should be published. The new system has resulted in some changes in the form of the citation. "Starred" decisions are still retained in the Commissioners' files, but the year in "starred" cases, *i.e.* those cases which are to be reported, is given in full, *e.g.* CS 61/1990, whilst unreported decisions have only the last two digits on the year, *e.g.* CS 10/89. The reported decision of the case, when it appears, is prefixed by R as previously.

Reported cases from 1948–50 had a different method of citation. They were prefixed by C, followed by a letter (*not* enclosed in brackets) representing the area of law covered. Thus, CI denotes an early decision on industrial injuries. Scottish or Welsh cases were prefixed with CS and CW respectively. The cases were numbered in sequence. However, only a minority were printed, which has resulted in gaps in the numerical sequence. For example, CWI 17/49 is followed by CWI 20/49. Cases numbered 18 or 19 of 1949 are unreported. The abbreviation (KL) after the citation is an indication that the case had been reported, whilst the suffix (K) denotes a decision of limited value.

Earlier reported decisions of the Commissioners were published in the *Reported Decisions of the Commissioner under the Social Security and National Insurance (Industrial Injuries) Acts*. The period from 1948–1976 was covered in seven volumes. They are known as the *Blue Books* because of their colour, and they contain decisions prefixed by R(I). Since 1976, these decisions appear in the bound volumes of the *Reported Decisions of the Social Security*

Commissioner, which cover all the different R series. The more recent decisions are available individually from HMSO; they are also summarised in the *Journal of Social Welfare Law* and in issues of the *Law Society Gazette*.

Decisions on a particular subject can be traced using D. Neligan, *Social Security Case Law: Digest of Commissioners' Decisions*, issued by the D.S.S. and published by HMSO. This publication summarises the majority of the reported decisions, under appropriate subject headings. The appendix provides a list of decision numbers, which will allow you to trace the summary of a particular case should the full report of the Commissioner's decision be unavailable.

Northern Ireland Commissioners' decisions are referred to in a similar fashion. For example, R 1/81 (I.I.) is a decision on industrial injuries benefit from Northern Ireland. Earlier reports were issued under the title *Reported Decisions of the Umpire*, published by HMSO, Belfast, and issued by the Northern Ireland Ministry of Labour and its successor bodies. The current decisions, issued by the Department of Health and Social Services for Northern Ireland, are available individually from HMSO, Belfast. The abbreviation for the series always follows the case number in Northern Ireland decisions; in more reent years, the year has preceded the case number. R 1989/2 (IS) is thus a Northern Ireland decision on income support, whilst R(SB) 2/84 is an English case on supplementary benefit. A list of Commissioners' decisions issued by both the Department of Social Security (previously called the Department of Health and Social Security) and the Department of Health and Social Services for Northern Ireland is found in the *HMSO Annual Catalogues* under the name of the relevant department.

HMSO publish a number of guides to social welfare law. *The Law relating to Social Security and Child Benefit*, issued by the D.S.S., contains the text of all relevant statutes and regulations. It is often refered to as the *Brown Book*. The *Yellow Book* is a reference to another D.S.S. publication, *The Law relating to Supplementary Benefits and Family Income Supplements*, which again reprints the relevant statutory material. Both publications are in a looseleaf format for easy updating.

2–19   Decisions of Other Tribunals

The wide range of tribunals makes a complete guide impossible within the available space. What follows is selective.

Immigration appeals are covered by *Immigration Appeals*,

published by HMSO. Also available from HMSO are the *Value Added Tax Tribunals Reports*.

Many Lands Tribunal cases appear in the *Property, Planning and Compensation Reports* and in the *Estates Gazette* and the *Estates Gazette Law Reports*. The latter series also covers leasehold valuation tribunals. Barry Rose published a series of volumes entitled *Lands Tribunal Cases*.

Most reported cases, in subjects other than welfare law, appear in standard series of law reports and are conventionally cited. *Current Law* contains references to many tribunal decisions, under appropriate subject headings, and provides a summary for each one. Looseleaf encyclopedias frequently refer to both published and unpublished decisions in the appropriate subject.

The *Industrial Tribunal Reports*, published until 1978, now form part of the *Industrial Cases Reports*. These contain many cases heard by the Employment Appeal Tribunal and many E.A.T. decisions also appear in the *Industrial Relations Law Reports*.

CHAPTER 3

Legislation

3–1 INTRODUCTION

When a Bill (para. 5–5) has been approved by both Houses of Parliament and has received the Royal Assent, it becomes an Act of Parliament. The first printed version of an Act to become available is the copy produced by the Queen's Printer (published by Her Majesty's Stationery Office (HMSO)), and is usually issued within a few days of the Act receiving the Royal Assent.

There are two types of Acts. Public General Acts deal with public policy and apply to the whole population, or a substantial part of it. Local and Personal Acts, on the other hand, affect only a particular area of the country, or a named organisation or group of individuals. This chapter will concentrate on Public General Acts, which you are more likely to use regularly. Local and Personal Acts will, however, be examined in para. 3–19.

3–2 THE STRUCTURE OF AN ACT

A copy of the Forestry Act 1991 is reproduced below. This is an unusually short Act, as most Acts are many pages in length. All Acts are structured in the same way, although some of the parts described below are not included in every Act.

The parts of an Act (see the illustration) are:

1. *Short title;*
2. *Official citation* (see para. 3–3);

The Structure of an Act

---

c. 43

Forestry Act 1991 ①

1991 CHAPTER 43 ②

An Act to increase from nine to twelve the maximum number of members of a regional advisory committee maintained under section 37 of the Forestry Act 1967. ③   [25th July 1991] ④

B E IT ENACTED by the Queen's most Excellent Majesty, by and with the advice and consent of the Lords Spiritual and Temporal, and Commons, in this present Parliament assembled, and by the authority of the same, as follows:— ⑤

1. In subsection (3) of section 38 of the Forestry Act 1967 (composition of regional advisory committees) for the word "nine" there shall be substituted the word "twelve". ⑥

Composition of regional advisory committees.
1967 c. 10.

2.—(1) This Act may be cited as the Forestry Act 1991.

(2) This Act shall come into force at the end of the period of two months beginning with the date on which it is passed. ⑧

(3) This Act shall not extend to Northern Ireland. ⑨

Short title, ⑦ commencement and extent.

---

3. *Long title*. This may give some indication of the purpose and content of the Act;
4. *Date of Royal Assent;*
5. *Enacting formula*. This is a standard form of words indicating that the Act has been approved by Parliament;
6. *Main body of the Act*. This is divided into sections, which are further divided into subsections and paragraphs. When referring to a section, it is usual to abbreviate it to "s." whilst subsections are written in round brackets. You would therefore write section 2, subsection 1 as s.2(1);

7. *Marginal note.* This gives a brief explanation of the contents
   of the section;
8. *Date of commencement.* A specific date may be set for the Act
   to come into force. Alternatively, the Act may give a
   Minister of the Crown the power to bring it into force at a
   later date. This will be done through a commencement
   order, which is a form of delegated legislation. If there is no
   commencement section at the end of an Act, it comes into
   force on the date of the Royal Assent;
9. *Extent.* Acts of Parliament usually apply to the whole of the
   United Kingdom, unless specified otherwise in an extent
   section.

Schedules and Tables are sometimes included at the end of an Act.
They may contain detailed provisions not included elsewhere in
the Act or may summarise and clarify the effect of the Act. They
help to prevent the main body of an Act becoming too cluttered
with detail and are used in the same way as appendices in a book.

3–3 CITATION OF STATUTES

Statutes (or Acts) are commonly referred to by a shortened version
of their title (the short title) and the year of publication, *e.g.* the
Theft Act 1968. Every Act published in a year is given its own
individual number and Acts may also be cited by the year in which
they were passed and the Act (or chapter) number. Thus the Theft
Act was the 60th Act passed in 1968 and is cited as 1968, c. 60.
"Chapter" is abbreviated to "c." when written, but it is spoken in
full.

The present system of citing statutes by their year and chapter
number began in 1963. Before that date, the system was more
complicated. Prior to 1963, statutes were referred to by the year of
the monarch's reign (the "regnal year") and the chapter number.
For example, a citation 3 Edw. 7, c. 36 is a reference to the Motor
Car Act 1903, which was the 36th Act passed in the third year of the
reign of Edward VII.

A session of Parliament normally commences in the autumn
and continues through into the summer of the following year. A
"regnal year" is reckoned from the date of the sovereign's
accession to the throne and a session of Parliament may therefore
cover more than one regnal year. In the case of Queen Elizabeth II,
who came to the throne in February, the first part of a
Parliamentary session, from the autumn until February, falls into
one regnal year, whilst the latter part of the session of Parliament
falls into a different regnal year. Statutes passed before February

bear a different regnal year to those passed after the anniversary of her accession to the throne. Two examples make this clearer:

1. The Children and Young Persons Act 1956 received the Royal Assent in March 1956, when the Queen had just entered the fifth year of her reign. It was the 24th Act to receive the Royal Assent during the Parliament which commenced sitting in the autumn of the fourth year of her reign, and which continued in session during the early part of the fifth year of her reign. The Act is therefore cited as 4 & 5 Eliz. 2, c. 24.
2. By contrast, the Air Corporations Act 1956 was passed during the following session of Parliament and it received the Royal Assent in December 1956, when the Queen was still in the fifth year of her reign. Since, at that time, there could be no certainty that the Queen would still be on the throne in two months' time or that Parliament would still be in session in February, when she would be entering the sixth year of her reign, the statute was cited as 5 Eliz. 2, c. 3 (*i.e.* the third Act passed in the Parliament held in the fifth year of the reign). When the Queen subsequently survived to enter her sixth year, the statute would henceforth be referred to as 5 & 6 Eliz. 2, c. 3.

Both these Acts are to be found in the 1956 volumes of the statutes, which contain all the Acts passed during that year, regardless of the session of Parliament in which they were passed.

Until 1939, the volumes of the statutes contained all the Acts passed in a particular session of Parliament. After that date, the annual volumes contain all the statutes passed in a calendar year. This can give rise to some confusion. For instance, the volume for 1937 contains the statutes passed in the parliamentary session which extended from November 1936 to October 1937. Thus, some Acts which actually bear the date 1936 are included in the 1937 volume. The volume for 1938 includes some statutes passed in December 1937 (which one might normally expect to find in the 1937 volume). The simple rule with older Acts is: if it is not in the volume you expect to find it in, look in the two volumes on either side of it!

Citation of the Names of Monarchs and their Regnal Years   3–4

The names of the monarchs are abbreviated as follows:

Anne	Ann.
Charles	Car., Chas. *or* Cha.
Edward	Edw. *or* Ed.
Elizabeth	Eliz.
George	Geo.
Henry	Hen.
James	Ja., Jac. *or* Jas.
Mary	Mar. *or* M.
Philip and Mary	Ph. & M. *or* Phil. & Mar.
Richard	Ric. *or* Rich.
Victoria	Vict.
William	Will., Wm. *or* Gul.
William and Mary	Wm. & M., Will. & Mar. *or* Gul. & Mar.

A list of the regnal year of monarchs showing the equivalent calendar year is found in *Sweet & Maxwell's Guide to Law Reports and Statutes* (4th ed.), pp. 21–33; in J. E. Pemberton, *British Official Publications* (2nd ed.), pp. 120–125 and at the back of *Osborn's Concise Law Dictionary*.

3–5 MODERN STATUTES

Official copies of the Public General Acts are published individually by HMSO as soon as they receive Royal Assent. The publication of new Acts is recorded in the *HMSO Daily Lists*. The Acts are then gathered together in two official collections: *Public General Acts and Measures* and *Statutes in Force*. Acts are also reprinted in a series called *Law Reports: Statutes*, which is published by the Incorporated Council of Law Reporting, the publisher of the *Law Reports*. In addition, there are three series which reprint the Acts with annotations. These are *Current Law Statutes Annotated*, *Halsbury's Statutes* and *Butterworths Annotated Legislation Service*. Such annotated versions of the statutes can be very helpful, although you should be aware that the notes have no official standing. The full text of Acts in force can also be found on LEXIS (see para. 7–9). The text of the Acts on LEXIS includes any amendments made by subsequent legislation, rather than just reprinting the text found in the Queen's Printer copy.

3–6 Public General Acts and Measures

At the end of the year, all Acts published during the year are bound together to form the official *Public General Acts and Measures of 19 . . .* This series of red volumes has been published since 1831 (originally under the title *Public General Acts*). At the front of the annual volumes will be found a list of all the Acts passed during the year, in alphabetical order, showing where they are to be found in the bound volumes. There is also a chronological list (*i.e.* a list in chapter number order), giving the same information. The General Synod Measures of the Church of England are also printed in full at the back of the annual volumes of the *Public General Acts*. A list of Local and Personal Acts published during the year is printed in the annual volumes, although the texts are not included.

Statutes in Force   3–7

Statutes in Force is an official collection of all Public General Acts of Parliament which are still law. The age of the Act is not important, for so long as it is still law then it is covered in this series. The series is arranged by subject, under broad headings, *e.g.* criminal law, employment. These general headings are further subdivided (*e.g.* criminal law has subdivisions for offences against the person, sexual offences, piracy and the slave trade, etc.). Within each subdivision, the Acts are arranged in date order.

The text of the Act is printed in the form in which it is currently in force: parts of an Act which have been repealed are omitted, and any amendments to an Act (made by subsequent Acts or delegated legislation) are incorporated into the Act as printed. Because it is in looseleaf form, it is possible for it to be kept up to date by the issue of replacement copies of Acts which have been revised. The looseleaf format also allows the subscribers to arrange the publication in several different ways, to suit their own needs. Therefore, the exact location of the *Cumulative Supplements*, referred to below, may vary from library to library. You may find that the *Cumulative Supplements* for each subject are filed at the end of that subject heading, or they may be in a separate set of volumes containing the supplements for all subjects.

Theoretically, *Statutes in Force* should be the first place to turn to for up-to-date information on a particular Act, or to trace all the Acts dealing with a specific subject. Unfortunately, in practice, it is often badly out of date and lacks a proper index. Students may well find it easier to consult *Halsbury's Statutes* (see para. 3–11) in preference to *Statutes in Force*.

How to Use Statutes in Force to Find a Particular Act of Parliament

1. Look at the volume containing the Alphabetical Lists of Groups, Acts and Measures. This is an alphabetical list of all Acts which are wholly or partly in force in the United Kingdom. The information gives the year of the Act, the

chapter number, the group (or subject) number which has been assigned it in *Statutes in Force*, the subject heading and, where there are several subdivisions of the subject, the appropriate subdivision. For example, if we are looking for the Sexual Offences Act 1956, the following entry appears in the Alphabetical List of Acts:

Sexual Offences Act 1956 (c. 69) ... 39 (Criminal Law): 5

This entry tells you that the Sexual Offences Act 1956 is found in group 39 of *Statutes in Force*, under the heading "Criminal Law". Criminal law is subdivided into various subgroups. This Act is printed in subgroup 5.

2: Go to the volumes of *Statutes in Force* and locate group 39, which is entitled "Criminal Law". This is a large subject and there are several volumes containing information on criminal law. Find the volume which contains subgroup 5—"Sexual offences and obscenity". Within the subgroup, the Acts are arranged in date order, from the earliest to the most recent. The text for the Sexual Offences Act 1956 is, at the time of writing of this book, that which was printed in 1978. (The date the text was printed is noted on the title page to the Act.) The text, therefore, incorporates all repeals and amendments made to the Act between 1956 and 1978. Parts of the Act which have been repealed are shown by a row of dots. The illustration on page 49 shows the first page of the text of the Sexual Offences Act 1956, as printed in *Statutes in Force*.

3. We need to find out if there have been any changes to the Act since 1978 (which was when the Act was printed in this series). Turn to the *Cumulative Supplement* and find the entries for group 39, "Criminal Law" subgroup 5, "Sexual offences and obscenity". Under the entries for the Sexual Offences Act 1956 we are informed, section by section, of any changes to the Act since 1978. It is important to see when the *Cumulative Supplement* was published, as it may also be out of date. Look at the title page to the section on "Criminal Law" for the publication date. If the information in the *Cumulative Supplement* is more than a few months old, we need to check for recent changes to the legislation, using another source. Consult *Halsbury's Statutes* (para. 3–11) or the Statute Citator section in the latest issue of the *Current Law Monthly Digest* (para. 3–13) for more up-to-date information.

If you are trying to trace which Acts deal with a particular

Example Page from Statutes in Force

An Act to consolidate (with corrections and improvements made under the Consolidation of Enactments (Procedure) Act 1949) the statute law of England and Wales relating to sexual crimes, to the abduction, procuration and prostitution of women and to kindred offences, and to make such adaptations of statutes extending beyond England and Wales as are needed in consequence of that consolidation.   [2nd August 1956]

PART I

OFFENCES, AND THE PROSECUTION AND PUNISHMENT OF OFFENCES

Intercourse by force, intimidation, etc.

1.—(1) It is felony for a man to rape a woman.   Rape.

(2) A man who induces a married woman to have sexual intercourse with him by impersonating her husband commits rape.

s. 1 amended by Sexual Offences (Amendment) Act 1976 (c. 82), s. 1 (1)

2.—(1) It is an offence for a person to procure a woman, by threats or intimidation, to have unlawful sexual intercourse in any part of the world.   Procurement of woman by threats.

(2) A person shall not be convicted of an offence under this section on the evidence of one witness only, unless the witness is corroborated in some material particular by evidence implicating the accused.

3.—(1) It is an offence for a person to procure a woman, by false pretences or false representations to have unlawful sexual intercourse in any part of the world.   Procurement of woman by false pretences.

(2) A person shall not be convicted of an offence under this section on the evidence of one witness only, unless the witness is corroborated in some material particular by evidence implicating the accused.

4.—(1) It is an offence for a person to apply or administer to, or cause to be taken by, a woman any drug, matter or thing with intent to stupefy or overpower her so as thereby to enable any man to have unlawful sexual intercourse with her.   Administering drugs to obtain or facilitate intercourse.

1

subject, turn to Chapter 6 (para. 6–16), where this is dealt with
more fully.

3–8 Law Reports: Statutes

The Incorporated Council of Law Reporting publishes, as part of
the *Law Reports*, a series entitled *Law Reports: Statutes*. These are
issued in several parts each year, each part containing the text of
one or more Acts. At the end of the year, the loose parts are
replaced by an annual volume or volumes. Unfortunately, the
loose parts are often not published until many months after the
Act receives the Royal Assent. For the text of recent Acts, you will
need to look in other sources, such as *Current Law Statutes
Annotated* or the Queen's Printer version of the Act.

3–9 Current Law Statutes Annotated

Current Law Statutes Annotated reprints the full text of all Public
General Acts soon after they receive the Royal Assent. They are
printed in booklet form on grey paper and are filed into a looseleaf
Service File in chapter number order. The grey paper denotes that
the Act is simply a reprint of the Queen's Printer copy. Some
months later, the Act printed on grey paper is replaced by the
annotated version which is printed on white paper. At the front of
the *Service File* are alphabetical and chronological lists of all the
Acts included. If the Act you want to look at is in *italic* type in the
contents list, it means that it has not yet been published in this
series.

The annotations give a detailed account of the background to
the Act, including references to discussions on the Bill in the
Houses of Parliament as reported in *Hansard*. The annotations also
include a summary of the contents of the Act, as well as definitions
and explanations of the meaning of individual sections of the Act.
The annotations are in smaller print to avoid confusion with the
Act itself. Although the annotations have no official standing, they
are extremely useful. The author is often a leading authority on the
subject matter and some Acts are later reprinted as books by the
publisher, Sweet & Maxwell.

The information in the *Service File* is reissued during the year in
bound volumes. *Current Law Statutes Annotated* covers all Public
General Acts since 1948, when the series commenced publication.
You may find that your library has subscribed to *Scottish Current
Law Statutes Annotated*. Despite the name, this contains
information on English as well as Scottish legislation and the
arrangement is the same as *Current Law Statutes Annotated*.

Butterworth's Annotated Legislation Service 3–10

Butterworth's Annotated Legislation Service was formerly called *Butterworth's Emergency Legislation Service*. It reprints the text of selected Acts, with notes. Many of the volumes cover only one Act, with detailed annotations. Every two years, a *Cumulative Index* volume is published, which lists all the Acts passed since 1939 when the service began, along with a list of Ecclesiastical Measures and certain private Acts. The index indicates where in the volumes to find each Act included in the series. A number of the titles in this series have also been published individually as books, *e.g.* R. M. Goode, *Introduction to the Consumer Credit Act 1974*. The emphasis is on statutes which will be of use to the practitioner.

Halsbury's Statutes of England 3–11

Halsbury's Statutes differs from the other annotated series of statutes. The series outlined above provide annotations to the Acts as they were originally printed. The purpose of *Halsbury's Statutes* is to provide the correct and amended text of all legislation in force, whatever the date of Royal Assent. It includes all Public General Acts in force in England and Wales, although the text of some Acts of limited importance are not printed. The text of each Act is accompanied by notes which provide, for example, judicial interpretation of words and phrases, details of statutory instruments made under the Act, case law and cross-references to other sections.

Halsbury's Statutes is in its fourth edition. The main work consists of 50 volumes, which are arranged alphabetically by subject. Hence, Volume 1 contains the Acts dealing with admiralty, agency and agriculture, whilst Volume 2 contains the law of allotments and smallholdings, animals, arbitration and so on. Legislation post-dating the volumes appears in the *Current Statutes Service* binders. The annual *Cumulative Supplement* summarises and explains the effect of new Acts, statutory instruments and case law on existing legislation and this in turn is kept up to date by a looseleaf *Noter-Up* service.

If you know the name of an Act, the easiest way to find it in *Halsbury's Statutes* is by looking in the Alphabetical List of Statutes in the front of the annual paper-covered *Tables of Statutes and General Index* volume. An example page from the Alphabetical Index is shown on page 52. The entry tells you the volume number (in bold type) and the page number in *Halsbury's Statutes* where you will find the full text of the Act. If the volume number in the Alphabetical List of Statutes is followed by (S), you will find

Example Page from the Alphabetical List of Statutes in Halsbury's Statutes Tables of Statutes and General Index

Example Page from Halsbury's Statutes, Volume 38

Traffic (Consequential Provisions) Act 1988, s 2(2) post, and the Interpretation Act 1978, s 17(2)(*b*), Vol 41, title Statutes, the Motor Vehicles (Driving Licences) Regulations 1987, SI 1987/1378, reg 24(5), has effect for those purposes.

Crown service; exemption for tramcars and trolley vehicles. See the notes to s 87 ante.

Definitions. For "disability", "prospective disability" and "relevant disability", see s 92(2) ante; for "licence", "prescribed", "provisional licence" and "test of competence to drive", see s 108(1) post; as to "class" of vehicle, see s 192(3) post.

95 Notification of refusal of insurance on grounds of health

(1) If an authorised insurer refuses to issue to any person such a policy of insurance as complies with the requirements of Part VI of this Act on the ground that the state of health of that person is not satisfactory, or on grounds which include that ground, the insurer shall as soon as practicable notify the Secretary of State of that refusal and of the full name, address, sex and date of birth of that person as disclosed by him to the insurer.

(2) In subsection (1) above "authorised insurer" means a person or body of persons carrying on insurance business within Group 2 in Part II of Schedule 2 to the Insurance Companies Act 1982 and being a member of the Motor Insurers' Bureau (a company limited by guarantee and incorporated under the Companies Act 1929 on 14th June 1946).

NOTES

Sub-s (1) contains provisions formerly in RTA 1972, s 92(2), as added by RTA 1974, s 13(1), Sch 3, para 7(2). Sub-s (2) contains provisions formerly in RTA 1972, s 145(2) (as amended by RTA 1974, s 20(1), the Insurance Companies Act 1981, s 36(1), Sch 4, Pt II, para 22, and by the Insurance Companies Act 1982, s 99(2), Sch 5, para 12), as applied by RTA 1972, s 92(3) (as added by RTA 1974, s 13(1), Sch 3, para 7(2)).

Part VI of this Act. Ie ss 143–162 of this Act.

Practicable. Cf the note "Reasonably practicable" to s 14 ante.

Secretary of State. See the note to s 8 ante.

Crown service; exemption for tramcars and trolley vehicles. See the notes to s 87 ante.

Insurance Companies Act 1982, Sch 2, Pt II. See Vol 22, title Insurance (Pt 2).

Companies Act 1929. Repealed by the Companies Act 1948, s 459(1), Sch 17. Incorporation of companies is now governed by the Companies Act 1985, Vol 8, title Companies.

96 Driving with uncorrected defective eyesight

(1) If a person drives a motor vehicle on a road while his eyesight is such (whether through a defect which cannot be or one which is not for the time being sufficiently corrected) that he cannot comply with any requirement as to eyesight prescribed under this Part of this Act for the purposes of tests of competence to drive, he is guilty of an offence.

(2) A constable having reason to suspect that a person driving a motor vehicle may be guilty of an offence under subsection (1) above may require him to submit to a test for the purpose of ascertaining whether, using no other means of correction than he used at the time of driving, he can comply with the requirement concerned.

(3) If that person refuses to submit to the test he is guilty of an offence.

NOTES

Sub-s (1) contains provisions formerly in RTA 1972, s 91(1). Sub-ss (2), (3) contain provisions formerly in RTA 1972, s 91(2).

Requirement as to eyesight prescribed . . . for the purposes of tests of competence to drive. See s 89(3), (4) ante. "Prescribed" means prescribed by regulations made under s 105 post; see s 108(1) post. Up to 1 March 1989 no requirement as to eyesight had been prescribed for the purposes of this Part of this Act, but, by virtue of the Road Traffic (Consequential Provisions) Act 1988, s 2(2) post, and the Interpretation Act 1978, s 17(2)(*b*), Vol 41, title Statutes, the Motor Vehicles (Driving Licences) Regulations 1987, SI 1987/ 1378, regs 20, 29, Sch 3, Sch 4, para 1, take effect for that purpose.

This Part of this Act. Ie Pt III (ss 87–109) of this Act.

Example Page from Halsbury's Statutes Cumulative Supplement

PAGE

Road Traffic Act 1988 (c 52)—*continued*

948   **Section 94A**
Inserted by the Road Traffic Act 1991, s 18(3), Vol 38, title Road Traffic.
Exemption for tramcars or trolley vehicles. See the note to s 12 ante.

Section 95
948n   *Exemption for tramcars or trolley vehicles.* See the note to s 12 ante.

Section 96
„   *Requirement as to eyesight prescribed . . . for the purposes of tests of competence to drive.* The Motor Vehicles (Driving Licences) Regulations 1987, SI 1987/1378, reg 20, Sch 3, are substituted by SI 1990/842 and amended (in the case of reg 20) by SI 1992/1318, reg 10, and (in the case of Sch 3) by SI 1992/3090.
The Motor Vehicles (Driving Licences) Regulations 1987, SI 1987/1378, Schs 3, 4, are amended by SI 1991/485, regs 8, 9.
Exemption for tramcars or trolley vehicles. See the note to s 12 ante.

949–   **Section 97**
950   Sub-ss (1) and (3) are amended and repealed in part, and sub-ss (3A) and (3B) are inserted, by the Road Traffic (Driver Licensing and Information Systems) Act 1989, ss 6(2), 7, 16, Sch 3, paras 9, 10, Sch 6, Vol 38, title Road Traffic.
In sub-s (1)(*c*), the words "and its counterpart" are inserted after the words "1st June 1970", and the word "them" is substituted for the word "it", by the Driving Licences (Community Driving Licence) Regulations 1990, SI 1990/144, reg 2(1), Sch 1, para 3.
Sub-s (7) is repealed by the Road Traffic Act 1991, ss 17(3), 83, Sch 8, Vol 38, title Road Traffic.

950n   *Such fee . . . as may be prescribed.* The Motor Vehicles (Driving Licences) Regulations 1987, SI 1987/1378, reg 7 (as substituted), is amended by SI 1990/842, reg 4, SI 1991/2493.
See the Motor Vehicles (Driving Licences) (Large Goods and Passenger-Carrying Vehicles) Regulations 1990, SI 1990/2612, as amended by SI 1991/515, SI 1991/1122, SI 1991/1541, SI 1991/2492, SI 1992/166, SI 1992/538, SI 1992/1356, SI 1992/1761, SI 1992/3089.
Sub-s (3): Prescribed conditions. The Motor Vehicles (Driving Licences) Regulations 1987, SI 1987/1378, reg 9, is amended by SI 1990/2385, reg 3(*b*).
See the Motor Vehicles (Driving Licences) (Large Goods and Passenger-Carrying Vehicles) Regulations 1990, SI 1990/2612, as amended by SI 1991/515, SI 1991/1122, SI 1991/1541, SI 1991/2492, SI 1992/166, SI 1992/538, SI 1992/1356, SI 1992/1761, SI 1992/3089.

951n   *Sub-s (4): Regulations may authorise, etc.* The Motor Vehicles (Driving Licences) Regulations 1987, SI 1987/1378, reg 6, is amended by SI 1990/842, reg 2, Sch 1, para 2.
Sub-s (7): Guilty of an offence. See the note to s 14 ante.
Exemption for tramcars or trolley vehicles. See the note to s 12 ante.

951–   **Section 98**
952   Sub-ss (1)–(4) are amended, and sub-s (4A) is inserted, by the Road Traffic (Driver Licensing and Information Systems) Act 1989, ss 5(10), 7, Sch 3, para 11, Vol 38, title Road Traffic.
In sub-s (1), the word "and" is inserted at the end of para (*b*), and the word "and" preceding para (*d*) is deleted, in sub-s (2), the words "person who holds a licence which", are substituted for the words "licence which, apart from this subsection", and the word "may" is substituted for the words "shall also authorise him to", and in sub-s (3), the words "Subsection (2) above does not", are substituted for the words "A licence shall not by virtue of subsection (2) above", by the Driving Licences (Community Driving Licence) Regulations 1990, SI 1990/144, reg 2(1), Sch 1, para 4.
In sub-s (4A) (as inserted by the Road Traffic (Driver Licensing and Information Systems) Act 1989, s 10(*b*)), the words "Subsection (2) above does

Modern Statutes   55

Example Page from Halsbury's Statutes Noter-Up Service

Vol 38	HALSBURY'S STATUTES FOURTH EDITION NOTER-UP

PAGE

Road Traffic Act 1988 (c 52)—*continued*

Section 41A

879n *Uses; causes or permits . . . to be so used.* See the corresponding note to s 40A ante.

Section 41B

„ *Uses; causes or permits . . . to be so used.* See the corresponding note to s 40A ante.

Section 42

879– *Uses; causes or permits . . . to be so used.* See the corresponding note to s 40A
880n ante.

Section 61

902n *Regulations under this section.* The Motor Vehicles (Type Approval and Approval Marks) (Fees) Regulations 1992, SI 1992/489, are revoked by SI 1993/630.

Add: the Motor Vehicles (Type Approval and Approval Marks) (Fees) Regulations 1993, SI 1993/630 (revoking and replacing SI 1992/489).

Section 80

931n *Regulations under this section.* The Motor Vehicles (Designation of Approval Marks) Regulations 1979, SI 1979/1088, are further amended by SI 1993/1710.

Section 88

938n *Sub-s (5): Regulations.* The Motor Vehicles (Driving Licences) (Large Goods and Passenger-Carrying Vehicles) Regulations 1990, SI 1990/2612, are further amended by SI 1993/1603.

Section 89

941n *Sub-s (3): Regulations.* The Motor Vehicles (Driving Licences) Regulations 1987, SI 1987/1378, are further amended by SI 1993/1602.

The Motor Vehicles (Driving Licences) (Large Goods and Passenger-Carrying Vehicles) Regulations 1990, SI 1990/2612, are further amended by SI 1993/1603.

Section 97

950n *Such fee . . . as may be prescribed.* The Motor Vehicles (Driving Licences) (Large Goods and Passenger-Carrying Vehicles) Regulations 1990, SI 1990/2612, are further amended by SI 1993/1603.

Sub-s (3): Prescribed conditions. The Motor Vehicles (Driving Licences) (Large Goods and Passenger-Carrying Vehicles) Regulations 1990, SI 1990/2612, are further amended by SI 1993/1603.

Section 98

952n *In such cases as the Secretary of State may prescribe.* The Motor Vehicles (Driving Licences) (Large Goods and Passenger-Carrying Vehicles) Regulations 1990, SI 1990/2612, are further amended by SI 1993/1603.

Section 101

956n *Regulations.* The Motor Vehicles (Driving Licences) (Large Goods and Passenger-Carrying Vehicles) Regulations 1990, SI 1990/2612, are further amended by SI 1993/1603.

Section 105

959n *Regulations under this section.* The Motor Vehicles (Driving Licences) Regulations 1987, SI 1987/1378, are further amended by SI 1993/1602.

The Motor Vehicles (Driving Licences) (Large Goods and Passenger-Carrying Vehicles) Regulations 1990, SI 1990/2612, are further amended by SI 1993/1603.

975– **Section 123**
976 In sub-s (7), after the word "licence", in both places where it occurs, there are inserted the words "or certificate", and sub-s (8) is substituted, by the Road Traffic (Driving Instruction by Disabled Persons) Act 1993, s 6, Schedule, para 2, Vol 38(S), title Road Traffic, as from a day to be appointed.

340

the Act printed in the looseleaf *Current Statutes Service* under the volume and page number given. Some Acts are not printed in full in one place, but are divided up, each portion of the Act being printed under the most appropriate subject title. If you want to look at the complete text of an Act which has been split up this way, it may be easier to find the Act in one of the other publications outlined above.

If you want to find the text of a very recent Act, look in the Alphabetical List of Statutes which appears in the first volume of the *Current Statutes Service* under the heading "Contents". The entries give the volume number and page where the text of the Act will be found in the *Current Statutes Service* binders.

Once you have located your Act, either in the main volumes or in the *Current Statutes Service* binders, you will find the official text of the Act. Following each section there are notes, in smaller type, giving the meaning of words or phrases used, referring to cases on the interpretation of that section and providing details of any amendments which have been made to the text of the Act since it was first passed. You will also find references to statutory instruments which have been passed under the authority granted by that Act. At the beginning of each Act, you are informed when it became law and provided with a summary of the main provisions of the Act. An example page from Volume 38 of *Halsbury's Statutes* is shown on page 53.

It is important to check that the information on the Act is still up to date (*i.e.* it has not been amended or repealed). To do this, you will need to consult both the *Cumulative Supplement* and the looseleaf *Noter-up* service.

Let us take an example to see how this works. Suppose you want to know whether there have been changes to the Road Traffic Act 1988 since it was passed. You have looked in the Alphabetical List of Statutes (see p. 52) and found the relevant part of the text of the Act in Volume 38 (see p. 53). To find out if this Act has been amended since Volume 38 was published, turn first to the *Cumulative Supplement* and look at the entries for Volume 38. The *Cumulative Supplement* lists, volume by volume and page by page, changes which have occurred in the law since each of the main volumes was published. There are a number of entries showing changes to the Road Traffic Act 1988 and references are provided to statutory instruments issued under authority granted by the Act (see p. 54).

The information in the *Cumulative Supplement* is up to date to the end of the preceding year. For more recent changes to the Act, you should consult the looseleaf *Noter-up* service under the appropriate volume and page number (see p. 55). This will tell you of any changes in the law in the last few months.

SUMMARY: FINDING UP-TO-DATE INFORMATION ON AN ACT USING HALSBURY'S STATUTES

1. Look for the name of the Act in the Alphabetical List of Statutes in the paper-covered *Table of Statutes and General Index* volume. This will refer you to the appropriate volume (in **bold** type) and page number. An (S) following the volume number refers you to the *Current Statutes Service*.
2. If the Act is more recent than the *Table of Statutes* volume, consult the Alphabetical List of Statutes at the front of Volume 1 of the *Current Statutes Service*.
3. Look up the Act in the appropriate volume, or the *Current Statutes Service*, and note the volume number and the page which contains the relevant information.
4. Look to see if there is an entry for your volume and page number in the *Cumulative Supplement*. If there is an entry, there has been a change in the law. Whether or not there is a relevant entry in the *Cumulative Supplement*, you should now turn to the *Noter-up* service (see below).
5. Finally, look for any entries for your volume and page number in the *Noter-up* service. Read this information (if there is any) in conjunction with the information in the main volume and the *Cumulative Supplement*.

Remember the stages:

main volume;
Cumulative Supplement;
Noter-up service;

and consult them in that order.

CHECKING WHETHER LEGISLATION IS IN FORCE OR   3–12
HAS BEEN AMENDED

The *Cumulative Supplement* and the *Noter-up* service in *Halsbury's Statutes* enable you to find out whether a statute has been repealed or amended (para. 3–11). In addition, *Halsbury's Statutes* also includes an annual paper-covered volume called *Is It In Force?*, which provides a quick alternative method of checking on the current status of any Act passed since 1961. The entry indicates the statutory instruments which brought the Act into force and, where applicable, the legislation through which the Act was repealed. To find out if an Act has recently come into force, consult the *Is It In Force?* update in the *Noter-up* service binder in *Halsbury's Statutes*.

Example Page from the Current Law Legislation Citator 1972–1988

1973   STATUTE CITATOR 1972–88

CAP.

1973—cont.

9. Counter Inflation Act 1973—*cont.*

s. 15, orders 73/662–664, 778, 784, 968, 1786–1789, 1840; 74/543, 775, 776, 840, 933, 1500, 2114, 2115; 75/865, 1294, 1295, 1948, 2209; 76/72, 1172, 1377; 77/1281; 78/1083; 79/60, 178, 568.

s. 23, regs. 77/1222; orders 73/645, 682, 741, 1065, 1717, 1741; 74/380–383, 434, 1030, 1294, 1482, 1924, 1928, 1988; 75/21, 590, 77/1223, 1225.

sch. 1, amended: 1977, c.33, s.1, sch.2; repealed in pt.: 1975, c.24, sch.3; c.25, sch.3; 1977, c.33, s.1, schs.2,3.

sch. 2, orders 73/616, 620, 646, 661, 662, 664, 784, 1786, 1788, 2118; 74/184, 543, 775, 840, 933, 1500, 2114; 75/1294; 76/73; 77/1281.

sch. 3, orders 73/659, 682, 741, 1717, 1741, 1801; 74/380–383, 434, 543, 775, 840, 933, 1030, 1223, 1294, 1482, 1500, 1793, 1924, 1928, 1988, 2114, 2116, 2195; 75/21, 590, 615, 1081, 1294, 1583, 1674, 1947, 2208; 76/496; 77/1225, 1281; 78/1083, 1454; 79/60, 178, 568; regs. 73/621, 660; 77/1222; amended: 1977, c.33, s.14; regs. 77/1220; repealed in pt.: 1977, c.33, sch.3.

sch. 4, orders 73/645, 1065; 77/1223, amended: regs. 77/1220; repealed in pt.: 1977, c.33, schs.2,3; c.42, sch.25.

sch. 5, repealed: 1977, c.42, sch.25.

10. Consolidated Fund (No. 2) Act 1973.
Royal Assent, March 29, 1973.
repealed: 1975, c.44, sch.C.

11. Fire Precautions (Loans) Act 1973.
Royal Assent, March 29, 1973.
s. 1, order 73/1271.

12. Gaming (Amendment) Act 1973.
Royal Assent, April 18, 1973.

→**13. Supply of Goods (Implied Terms) Act 1973.**
Royal Assent, April 18, 1973.
ss. 1–7, repealed: 1979, c.54, sch.3.
s. 3, see *Smith* v. *Park,* 1980 S.L.T. (Sh.Ct.) 62.
s. 4, see *White Cross Equipment* v. *Farrell* (1983) 2 Tr.L. 21, Garland Q.C.
ss. 8, 9, amended: 1974, c.39, sch.4.
s. 10, see *Laurelgates* v. *Lombard North Central* [1983] 133 New L.J. 720, Webster J.
s. 10, amended: 1974, c.39, sch.4; 1982, c.39, s.17.
ss. 10, 12, see *McCann* v. *Patterson* [1984] 16 N.I.J.B., Lord Lowry L.C.J.
s. 11, amended: 1974, c.39, sch.4.
s. 12, see *Robotics* v. *First Co-Operative Finance,* November 1, 1982, Assistant Recorder G. G. Brown, Poole County Ct.
s. 12, amended: 1974, c.39, sch.4; repealed in pt.: 1977, c.50, sch.4.
s. 13, repealed: 1977, c.50, sch.4.
s. 14, repealed in pt.: 1981, c.19, sch.1.
s. 15, amended: 1977, c.50, sch.3; 1979, c.54, sch.3; repealed in pt.: 1977, c.50, sch.4.
s. 17, amended: 1973, c.36, sch.6.
s. 18, repealed in pt.: 1979, c.54, sch.3.

CAP

1973—cont.

14. Costs in Criminal Cases Act 1973.
Royal Assent, April 18, 1973.
repealed: 1985, c.23, sch.2.

s 1, see *R.* v. *Stockport Magistrates' Court, ex p. Cooper* [1984] Crim.L.R. 233, D.C.; *R.* v. *Stafford Stone and Eccleshall Magistrates' Court, ex p. Robinson* [1988] 1 All E.R. 430, Simon Brown J.

s 2, see *R.* v. *Tottenham JJ., ex p. Dwarkados Joshi* [1982] 1 W.L.R. 631, D.C.; *Bunston* v. *Rawlings* [1982] 2 All E.R. 697, D.C.; *Sierzant* v. *Anderton* [1982] Crim.L.R. 823, D.C.; *Neville* v. *Gardner Merchant* (1984) 5 Cr.App.R.(S.) 349, D.C.; *R.* v. *Scunthorpe Justices, ex p. Holbrey, The Times,* May 24, 1985 D.C.; *R.* v. *Nottingham JJ., ex p. Fohmann* (1987) 84 Cr.App.R. 316, D.C.

s 3, see *R.* v. *Michael* [1975] 3 W.L.R. 731; Practice Direction (Costs: Acquittal of Defendants) [1981] 1 W.L.R. 1383, C.A.; *R.* v. *Miller (Raymond)* [1983] 3 All E.R. 186; (1984) 78 Cr.App.R. 71, Lloyd J.; *R.* v. *Maher* (1983) 5 Cr.App.R.(S.) 39, C.A.

ss. 3, 4, see *Sampson, Re, The Independent,* February 12, 1987, H.L.

s. 4, see *R.* v. *Hayden* [1975] 1 W.L.R. 852, C.A.; *R.* v. *Rowe (Frederick)* [1975] R.T.R. 309, C.A.; *R.* v. *Hier* (1976) 62 Cr.App.R. 233, C.A.; *R.* v. *Newlove* [1978] R.T.R. 150, C.A.; *R.* v. *Smith* (1978) 67 Cr.App.R. 332, C.A.; *R.* v. *Mountain; R.* v. *Kilminster* (1978) 68 Cr.App.R. 41, C.A.; *R.* v. *Lewes Crown Court, ex p. Castle* (1979) 70 Cr.App.R. 278, D.C.; *R.* v. *Maher, Barclay, Russell and Sinclair* [1983] 2 W.L.R. 764, C.A; (1983) 5 Cr.App.R.(S.) 39, C.A.

s. 5, see *Cannings* v. *Houghton (No. 2)* [1977] R.T.R. 507, D.C.

s. 7, see *R.* v. *Whitby* (1977) 65 Cr.App.R. 257, C.A.; *R.* v. *Agritraders* [1983] 2 W.L.R. 412, C.A.

s. 9, see *R.* v. *Howitt* (1975) 61 Cr.App.R. 327, C.A.

s 12, see *R.* v. *Bolton JJ., ex p. Wildish* (1983) 147 J.P. 309, D.C.; *Patel* v. *Blakey* [1977] Crim.L.R. 683, D.C.; [1988] R.T.R. 65, D.C.

s. 17, regs. 73/1172, 1745; 74/831, 1580; 75/2067; 77/248, 407, 709, 2069; 84/330.
sch. 1, repealed in pt.: 1988, c.33, sch.16.

15. Administration of Justice Act 1973.
Royal Assent, April 18, 1973.
s 1, repealed in pt.: 1979, c.55, sch.3.
s. 2, amended: *ibid.,* sch.2; repealed in pt.: *ibid.,* sch.3; 1981, c.20, sch.4.
s. 3, repealed: *ibid.*
s. 4, repealed: 1974, c.47, sch.4.
s. 5, substituted: 1979, c.55, sch.2.
s. 7, repealed: 1984, c.28, sch.4.

s 8, see *Centrax Trustees* v. *Ross* [1979] 2 All E.R. 952, Goulding J.; *Habib Bank* v. *Taylor* [1982] 1 W.L.R. 1218, C.A.; *Bank of Scotland* v. *Grimes* [1985] 2 All E.R. 254, C.A.; *Citibank Trust* v. *Ayivor* [1987] 1 W.L.R. 1157, Mervyn Davies J.

In addition to *Halsbury's Statutes*, there are other publications which provide information on whether legislation has been amended or repealed. The *Chronological Table of the Statutes* (described in para. 3–14) is the easiest place to look if you wish to check whether a very old statute is still in force. For up-to-date information, however, the most useful alternative to *Halsbury's Statutes* is the *Current Law Statute Citator*, described in para. 3–13.

Both *Halsbury's Statutes* and *Current Law* are updated monthly. The most up-to-date information is to be found in Lawtel, which provides details of commencements, repeals and amendments to Acts passed in or after 1984. For further information on Lawtel, see para. 7–10. If Lawtel is not available, you can update the information found in *Current Law* or *Halsbury's Statutes* by consulting the weekly practitioners' journals, such as the *New Law Journal* and the *Solicitors' Journal*, or glance through the latest issues of the *HMSO Daily List*.

Current Law Statute Citator   3–13

The *Current Law Statute Citator* enables you to check whether any statute has been repealed, amended or interpreted by the courts since 1947. The *Citator* is divided into several volumes, entitled either *Statute Citator* or *Legislation Citator*. The oldest volume details changes to Acts (of whatever age) taking place between 1947 and 1971. A second bound volume covers changes to Acts taking place between 1972 and 1988, while changes which have happened between 1989 and the end of last year are published in an annual paper-covered volume. For the most recent developments, you will need to look in the Statute Citator section in the most recent issue of the *Current Law Monthly Digest*.

Entries in the *Citators* are arranged by year and chapter number of the legislation and cover Acts which have been altered or amended between the dates mentioned in the title of the *Citator*. The *Statute Citator 1947–1971*, for example, includes Acts as far back as the thirteenth century, provided they were amended or cited in court during the years 1947–1971. The entries indicate which statutes have amended the Act, any statutory instruments which have been made under the Act and any judgments which have interpreted the meaning of the Act. At the front of the *Legislation Citator 1972–1988*, there is an Alphabetical List of Statutes. This is very useful if you are unsure of the year or chapter number of an Act, and wish to locate it in the *Citator*.

The entry from the *Legislation Citator* on page 58 shows that the Supply of Goods (Implied Terms) Act 1973, which was chapter 13 in the Statute Book, received Royal Assent in April 1973. Sections

1–7 of the Act were repealed by the 1979 Act numbered chapter 54. (To find the name of this Act, move forward in the *Citator* to the entries for 1979, and locate chapter number 54 within that year.) The meaning of sections 3 and 4 of the Supply of Goods (Implied Terms) Act 1973 was interpreted in two cases. Sections 8–11 have been amended by subsequent legislation, in 1974. If any statutory instruments had been passed under the Act, the year and the statutory instrument number would be given, preceded by the words "order" or "regs.".

To find any amendments to the Supply of Goods (Implied Terms) Act 1973 since 1988, you would need to look next in the paperback *Legislation Citator* dated 1989 to the end of last year. The entries are ordered in the same way, so look for the year 1973 and then chapter 13 within that year. If there have been any changes, the Act will be included and any amendments outlined.

Finally, you may need to find the latest changes to the Act. Look in the Statute Citator section of the latest issue of the *Current Law Monthly Digest* for changes which have taken place in the current year.

The *Current Law Statute Citator* is a quick and simple way to find current information on the status of an Act. Remember to use the volumes in chronological order, to ensure you do not miss the vital amendment or repeal. Since, however, *Current Law* only covers amendments since 1949, any amendments or repeals to Acts prior to that date must be traced using other sources. The most comprehensive method to trace older amendments or repeals is to use the *Chronological Table of the Statutes*.

3–14   Chronological Table of the Statutes

The *Chronological Table of the Statutes* is an official publication which lists every statute which has been passed since 1235, and shows, for each one, whether it is still law. This is done by the use of different type faces—an entry in *italic* type indicates that the statute in question is no longer law, whilst entries in **bold** type represent Acts which are still wholly or partly in force. The use of a number of abbreviations can make the entries appear a little confusing.

The entries are arranged in date order in the two volumes. Let us suppose that you wish to discover if any part of the Children and Young Persons Act 1956 is still law. Turn to the entries for 1956, and locate the relevant entry (4 & 5 Eliz. 2, c. 24). The entry, which is reproduced on page 61, is printed in *italic* type. This is an indication that the Act is *not* in force. The entry tells us that the

Example Page from the Chronological Table of the Statutes, Part II 1951–1990

CHRONOLOGICAL TABLE OF THE STATUTES   929

1955 (4 & 5 Eliz. 2).
c. 20   ..   *Agriculture (Improvement of Roads).*—**r.** S.L. (Reps.), 1986 (c. 12), s. 1 (1), sch. 1 pt. II.
c. 21   ..   *Diplomatic Immunities Restriction.*—**r.,** Diplomatic Privileges, 1964 (c. 81) s. 8 (4), sch. 2.
c. 22   ..   *E.L.C.*—**r.,** S.L.R., 1963.

1956 (4 & 5 Eliz. 2).
c. 23   ..   *Leeward Islands.*—**r.,** S.L. (Reps.), 1986 (c. 12), s. 1 (1), sch. 1. pt. IX.
➤ c. 24   ..   *Children and Young Persons.*—**r.** (S.) Social Work (S.), 1968 (c. 49), s. 95 (2), sch. 9 pt. I; (E.), Children and Young Persons, 1969 (c. 54), s. 72 (4), sch. 6.
c. 25   ..   **Therapeutic Substances.**
    r. *(prosp.*(exc. s. 1 pt., ss. 2, 8–15, pt. sch. 1)—Medicines, 1968 (c. 67), s. 135 (2), sch. 6.
    s. 1 **r.** in pt.—Medicines, 1968 (c. 67), s. 135 (2), sch. 6.
    4 am.—S.I.s 1968/1699; 1969/388; Biological Standards, 1975 (c. 4), s. 6 (1); S.I. 1988/1843.
    transfer of functions—Biological Standards, 1975 (c. 4), s. 6; S.I. 1988/1843.
    5 transfer of functions—S.I. 1988/1843.
    17 **r.**—N.I., 1962 (c. 30), ss. 7 (9), 30 (2), schs. 1, 4 pt. IV; N.I. Constitution, 1973 (c. 36), s. 41 (1), sch. 6 pt. I.
    sch. 1 am.—S.I.s 1963/1456; 1966/501, 502, 505, 506; 1967/1195.
c. 26   ..   *Police (S.).*—**r.,** Police (S.), 1967 (c. 77), ss. 52 (2), 53, sch. 5 pts. I, II.
c. 27   ..   *Charles Beattie Indemnity.*—**r.,** Representation of the People, 1969 (c. 15), s. 24 (4), sch. 3 pt. I.
➤ c. 28   ..   **Agricultural Research.**
    expld.—Science and Technology, 1965 (c. 4), s. 2 (5).
    s. 1 **r.** (exc. subs. (1))—Science and Technology, 1965 (c. 4), ss. 2 (4), 6 (3), sch. 4.
c. 29   ..   *Dentists.*—**r.,** Dentists, 1983 (c. 38), s. 33 (2), sch. 3 pt. I.
c. 30   ..   **Food and Drugs (S.).**
    r. (1991)—Food Safety, 1990 (c.16), s.59(4), sch.5.
    saved—Trade Descriptions, 1968 (c. 29), s. 2 (5); Agriculture, 1970 (c. 40), s. 25 (5).
    appl.—Weights and Measures, 1985 (c. 72), s. 94 (1).
    s. 1, 2 **r.** in pt.—Medicines, 1968 (c. 67), s. 135 (2), sch. 6.
    3 **r.** in pt.—Medicines, 1968 (c. 67), s. 135 (2), sch. 6; Finance, 1981 (c. 35), s. 139 (6), sch. 19 pt. III, Note I; S.I.1990/1196;
    am.—Alcoholic Liquor Duties, 1979 (c. 4), s. 92 (1), sch. 3 para. 2.
    4 am.—European Communities, 1972 (c. 68), s. 4, sch. 4 para. 3.
    6 am.—Agriculture, 1967 (c. 22), s. 7 (3).
    r. in pt.—Medicines, 1968 (c. 67), s. 135 (2), sch. 6.
    appl. (mod.)—Agriculture, 1970 (c. 40), s. 25 (4).
    7 **r.** in pt.—Weights and Measures, 1963 (c. 31), s. 63 (1), sch. 9 pt. II.
    9 ext.—S.I. 1979/1641.
    appl.(mods.)—S.I.1989/2157.
    11 am.—Transport, 1962 (c. 46), s. 32 sch. 2; Transport, 1968 (c. 73), s. 156 (2), sch. 16 para. 7.
    12 am.—Slaughter of Animals (S.), 1980 (c. 13), s. 23, sch. 1 para. 1.
    16 **r.** in pt.—European Communities, 1972 (c. 68), s. 4, sch. 4 para. 3.
    17 am.—Food and Drugs (Milk), 1970 (c. 3), s. 1 (2).
    r. in pt.—European Communities, 1972 (c. 68), s. 4, sch. 4 para. 3; S.I. 1990/816.
    20 am.—Local Govt. (S.), 1973 (c. 65), s. 214 (1), sch. 27, pt. II para. 121.
    21 am.—Local Govt. (S.), 1973 (c. 65), s. 214 (2), sch. 27 pt. II para. 122.
    r. in pt.—Local Govt. (S.), 1973 (c. 65), ss. 209 (1), 237 (1), sch. 25 para. 27, sch. 29.
    22 am.—Nat. Health Service (S.), 1972 (c. 58), s. 64 (1), sch. 6 para. 95; Nat. Health Service (S.), 1978 (c. 29), s. 109, sch. 15 para. 10.
    r. in pt.—Local Govt. (S.), 1973 (c. 65), ss. 209 (1), 237 (1), sch. 25 para. 28, sch. 29.
    24 am.—Nat. Health Service (S.), 1972 (c. 58), s. 64 (1), sch. 6 para. 96; Nat. Health Service (S.), 1978 (c. 29), sch. 15 para. 10.
    Pts. II, III (ss. 25–51) appl. (mod.)—Weights and Measures &c., 1976 (c. 77), s. 12, sch. 6 para. 3 (2).
    s. 25 **r.**—Local Govt. (Misc. Provns.) (S.), 1981 (c. 23), ss. 30, 41, sch. 4.

[See next page.]

statute was repealed (r.) in respect of Scotland (S.) by the Social Work (Scotland) Act 1968 (c. 49), s.95(2) and Schedule 9, Part I; and in England (E.) the Act was repealed by the Children and Young Persons Act 1969, s.72(4).

The entry for the Agricultural Research Act (4 & 5 Eliz. 2, c. 28) is printed in **bold** type. This indicates that part of this Act is still law, although the entry tells you that most of section 1 was repealed by the Science and Technology Act 1965. A list of the abbreviations used will be found at the front of the volume.

The *Chronological Table* also includes a list of Acts of the Parliament of Scotland 1424–1707, and of Church Assembly Measures, showing if they are still law.

Unfortunately, the *Chronological Table* is usually two or three years out of date. It is updated by the annual publication entitled *The Public General Acts and General Synod Measures: 19 . . .: Tables and Index*, under the heading "Effect of legislation". This shows whether the Acts passed during that year have amended or repealed any previous legislation. Like the *Chronological Table*, the entries in this index are arranged by the date of the original Act, so that it is possible to tell at a glance if there has been any change to a particular statute. The *Public General Acts: Table and Index* is published separately by HMSO and it is also printed at the end of the annual volumes of the *Public General Acts and Measures*.

A quicker method of bringing the information in the *Chronological Table* up to date is to look in the latest *Current Law Statute Citator* (para. 3–13).

3–15 OLDER STATUTES

Through the *Chronological Table of the Statutes*, you will be able to discover whether an Act is still in force. Acts, or sections of Acts, which are in force, whatever their date, can be found in *Halsbury's Statutes* (para. 3–11) and *Statutes in Force* (para. 3–7). However, it will sometimes be necessary to look at an Act of Parliament which is no longer in force and dates back beyond 1831 when the *Public General Acts* series (para. 3–6) was first published. These can be found in the collections described below.

The earliest statute which is still part of the law of the land was passed in 1267. The first parliamentary statute dates from 1235 (the Statute of Merton), although some collections of the statutes commence in 1225. Collections of the legislation prior to 1225 do exist (*e.g.* A. J. Robertson, *The Laws of the Kings of England from Edmund to Henry I*) but they are not regarded as forming part of the statutes of the realm.

Statutes of the Realm 3–16

Produced by the Record Commission, *Statutes of the Realm* is generally regarded as the most authoritative collection of the early statutes. It covers statutes from 1235 to 1713, including those no longer in force, and prints the text of all Private Acts before 1539. There are alphabetical and chronological indexes to all the Acts and there is a subject index to each volume, as well as an index to the complete work.

Statutes at Large 3–17

The title of *Statutes at Large* was given to various editions of the statutes, most of which were published during the eighteenth century. They normally cover statutes published between the thirteenth and the eighteenth or nineteenth centuries.

Acts and Ordinances of the Interregnum 3–18

Acts passed during the Commonwealth are excluded from the collections of the statutes mentioned above. They can be found in C. H. Firth and R. S. Rait, *Acts and Ordinances of the Interregnum 1642–1660*.

LOCAL AND PERSONAL ACTS 3–19

In addition to Public General Acts, which apply to the whole population or a substantial part of it, there are also passed each year a few Local and Personal Acts. These Acts affect only a particular area of the country or a particular individual or body, *e.g.* Penzance Albert Pier Extension Act 1990; Valarie Mary Hill and Alan Monk (Marriage Enabling) Act 1985.

The chapter number of a Local Act is printed in roman numerals, to distinguish it from the Public General Act of the same number. Thus the Penzance Albert Pier Extension Act may be cited as 1990, c. viii (*i.e.* the eighth Local Act passed in 1990), whilst 1990, c. 8 is the citation for a Public General Act, the Town and Country Planning Act.

Personal Acts are cited in the same way as Public General Acts, but with the chapter number printed in italics, *e.g. c. 3*. The citation of Local and Personal Acts was amended in 1963. Prior to that date, they are cited by regnal years, in the same way as Public General Acts, *e.g.* 12 & 13 Geo. 5, c. xiv relates to a Local Act, whilst 12 & 13 Geo. 5, c. 14 is a Public General Act (para. 3–3).

Local and Personal Acts are listed in alphabetical order in the annual *Local and Personal Acts 19 . . .: Tables and Index*, which can also be found in the bound volumes of the *Public General Acts and Measures*. In addition, HMSO has published two cumulative indexes: the *Index to Local and Personal Acts 1801–1947* and the *Supplementary Index to the Local and Personal Acts 1948–1966*.

Although most libraries will possess copies of the Public General Acts in some form, the Local and Personal Acts are not so widely available. Those which are published are listed in the *HMSO Daily Lists*, which are cumulated in the monthly and annual *HMSO Catalogues*. Local Acts since 1992 are printed in the final Volume of *Current Law Statutes Annotated* each year. To obtain a copy of the text of an older Local Act or a Personal Act, you may need to contact the local library or the organisation affected by the legislation.

3–20   STATUTORY INSTRUMENTS

In order to reduce the length and complexity of statutes and increase flexibility in the light of changing circumstances Parliament may include in an Act an "enabling" section, which grants to some other authority (usually a Minister of the Crown) power to make detailed rules and regulations on a principle laid down in general terms by the Act. The various Road Traffic Acts, for example, give the Secretary of State for Transport power, amongst other things, to impose speed limits on particular stretches of road, to vary these limits at any time, to create experimental traffic schemes, to introduce new road signs, to control the construction and use of vehicles and to impose regulations concerning parking, pedestrian crossings, vehicle licences, insurance and numerous other aspects of the law relating to motor vehicles. An advantage of this power is that the rules can be readily changed, without the necessity for Parliamentary debate and approval of every amendment.

Statutory instruments, together with statutory codes of practice and by-laws, form what is called *secondary* or *subordinate* legislation, often also called *delegated* legislation, since Parliament has delegated the power to make this legislation to another authority.

The term *statutory instruments* is a generic one, and includes rules, regulations and orders. Commencement orders are a particularly important type of statutory instrument, since they set the date for the commencement of an Act or bring certain provisions of an Act into force (see point 8 of para. 3–2). Like statutes, statutory instruments may be of general or of purely local interest. Local instruments are not always printed and published in the normal way. An Order of Council, made by the Queen and her Privy Council, is also a form of statutory instrument. These are printed as an appendix to the annual volumes of statutory instruments, together with Royal Proclamations and Letters Patent.

Citation of Statutory Instruments   3–21

Each statutory instrument published during the year is given its own number. The official citation is: S.I. year/number. For example, the Genetically Modified Organisms (Contained Use) Regulations 1993 was the 15th statutory instrument to be passed in 1993 and its citation is therefore S.I. 1993/15.

Statutory instruments typically have a title which includes the word "Rules", "Regulations" or "Order", *e.g.* Rules of the Supreme Court, the Safety of Sports Grounds (Designation) Order, the Registration of Births and Deaths Regulations. If you are undecided whether the document you are seeking is a statutory instrument, check in the Alphabetical List of Statutory Instruments in *Halsbury's Statutory Instruments*.

Tracing Statutory Instruments   3–22

The statutory instruments published each day are listed in the *HMSO Daily Lists*. Every week, a summary of the most important new instruments is printed in the *New Law Journal*. The *Solicitors' Journal*, many specialist journals and *Current Law* all note recent changes in the law which have been brought about by statutory instruments.

A monthly publication called the *List of Statutory Instruments* summarises the statutory instruments published during a particular month, along with alphabetical and numerical lists. A detailed subject index cumulates during the year and an annual *List of Statutory Instruments* replaces the monthly parts.

Individual statutory instruments can be bought from HMSO. In many libraries, these are replaced at the end of the year by a number of bound volumes. The instruments are now printed in these volumes in numerical order, although, until 1961, they were arranged by subject. The last volume of each yearly set contains a subject index to all the instruments published during the year.

All the statutory instruments which were still in force at the end of 1948 were reprinted in a series of volumes entitled *Statutory Rules and Orders and Statutory Instruments Revised*. This was arranged in subject order, showing all the instruments which were then in force.

If your library does not possess a complete set of statutory instruments, you may be able to trace the text of the instrument in *Halsbury's Statutory Instruments* (see para. 3–23) or in one of the many specialist looseleaf encyclopedias, *e.g.* the *Encyclopedia of Housing Law and Practice*. Failing this, a summary may often be found in the *Current Law Year Book* or the *Current Law Monthly Digest* under the appropriate subject heading. There are chronological, alphabetical and subject lists at the beginning of each *Year Book* showing where each instrument appears in the volume. An alphabetical list in the *Monthly Digest* covers statutory instruments digested during the year, with a reference to the relevant *Monthly Digest* issue and paragraph number. Statutory instruments enforcing European legislation are ordered chronologically in another list, which includes a reference to the legislation which the statutory instrument implements and where to find a summary of the instrument in *Current Law*. The annual *Current Law Statutory Instrument Citator* brings together a full list of statutory instruments enforcing European legislation.

The text of statutory instruments can be found also in electronic sources. LEXIS (see para. 7–9) includes the text of statutory instruments in force. Where an instrument has been amended by another instrument, the amended text is included. Statutory instruments from January 1987 can also be found on CD-ROM. The Justis Statutory Instruments CD-ROM (SI-CD) does not amend the statutory instruments like LEXIS, so the text appears as when first published by HMSO, although tables are excluded. SI-CD is updated every six months, so you will not find the most recent statutory instruments here. The advantage of LEXIS and SI-CD over printed sources is the ability to search for any word in the text of a statutory instrument. For more information on full-text searching, refer to para. 7–1.

3–23 Halsbury's Statutory Instruments

Halsbury's Statutory Instruments provides up-to-date information on every statutory instrument of general application in force in England and Wales. It reproduces the text of a selected number and provides summaries of others. The work consists of 22 volumes, in which the statutory instruments are arranged in broad subject categories. The service is kept up to date by two looseleaf *Service* binders containing, in Binder 1, notes of changes in the law and, in Binder 2, the text of selected new instruments.

If you know the year and number of a statutory instrument, the easiest way to locate it in *Halsbury's Statutory Instruments* is through the Chronological List of Instruments in Binder 1.

Example Page from the Consolidated Index and Alphabetical List of Statutory Instruments

Example Page from the Annual Supplement in Binder 1 of Halsbury's Statutory Instruments

VOL 16 REAL PROPERTY (PART 3)

PAGE
339–340—contd
Act, Sch 8, para 3 may make provision with respect to applications for composite licences (as to which see the 1990 Act, s 53 (4)). These provisions take effect partly as from a day to be appointed (see SI 1991/608, in the title Courts (Pt 1)).

The 1985 Act, s 32 has effect as if the reference to conveyancing services included references to advocacy, litigation or probate services, by virtue of the Courts and Legal Services Act 1990, s 53(7)–(9), Sch 8, para 11, partly as from a day to be appointed (see SI 1991/608, in the title Courts (Pt 1)).

PART 4 ESTATE AGENTS

CHRONOLOGICAL LIST OF INSTRUMENTS

PAGE
348—contd

SI	Description	Remarks	Page in Supp
1991/859	Estate Agents (Provision of Information) Regulations 1991	—	16/38
1991/1032	Estate Agents (Undesirable Practices) (No 2) Order 1991	—	16/38
1991/1091	Estate Agents (Specified Offences) (No 2) Order 1991	—	16/39

INSTRUMENTS NO LONGER IN OPERATION

The following instruments, formerly included in this Part of the title, are no longer in operation:

SI		SI		SI		SI
1991/860	revoked by	1991/1091		1991/861	revoked by	1991/1032

NOTER-UP

PAGE
348—Introductory Note. The Property Misdescriptions Act 1991 makes estate agents and others who market property in the course of their business criminally liable for statements about prescribed matters which are false or misleading to a material degree; orders may be made under s 1 thereof prescribing matters to which the offence relates.

For orders under the 1979 Act, s 3 specifying certain undesirable practices and offences, see SI 1991/1032 and 1091 respectively, both summarised post. SI 1991/859, summarised post, is made under s 18(4) of the 1979 Act, which empowers the Secretary of State to require that additional information be given to the clients of persons engaging in estate agency work and to stipulate the time and manner in which that obligation, as well as the obligation to give other information required by s 18, is to be performed.

SUMMARIES

SI 1991
No

859 ESTATE AGENTS (PROVISION OF INFORMATION) REGULATIONS 1991
Authority These regulations were made on 28 March 1991 by the Secretary of State under the Estate Agents Act 1979, s 18(4), and all other enabling powers.
Commencement 29 July 1991.
Summary The Secretary of State is empowered under the Estate Agents Act 1979, s 18(4) to require that additional information be given to clients of persons engaging in estate agency work, and to stipulate the time and the manner in which that obligation, as well as the obligation to give any other information required by s 18, is to be performed. These regulations provide that information as to the services being offered to prospective purchasers be given, and that this information, as well as information about remuneration, be given before the client becomes committed to the estate agent, and that it be given in writing. Further provision is made for the form in which certain terms used by estate agents in connection with their entitlement to remuneration are to be explained and as to the prominence and legibility of those explanations.

1032 ESTATE AGENTS (UNDESIRABLE PRACTICES) (NO 2) ORDER 1991
Authority This order was made on 19 April 1991 by the Secretary of State under the Estate Agents Act 1979, s 3(1)(d), and all other enabling powers.

Alternatively, if you know the name of a statutory instrument, look in the Alphabetical List in the back of the annual paper-covered volume of the *Consolidated Index and Alphabetical List of Statutory Instruments*. You may, for example, be looking for information on the Estate Agents (Provision of Information) Regulations 1991. The relevant page from the Alphabetical List is shown on page 67. The list tells us that the number of the statutory instrument is 859 and that it has been allocated the subject title "Real Property (Part 4)" in *Halsbury's Statutory Instruments*. (Entries in the Chronological List in Binder 1 are displayed in the same way.)

On the inside front cover of each of the main volumes, there is a list of subject titles, indicating in which volume they are printed. "Real Property" is located in Volume 16. Consult the Chronological List of Instruments at the beginning of the section headed "Real Property (Part 4)" in Volume 16. At the time of the writing of this book, S.I. 1991/859 does not appear in this list, and by looking at the title page of the volume, we find that the volume contains only those statutory instruments which became available before December 1, 1989. To find information on instruments published after that date, look in the *Annual Supplement* in Binder 1. The arrangement is the same as in the main volumes. The entry under the heading "Real Property (Part 4)", at the time of writing this book, is shown on page 68. The Chronological List of Instruments at the beginning of the section lists the statutory instrument we want and indicates on which page it can be found. If a line appears instead of a number in the "Page in Supp" column, the statutory instrument described cannot be found in *Halsbury's Statutory Instruments*. S.I. 1991/859 is summarised on the same page. The summary indicates the Act under which the instrument was made and the date the instrument came into force.

Changes subsequent to the *Annual Supplement* are recorded in the Monthly Survey—Key in Binder 1. The Monthly Survey is arranged by subject titles as in the main volumes. Look for the number of the instrument in the "Amendments and Revocations" section in "Real Property (Part 4)". This will tell you if the instrument has been revoked, superseded or amended. The Monthly Survey—Summaries pages in Binder 1 give summaries of the new statutory instruments mentioned in the Key.

An explanation of how to use *Halsbury's Statutory Instruments* to find statutory instruments on a subject is given in para. 6–22.

Example page from the Table of Government Orders 1671–1990

1989

276   *Plant Breeders' Rights (Fees) (Amdt.) Regs.* **r.**, 1990/618
282   **Education (Designated Institutions) O.**
    Sch., Pt. I am., 1989/2055
285   **Zoonoses O.**
286   **Statutory Maternity Pay (Compensation of Employers) and Statutory Sick Pay (Addnl. Compensation of Employers) Amdt. Regs.**
287   *Admin. of Justice Act* 1985 *(Commencement No. 6) O.* spent
288   *Legal Aid Act* 1988 *(Commencement No. 3) O.* spent
289   **Confirmation to Small Estates (S.) O.**
291   **Finance Act 1986 (Stamp Duty Repeals) O.**
292   **Industrial Training Levy (Engineering Bd.) O.**
293   *Insurance (Fees) Regs.* **r.**, 1990/550
294   *Gaming Act (Variation of Fees) O.* **r.**, 1990/386
295   *Lotteries (Gaming Bd. Fees) O.* **r.**, 1990/387
296   **London Regional Transport (Levy) O.**
298   **Teachers (Compensation for Redundancy and Premature Retirement) Regs.** applied with mods., 1989/1139
299   **Crown Ct. (Amdt.) Rules**
300   **Magistrates' Ct. (Amdt.) Rules**
301   *Local Authies. (Allowances) (S.) Amdt. Regs.* **r.**, 1990/1713
302   **Education (Prescribed Courses of Higher Education) (E.) Regs.**
303   **Civil Aviation (Route Charges for Navigation Services) Regs.**
    gen. am., 1989/2257
    reg. 3 am., 1989/2257
        5, 8 replaced, 1989/2257
    sch. 2, 3 replaced, 1989/2257, 1990/2482
304   **London Govt. Reorganisation (Hampstead Heath) O.**
305   *Merchant Shipping (Light Dues) Regs.* **r.**, 1990/364
306   **N.H.S. (Charges to Overseas Visitors) Regs.**
307   **Nat. Assistance (Charges for Accommodation) Regs.**
    reg. 2, 3 am., 1990/498
308   **Education (Nat. Curriculum) (Attainment Targets and Programmes of Study in Mathematics) O.**
309   **Education (Nat Curriculum) (Attainment Targets and Programmes of Study in Science) O.**
317   **Air Quality Standards Regs.**
318   **Control of Industrial Air Pollution (Registration of Works) Regs.**
319   **Health and Safety (Emissions into the Atmosphere) (Amdt.) Regs.**
320   **Goods Vehicles (Plating and Testing) (Amdt.) Regs.**
321   **Motor Vehicles (Tests) (Amdt.) Regs.**
322   **Public Service Vehicle (Conditions of Fitness, Equipment, Use and Certification) (Amdt.) Regs.**
323   *Merchant Shipping (Fees) Regs.* **r.**, 1990/555
324   *Education (Grants) (Royal Ballet School) Regs.* **r.**, 1990/1989
325   **Wireless Telegraphy (Broadcast Licence Charges and Exemption) (Amdt. No. 2) Regs.**
326   **N.H.S. (Charges for Drugs and Appliances) (S.) Regs.**
    reg. 3 am., 1990/468
        7, 8 am., 1990/468
    sch. 1–3 replaced, 1990/468
327   **Registered Housing Assocns. (Accounting Requirements) (Amdt.) O.**
328   *Industrial Assurance (Fees) Regs.* **r.**, 1990/539
329   *Education (Teachers) (Amdt.) Regs.* **r.**, 1989/1319
330   **Prison (Amdt.) Rules**
331   **Young Offenders Institution (Amdt.) Rules**
335   **London Govt. Reorganisation (Pipe Subways) O.**
336   **Water Resources (Licences) (Amdt.) Regs.**

Finding Out whether a Statutory Instrument is Still in Force   3–24

Halsbury's Statutory Instruments collects together all the statutory instruments which are still in force. The information in *Halsbury's* is likely to be more up to date than information provided in other printed sources. Using *Halsbury's Statutory Instruments* to find out if an instrument is in force is described in para. 3–23.

If you know the number of a statutory instrument, you can check whether it is still in force by consulting the *Table of Government Orders*. This is a list, in date order, of all instruments passed since 1671, and it shows, for each one, whether it was still in force when the volume was published. If the entry is in **bold** type, it is wholly or partly in force; if it appears in *italic* type, then the instrument is no longer law. Entries in **bold** type also include any changes to the instrument since 1948 (the text as it stood in December 1948 will be found in *Statutory Rules and Orders and Statutory Instruments Revised*). Full details of the abbreviations used will be found in the introduction to the volumes. The *Table of Government Orders* is produced annually and the information is brought up to date between editions by a *Noter-up* service. An example page is reproduced on page 70.

The *Current Law Statutory Instrument Citator* notes all amendments and revocations during the year indicated on the cover. It also usefully notes whether the instrument has been cited in court during the year. The citator is arranged in year and S.I. number of the instrument. If you are unsure of the year or number there is an alphabetical list of all instruments mentioned in the citator at the front of the volume.

Tracing Statutory Instruments Made Under a Particular Act   3–25

If you know the name of an Act and you wish to find out if any statutory instrument has been made under that Act, you should turn to either *Halsbury's Statutes* (see para. 3–11) or the *Current Law Statute Citator* (see para. 3–13).

The *Index to Government Orders* is an alternative method of finding statutory instruments made under an Act. Consult the Table of Statutes on the green pages at the front of the first volume. This will indicate under which subject heading(s) entries relating to that Act appear in the *Index to Government Orders*. For instance, suppose you wish to trace what instruments were made under the powers conferred by the Local Government Act 1972, s.184(2). The Table of Statutes at the front of the first volume informs you that the powers conferred under this Act are dealt with under the heading "Countryside" section 3. The relevant entry in the *Index to*

Example Page from the Index to Government Orders in Force on December 31, 1989

INDEX TO GOVERNMENT ORDERS 1989

COUNTRYSIDE—*cont.*

1 Preliminary—*cont.*

(3) EXTENSION TO SCILLY ISLES—*cont.*

Power
1981   Secy. of State may, after consultation with Council of Is. of Scilly, by O. by S.I. apply Pts. II, III of Act of 1981 to Is. of Scilly as separate county, subject to any mods.
Wildlife and Countryside Act 1981 (c. 69) s. 68

Exercise
1983/512   Wildlife and Countryside (Is. of Scilly) O.

(4) COMMENCEMENT OF ACT

Power
1981   Secy. of State may by O. by S.I. prescribe date for commct. of Act of 1981
Diff. dates may be prescribed for diff. enactments   Countryside (S.) Act 1981 (c. 44) s. 18 (2)

Exercise
1981/1614   Countryside (S.) Act 1981 (Commct.) O.

(5) PLANNING BOARDS

Power
1972   Secy. of State to make O. reconstituting joint planning bds. constituted by O. under s. 1 of *Town and Country Planning Act 1971* (c. 78) (*see* TOWN AND COUNTRY PLANNING, E. & W., 2) for discharging functions to which Pt. I [planning and countryside functions in Nat. Parks] of sch. 17 to Act of 1972, sch. 1 to Act of 1971 to apply
Local Govt. Act 1972 (c. 70) sch. 17 para. 1
1972   O. under s. 1 of 1971 Act constituting new joint bd. for united district consisting of whole or pt. of Nat. Park may confer on bd. other functions to which Pt. I of sch. 17 to 1972 Act applies
Ibid. sch. 17 para. 2
1972   Secy. of State by O. to reconstitute joint planning bd. for Nat. Park comprised in 2 or more counties, which on 1.4.74 wil be wholly comprised in one county, as special planning bd. to discharge functions to which Pt. I of sch. 17 to Act of 1972 applies. Enactments relating to joint bds. constituted under s. 1 of Act of 1971 to apply .. .. *Ibid.* sch. 17 para. 3
1972   Secy. of State may by O. confer on joint or special planning bds. for Nat. Park, or pt. thereof, additional countryside functions .. .. *Ibid.* sch. 17 para. 4

Exercise
Such O., being classified as local, are not indexed in this work
Parliamentary control *See* LOCAL GOVERNMENT, E. & W., 1 (2)

2 Countryside Commission

Power
1981   Secy. of State may by regs. prescribe etc. terms of holding and vacating office of members of Countryside Commn. Regs. to be by S.I. subject to annulment on resolution of either House
Wildlife and Countryside Act 1981 (c. 69) sch. 13 para. 3

Exercise
Power not yet exercised
Commct. of *Wildlife and Countryside Act 1981* (c. 69) *See* WILDLIFE, 1

3 Access to open country

Power
1949, 1972   Min. may by regs. prescribe scale, manner of describing land, etc., (*a*) of maps for purpose of notification to Min. by county planning authorities of action taken to secure public access; (*b*) of maps to be contained in access orders; (*c*) of maps to be kept by county planning authorities showing land subject to public access; and descriptive matter to be included in access orders
National Parks and Access to the Countryside Act 1949 (c. 97) ss. 63 (1), 65 (3), 78 (1)
Local Government Act 1972 (c. 70) s. 184 (2)

Exercise
1950/1066   National Parks and Access to the Countryside Regs.

Power
1949   Min. may by regs. prescribe manner and time for making applications for compensation for depreciation due to the making of an access order; payment of compensation; recording of claims; rate of interest, etc.   .. National Parks and Access to the Countryside Act 1949 (c. 97) s. 72

Exercise
1950/1066   National Parks and Access to the Countryside Regs.

Government Orders is reproduced on page 73. It is still necessary, however, to use either the *Current Law Statute Citator* or *Halsbury's Statutes* to bring the information in the *Index to Government Orders* up to date.

The most recent information on statutory instruments made under a particular Act is to be found on Lawtel, which is described in para. 7–10. Lawtel lists statutory instruments created since 1984 under the name of the "enabling" Act.

CHAPTER 4

Journals

4–1 TYPES OF JOURNALS

Journals (or periodicals) are important to lawyers: they keep you up to date with the latest developments in the law, and provide comments and criticisms of the law. In your preparations for seminars, essays and moots, it is essential to show that you are aware of what has been written in journals. You cannot rely exclusively on textbooks which are always, to some degree, out of date, and which may provide inadequate information on some topics. You should develop the habit of glancing at the title pages of recently published journals, which are normally kept on a separate display shelf. This will help to keep you up to date with recent cases, statutes, official publications, comments and scholarly articles.

For convenience, we can divide journals into four different types, although there is some overlap between them. However, they are treated similarly in libraries. There are a number of weekly publications, such as the *New Law Journal, Justice of the Peace*, the *Solicitors' Journal* and the *Law Society Gazette*, which aim to keep practitioners and students up to date. They provide reports and comments on recent cases, statutes, statutory instruments and the latest trends and developments in the law, together with some longer articles, usually on topical or practical subjects. In contrast are the academic journals, which are published less frequently. They contain lengthy articles on a variety of topics, comments on recent cases, statutes and government publications, and book reviews. Some examples are the *Law Quarterly Review*, the *Modern Law Review* (six issues a year) and the *Journal of Law and Society* (four issues a year). The third category is the specialist journal dealing with particular aspects of the law. Some specialist journals combine notes of recent developments with longer articles on aspects of that area of the law. Examples of these journals include the *Criminal Law Review* (monthly), *Legal Action* (monthly) and *Family Law* (ten issues a year). Other specialist journals are more like newsletters and are designed as current awareness bulletins for practitioners. These journals (*e.g.* the *Property Law Bulletin, Simon's Tax Intelligence*) are only a few pages in length and summarise and briefly comment on the latest developments. The final category is foreign journals. English language publications, particularly from common law jurisdictions, are of assistance in providing a comparative view of similar United Kingdom issues. Examples of this group are the *Yale Law Journal* (eight issues a year), the *Harvard Law Review* (eight issues a year), the *Canadian Bar Review* (four issues a year) and the *Australian Law Journal* (monthly).

TRACING ARTICLES IN LEGAL JOURNALS   4–2

There are several indexes you can use to find journal articles on a subject or on a particular case, statute or other document. The most relevant indexes are described below. Although you would not need or wish to consult every indexing publication every time you require articles on a topic, you should remember that the information given and the journals covered vary and by using only one index you may miss helpful material.

As an alternative to looking in indexes, you could rely on footnotes in recent books or journal articles which discuss your topic. If the article is well researched, it may give you numerous citations to read. You are likely, however, only to get coverage of those articles which support the view of the author. Using footnotes from key texts is a good way to widen your search for documents on a subject but for the most comprehensive and recent coverage, you must also look in the indexes of journal articles.

Legal Journals Index and European Legal Journals Index   4–3

The *Legal Journals Index* began publication in 1986 and is the most useful source for tracing law articles in British journals. It covers articles from approximately 260 legal journals published in the United Kingdom and is more comprehensive than *Current Law*, the *Index to Legal Periodicals* and other titles mentioned later in this chapter.

Sample entry from Legal Journals Index

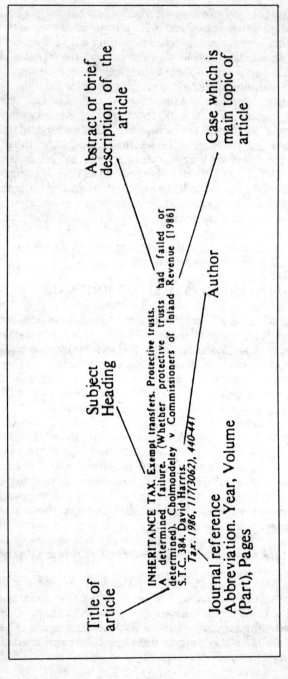

Since the beginning of 1993, articles on E.C. (*i.e.* European Communities) law have been excluded from the *Legal Journals Index* and can be found in a separate publication called the *European Legal Journals Index*. This publication also indexes articles on E.C. law from journals published in other European countries.

The largest section of the *Legal Journals Index* is the subject index. Each article may have been given several subject headings by the indexers and the reference to the article will be printed under each of the headings. The example entry on page 76 is found in the subject index under "Inheritance Tax" in the 1986 volume of the *Legal Journals Index*. The same article could also be found under the headings "Exempt Transfers" and "Protective Trusts". Where the title of the article does not clearly indicate its content, a brief description is added in parentheses.

In addition to the subject index, articles can be located through the separate indexes of authors, names of cases, books reviewed and titles of Acts and other legislation. The case index is particularly useful, since there is a reference from the defendant's name to the entry under the plaintiff: so if you only know the name of the defendant and are therefore unable to trace the case in the *Current Law Case Citators*, this index may enable you to locate it. You may also find commentaries on a case which has not been reported in any of the series of law reports. The entry on page 76, therefore, could not only be located through the three subject headings it was given but under Harris, David in the Author Index and under the names of both parties in the case index of 1986. At the end of the entry, details of where the article is published are given in italics. A list of abbreviations is printed at the front of every issue.

The *Legal Journals Index* and the *European Legal Journals Index* are printed monthly, with quarterly and annual cumulative volumes. The publishers, Legal Information Resources Ltd., also provide the information in electronic format. The database includes not only these two titles, but all the indexes they produce, including the *Financial Journals Index* (pensions, insurance and banking articles) and the index of newspaper law reports, the *Daily Law Reports Index*. You may find the database is stored on a computer and updated fortnightly, or it may be on a CD-ROM, updated every four months.

Current Law   4–4

Current Law commenced in 1947 and entries are arranged by subject (see para. 6–8). At the end of each subject heading in the *Monthly Digest* is a list of recent books and journal articles which have been published on that subject. All the books listed separately under the relevant subject headings are brought together in the list of new books at the back of the issue.

When the *Current Law Year Book* is published, the index to articles is found at the back of the volume. (Before 1956, journal articles were listed at the end of each subject heading.) The *Current Law Year Books* are useful for tracing older articles, but for a full list of recent articles written in British journals it is advisable to consult the *Legal Journals Index* (para. 4–3).

4–5   Index to Legal Periodicals

The *Index to Legal Periodicals*, which commenced in 1908, is published in the United States. It also includes some journals from Britain, Canada, Ireland, Australia and New Zealand. If in doubt about the journals covered, consult the list of periodicals indexed. This list appears in each issue.

Entries are arranged under author and also under the subject, in one single alphabetical sequence. There are separate indexes at the back of each issue which give cases and statutes which have been commented upon in periodical articles, and book reviews. The headings use American terminology and spelling and this may cause occasional difficulties. This is a useful index for overseas commentaries on English law and for information for comparisons of English law with other common law jurisdictions. For recent material relating to U.K. law, however, the *Legal Journals Index* is more comprehensive. A typical subject entry from the *Index to Legal Periodicals* is printed below, with numbered explanations:

CONTRACTS[1]: consideration
Bankers' commercial credits among the High Trees.[2] M. Clarke.[3]
    Camb. L.J. 33: 260–92 N '74[4]
Contract restitution and total failure of consideration.[2] C.P.
    Seepersad.[3] New L.J. 123: 435–8 My 10 '73.[5]

[1] subject heading;
[2] title of article;
[3] author;
[4] article in the *Cambridge Law Journal*, Vol. 33, pp. 260–292 (dated November, 1974);
[5] article in the *New Law Journal*, Vol. 123, pp. 435–438 (dated May 10, 1973).

Since 1983, entries under the authors' names also provide a full reference to the article, similar to the entries under the subject heading, as shown above. The examples above, however, were indexed before 1983 and the author entry therefore appears as:

SEEPERSAD, C.P.[1]
Contracts: consideration[2] (C)[3]
Restitution[2] (C)[3]

[1] author entry for the second of the specimen subject entries (above);
[2] headings under which articles by Seepersad appear;
[3] first letter of first word of the title (*i.e.* Contract ...) of the article. The same article may appear under several subject headings. In this example it occurs under two headings: "Contract" and "Restitution".

A list of the subject headings used in the *Index to Legal Periodicals*, and all of the abbreviations used, is found at the beginning of the volume. It is published 11 times a year. There is a quarterly cumulative edition but these are later replaced by an annual volume containing all the periodical articles for that year.

Index to Foreign Legal Periodicals   4–6

The *Index to Foreign Legal Periodicals* commenced in 1960. It indexes articles on international and comparative law and the municipal law of countries other than the United States, the United Kingdom and the common law of Commonwealth countries. Many of the articles are not in English. The series contains subject, geographical, book reviews and author indexes. Until the end of 1983, publication was in a three-year cycle, at the end of which a cumulative volume was produced. Since 1984, cumulations have been annual. It is also available on CD-ROM.

Legal Resource Index   4–7

The *Legal Resource Index* indexes over 800 legal publications, most of which are American, although a few U.K. journals are included. The index can be accessed online via DIALOG (*i.e.* the database is mounted on DIALOG's computer and can be accessed through telecommunications links. For more information, see para. 7–3.) and LEXIS, or on Legaltrac, the CD-ROM version. Coverage is from 1980.

4–8 Halsbury's Laws

Halsbury's Laws includes a Table of Articles in Binder 2. Only a relatively small range of journals is covered. References to articles are arranged alphabetically by title within broad subject areas. As a result, this is not the easiest way to locate specific articles.

The Table of Articles in Binder 2 is updated by the latest copy of the Monthly Review in Binder 1. The *Monthly Review* summarises changes in the law by broad subject area and new articles are listed at the beginning of each section.

The *Annual Abridgement* to *Halsbury's Laws* includes a Table of Articles. This gives a selection of the journal articles written on a subject during that year. The *Annual Abridgement* replaces the information in the Table of Articles in Binder 2. *Halsbury's Laws* is described in more detail in para. 6–3.

4–9 TRACING LAW-RELATED JOURNAL ARTICLES

The effective study of law will of necessity take you into other disciplines. Articles on subjects such as housing, delinquency, sentencing, families and town and country planning are found in a wide range of journals, many of which are not solely concerned with law and which as a consequence are not usually found in a law collection. You may wish to consult journals which carry articles by sociologists, economists, criminologists, social administrators or historians. To trace social science and arts material on law-related topics, you will need to use a different selection of indexes, most of which will be housed outside the law collection.

4–10 Index to Periodical Articles Related to Law

This index commenced in 1958. It contains a selective coverage of English-language articles not included in the *Legal Journals Index*, the *Index to Legal Periodicals* or the *Index to Foreign Legal Periodicals*. There is an index to articles by subject, a list of journals indexed and an author index. All the entries from 1958 to 1988 have been published in one cumulative volume. Thereafter, the index appears quarterly, with the last issue of the year being an annual cumulation.

4–11 Applied Social Sciences Index and Abstracts

Articles from approximately 550 journals are indexed in one alphabetical subject sequence. ASSIA is aimed at those in practice in the social services, prison services, employment, race relations, etc., and includes articles on many aspects of the law. Although published in Britain, the index covers English-language journals from 16 countries. It commenced in 1987 and is published bi-monthly, with a bound annual cumulation. ASSIA can also be searched electronically, either on CD-ROM or online via Data-Star.

British Humanities Index   4–12

This covers a broad range of subjects and includes articles from British newspapers and popular weekly journals, as well as more scholarly periodicals. Entries are indexed by subject and author. It is printed quarterly with bound annual cumulations. The *British Humanities Index* is also available as a CD-ROM with entries from 1985.

Social Sciences Index   4–13

This index, which replaces the *Social Sciences and Humanities Index*, includes articles on law, criminology, sociology, political science, sociological aspects of medicine and other socio-legal topics. Entries are indexed under authors and subjects. A CD-ROM of the *Social Sciences Index* has been produced and it can also be searched online via Wilsonline.

Criminology and Penology Abstracts   4–14

Detailed subject and author indexes refer to individually numbered entries. The entries themselves are arranged by subject, and include abstracts (*i.e.* summaries) of the articles.

Psychological Abstracts   4–15

The scope of this is far wider than the title suggests, covering abortion, drug use, alcoholism, etc. Entries are arranged by subject and there are detailed subject and author indexes. The publication indexes and summarises articles from over 1,300 journals. Books and book chapters are also indexed. The PsycLIT CD-ROM contains *Psychological Abstracts* from 1974. *Psychological Abstracts* can also be searched online under the name PsycINFO through several services, *e.g.* DIALOG, BRS and Data-Star.

Current Contents: Social and Behavioural Sciences   4–16

This is published weekly and contains the contents pages of recent issues of 1,160 journals in the social and behavioural sciences, including law. The journals are arranged in subject order, with author and "key word" subject indexes. It is available on diskette, updated weekly, and online via BRS.

4–17 The Philosopher's Index

This is a subject and author index with abstracts. Philosophy and inter-disciplinary periodicals and books are indexed. The index from 1940 is also available on CD-ROM. It can be searched online via DIALOG.

4–18 Sociological Abstracts

This abstracting service is indexed by subject and author. It includes sections on the sociology of law, the police, penology and correctional problems. The CD-ROM version is called Sociofile and contains *Sociological Abstracts* from 1974, along with dissertation citations from the SOPODA database. *Sociological Abstracts* is available online via a number of services, including DIALOG and Data-Star.

4–19 Social Sciences Citation Index

The *Citation Index* is so called because, in addition to author and subject indexes to articles, it contains an index of all the footnotes and references given at the end of the articles. As a result, you can find out who has cited an article. This is especially useful if you wish to find the latest articles contributing to a long-running debate in the literature, or if you have found a key article and have traced the footnotes in it, but now wish to find more recent articles.

The printed *Index* is more complicated to search than many of the indexes mentioned above. The *Index* can, however, be searched with more ease electronically. It is available on CD-ROM, online via DIALOG and several other services and through JANET (para 7–5).

These are by no means the only subject indexes to the contents of journals. Indexes exist covering many different subjects. The library staff will help you find out which indexing or abstracting services are available to cover the subjects which interest you.

4–20 NEWSPAPER ARTICLES

In addition to factual reporting, newspapers often contain commentary, analysis and background information on recent legal developments and controversial topics. Some libraries operate a cutting service of articles from the "quality" newspapers such as *The Times* and *The Guardian*, as well as cutting out the law reports. Many libraries keep back copies of newspapers or have them on microfilm. The "quality" newspapers are now also available in full text on CD-ROM, although advertisements and crosswords are usually excluded.

Newspapers such as *The Times* and *The Guardian* publish printed subject indexes. Other indexes, *e.g.* the *Clover Newspaper Index*, cover a range of papers. To find articles from these indexes, you need to know which subject heading to use. The CD-ROMs, on the other hand, will search for a word anywhere in the article and are not dependent on subject headings or titles. Searching "full-text" will therefore give you a more comprehensive result (para. 7–1). Newspapers can also be searched online. FT Profile, for example, provides access to all the quality newspapers in full-text and is updated every day. Many newspapers can also be accessed in full-text or summary form over the Internet (see para. 7–5).

LOCATING JOURNALS IN THE LIBRARY 4–21

Having traced a reference to an article, how do you locate the relevant copy of the journal? The first problem may be to decipher the abbreviation which has been used for the name of the journal. If you obtained your information from a periodical index or from the *Current Law Case Citators*, a list of the abbreviations will be found at the front of the volume. If the information was obtained from elsewhere, *e.g.* from a footnote in a textbook, look up the abbreviation in the *Legal Journals Index*, or D. Raistrick, *Index to Legal Citations and Abbreviations*.

Once the full title of the journal is known, look up the name of the journal in the library's periodicals catalogue. The catalogue entry will guide you to the part of the library in which the journal is to be found, and will indicate which volumes of the journal are available in your library. Law journals are often arranged in alphabetical order (see para. 1–9).

LOCATING JOURNALS FROM OTHER LIBRARIES 4–22

If the journal is not available in your library, you may wish to try to obtain it from elsewhere. Legal periodicals can be traced by consulting the *Union List of Legal Periodicals* (published by the University of London Institute of Advanced Legal Studies), which give the location of journals in libraries throughout the United Kingdom. Similar union lists are published covering more specialised subjects, such as air law literature, West European legal literature, Commonwealth and South African law and United States legal literature. If you wish to consult a large number of journals or reports, it may be more convenient to go to another library and use the material there. Your library may hold information on the periodical holdings of local libraries. Alternatively, most British university library catalogues can be searched through JANET, the computer network which links academic institutions. The librarians will be able to explain how to access other libraries' catalogues and be able to tell you which institutions have included periodicals in their computerised catalogues.

If only a few articles are required, it may be easier to ask your library to obtain them through the inter-library loan service. Details of this service may be obtained from the librarians. If you wish to use this service, plan ahead and allow time for your request to be processed and for the material to arrive.

Legal Information Resources Ltd, the publisher of the *Legal Journals Index*, provides an alternative to the inter-library loan service. The service is also available for commercial organisations unable to use inter-library loans. The price of a photocopied article depends on the number of pages it contains. If you have to pay for inter-library loans, you may find it cheaper, as well as much quicker, to request short articles from Legal Information Resources. Further details can be found at the front of any issue of the *Legal Journals Index*.

CHAPTER 5

Government Publications

INTRODUCTION 5–1

Government publications are notoriously difficult to trace. Some of them are issued by HMSO (Her Majesty's Stationery Office) and thus appear in the official *HMSO Lists*. Other publications are issued directly by government departments, such as the DSS, and cannot readily be traced except through the *Catalogue of British Official Publications Not Published By HMSO*.

In this chapter, we look at those government publications most likely to be encountered by law students, *e.g.*:

Command Papers;
Bills;
House of Commons and House of Lords Papers;
Official Reports of Parliamentary Debates (*Hansard*).

Acts of Parliament, which are, of course, government publications were covered in Chapter 3.

HMSO publishes approximately 9,000 items each year. This represents less than half the vast number of official documents issued annually. HMSO divides publications into two groups: parliamentary publications and non-parliamentary publications.

Parliamentary publications are those documents which are required by Parliament in the course of its work, *e.g.* Bills, records of proceedings in the House and information papers on a wide variety of topics. All parliamentary publications are published by HMSO. Documents other than parliamentary publications, published on behalf of government departments or other official bodies, are called non-parliamentary publications. These items vary considerably and include, for example, public information pamphlets such as the *Highway Code* and directories such as the *Civil Service Yearbook* which lists civil service departments, telephone numbers and names of senior civil servants. Some non-parliamentary publications are published by HMSO, but many are published by the department or organisation itself.

This is a field in which you should not hesitate to seek the advice of library staff whenever you are in difficulty. Most libraries which have a collection of government publications have at least one person who is responsible for helping readers to use this material. For more detailed information on government publications, refer to D. Butcher, *Official Publications in Britain* (2nd ed.).

5–2 PARLIAMENTARY PUBLICATIONS

If your library has a complete collection of parliamentary publications, they may be bound together in volumes containing all the material produced during a particular session of Parliament. These volumes are known as *sessional papers* or *sessional sets*. A Sessional Index provides a subject approach to the material. The sessional papers are also available on microfiche. These are arranged by type of material (Bills, Command Papers, etc.) and then in numerical order within each session.

Libraries with large collections of government publications do not usually enter parliamentary publications in the library catalogues, relying instead on the indexes produced by HMSO (para. 5–14) to trace relevant material. If, however, your library has only a small collection of parliamentary publications, they may be catalogued individually. Libraries with card catalogues usually index these items under the heading "Great Britain".

In many libraries, recent parliamentary publications are gathered together in boxes. Every parliamentary paper has its own individual number and the papers will usually be arranged by these numbers in boxes comprising:

House of Commons Papers;
House of Commons Bills;
House of Lords Papers and Bills;
Command Papers.

These recent publications can also be traced through the various HMSO indexes (para. 5–14). You will probably find that all the parliamentary publications have been housed in an official publications collection, in a separate area of the library (which may not form part of the law library). In some libraries, government publications' collections may be held on microfiche or microfilm. Therefore, you should ask the librarians whether there is a collection of government publications available and get them to show you where they are located and how they are arranged.

Older parliamentary papers may only be available in your library on microfiche or microfilm (para. 5–18) or in the form of reprints published by bodies such as the Irish University Press. (These reprints are arranged in subject order.) If your library does not have a complete collection of older material, it may be possible to trace a summary of a report in the *Breviates of Parliamentary Papers*, produced by P. & G. Ford. Material which is still in print may be purchased from any branch of HMSO (addresses appear on the *Daily Lists* and in the monthly and annual *HMSO Catalogues*) or through any bookseller. Photocopies of out of print publications can be purchased from HMSO. The current cost of new publications is given in the catalogue *HMSO in Print* (on microfiche). Publications may also be available on loan through the inter-library loan service.

We shall now look in more detail at some of the most important types of parliamentary publications and how they are arranged in the library.

Command Papers   5–3

This is a very important category of parliamentary papers and one to which you may frequently be referred. It includes many major government reports, *e.g. The Health of the Nation: a Strategy for Health in England* (1992), some, but not all, of the reports of the Law Commission and the reports of all Royal Commissions. A Command Paper is, as it states on the front cover, presented to Parliament "By Command of Her Majesty." In practice, this means that it is presented to Parliament by a Minister of the Crown on his own initiative; its preparation has not been requested by Parliament. Command Papers are often statements of government policy, which are likely to be the subject of future legislation, or they are presented for the information of the Members of Parliament. Command Papers include:

   statements of government policy (often referred to as *White Papers*);
   some annual statistics and annual reports (many more are issued as non-parliamentary publications);
   reports of Royal Commissions;

reports of some committees (other committee reports may be
issued as non-parliamentary publications);
reports of tribunals of inquiry, *e.g. Report of the tribunal appointed
to inquire into the Vassall Case* (Cmnd. 2009);
state papers (including the Treaty Series—para. 12–7).

5–4   Citation and location of Command Papers
Command Papers are each given an individual number, prefaced
by an abbreviation for the word "command". This abbreviation
and the number are printed at the bottom left-hand corner of the
cover of the report. The numbers run on continuously from one
session of Parliament to another. The present abbreviation "Cm."
has been used for publications issued since 1986. Prior to 1986,
different abbreviations of the word "command" were used. They
are:

1st series 1833–1869	[1]–[4222] (the abbreviation for "Command" was omitted in the first series)
2nd series 1870–1899	[C. 1]–[C. 9550]
3rd series 1900–1918	[Cd. 1]–[Cd. 9239]
4th series 1919–1956	[Cmd. 1]–Cmd. 9889
5th series 1956–1986	Cmnd. 1–Cmnd. 9927
6th series 1986–	Cm. 1–

(The use of square brackets was abandoned in 1922). It is
important to note exactly the form of the abbreviation so that you
have some idea of the date of the report. For instance, Cmd. 6404,
which relates to social insurance and allied services (the Beveridge
Report), is a different item from Cmnd. 6404, which is an
international agreement relating to pensions. One was published
in 1942 and the other in 1976.

If your library keeps all the Command Papers together in boxes
arranged by command numbers, you will have no difficulty in
tracing the report you want. However, if the publications are
arranged by sessions or are bound into sessional sets (see para.
5–2), it will be necessary to have some idea of the date of the
Command Paper. You may find the *Concordance of Command Papers
1833–1972*, which is in J. E. Pemberton, *British Official Publications*
(2nd ed.), pp. 65–66, of help. Occasionally, a report is published
later than the Command Papers with adjoining numbers, with the
result that it appears in a different session of Parliament (and is
therefore in a different sessional set (para. 5–2)). If you know the
Command Paper number of a publication issued before 1979–80
and wish to locate it in the bound sessional sets, first ascertain the

correct session by consulting Pemberton's list or the *HMSO Annual Catalogues* (see para. 5–14). Until the 1979–80 session, Command Papers were not arranged in number order in the sessional sets. They were arranged alphabetically by subject in a sequence with all reports, accounts and papers. To find a Command Paper in the sessional sets before 1979–80 therefore, you need to consult the Sessional Index at the back of the last volume of the session. There you will find a list of Command Paper numbers indicating, for each one, the volume and page within the sessional set where it can be found. Command Papers bound in the sessional sets since 1979–80 can be readily traced under the Command Paper number.

Some Command Papers also form part of another series. For instance, some of the reports of the Law Commission (but not all) are Command Papers: but each Law Commission report also bears its own running number. For convenience, law libraries may keep all Law Commission reports together, regardless of whether they are issued as Command Papers, House of Commons Papers, or non-parliamentary papers (and some of the series have been issued in all these categories). Another major series within the Command Papers are the state papers know as the Treaty Series (para. 12–7). These are Command Papers and each has a number, but, in addition, each has its own Treaty Series number. If they are not bound into the sessional sets, the library may keep all the Treaty Series together. There are separate annual and three- or four-yearly consolidated indexes to the series; in addition, they also appear in the monthly and annual *HMSO Catalogues*. Both the Treaty Series number and the Command Paper numbers are given. In 1970, HMSO published an *Index of British Treaties 1101–1968* (complied by Clive Parry and Charity Hopkins) (see para. 12–14). There are entries under subjects (Volume 1) and by the date of the treaties (Volumes 2 and 3).

Bills   5–5

Bills are the draft versions of Acts, laid before Parliament for its consideration and approval. If your library has a complete collection of parliamentary papers, the Bills will be shelved with this collection; if not, they may be available in the law library. If the library's parliamentary papers are bound up into sessional sets, the Bills will form the first volumes of each set. The most recent Bills are likely to be shelved separately in boxes.

A Bill may be introduced into Parliament by a Member of Parliament (or by a peer) as an independent action (called a Private Member's Bill), or it may be introduced by a Minister as a

Government Bill. Ultimately, however, if it is passed, it becomes a Public General Act whoever introduces it. Private Members' Bills are not always published by HMSO: if not otherwise available, they can usually be obtained by writing directly to the Member of Parliament concerned.

5–6   Stages in the passage of a Bill
Before a Bill can become law, it passes through a number of stages. The exact stage which any Bill has reached on its passage through Parliament can be discovered by consulting the *House of Commons Weekly Information Bulletin* (para. 5–7). A Bill may be introduced into the House of Lords or the Commons. If they commence in the House of Commons, Bills progress through the following stages. Bills fail if they do not pass through all these stages before the end of the parliamentary session.

(i)   *First Reading*—a purely formal reading of the Bill's title by the Clerk of the House; after this, the Bill is printed, a day is fixed for its Second Reading and it becomes available to the public.

(ii)   *Second Reading*—the principles of the Bill are debated. If the Bill fails to gain the approval of the House at this stage, it cannot proceed. The debate is reported in *Hansard* (see para. 5–11).

(iii)   *Committee stage*—the whole House may sit in committee to examine the clauses of a Bill. More usually, the Bill is discussed in a Standing Committee consisting of approximately 20 Members of Parliament. The *Parliamentary Debates: House of Commons: Official Reports of Standing Committees* are published separately from *Hansard*. They are issued daily and each issue covers the discussions on one Bill. The daily copies are later replaced by bound volumes. There are various Standing Committees and when using the unbound copies it is necessary to find out which committee discussed the particular Bill you are interested in. This may be done by looking in the *House of Commons Weekly Information Bulletin* (para. 5–7) or in the monthly and annual *HMSO Catalogues* (para. 5–14) under the heading "House of Commons Papers: Minutes of Proceedings".

(iv)   *Report stage*—if the Bill has been amended by the Standing Committee, this stage gives the House an opportunity to consider the changes. If necessary, the Bill may be referred back to the committee. (If the Bill was debated and approved without amendment in a Committee of the whole House, then this stage is a formality.)

(v) *Third Reading*—a general discussion of the Bill as amended, after which it is passed to the House of Lords for its approval.

(vi) *Lords' stages*—The Bill is reprinted when it is passed to the Lords for their consideration and approval. If the Lords make any amendments, these are referred back to the Commons for their approval. Normally, both Houses must be in agreement on the text before the Bill can receive the Royal Assent. The Parliament Acts 1911 and 1949 provide for certain exceptions to this rule. Finance Bills are the standard exception.

Citation of Bills   5–7

Most Bills submitted to Parliament are printed and placed on sale to the public by HMSO as soon as they are given their first reading. The *House of Commons Weekly Information Bulletin* states if the Bill has been printed. The Bill is given a number, which appears in the bottom left-hand corner of the first page. If the number is printed enclosed in *square* brackets, this indicates that the Bill is a House of Commons Bill, *i.e.* it is at present being considered by the House of Commons. If the number is enclosed in *round* brackets, this indicates a Bill which is at present under consideration by the House of Lords. It is important to notice whether round or square brackets are used, as this will enable you to trace the correct Bill. The initials H.C. or H.L. are used to indicate the two different Houses of Parliament and the parliamentary session is also given. Without this information, it is difficult to trace the Bill. A citation to a Bill therefore gives: the initials of the House; the session of Parliament; the Bill number in round (Lords) or square [Commons] brackets, *e.g.* H.L. Bill 1993–94 (11) Police and Magistrates' Courts Bill; H.C. Bill 1992–93 [130] Education Bill. When Parliament discusses the Bill, some amendments may be incorporated. If these are only minor amendments, this is done by issuing a sheet of paper stating the amended version of the text. This bears the same number as the original Bill but with the addition of a lower case letter, *e.g.* (38a). If a major alteration is made, the complete text of the Bill is reprinted and this reprinted version is given a completely new number. If there have been a number of amendments, a marshalled list of amendments may be published which bears the same number as the original Bill but with the addition of a roman number, *e.g.* [123 II].

Most Bills require the approval of both Houses of Parliament. The Bill is again reprinted, with a new number, when it is passed to the other House for approval. Thus, there may be several versions of the same Bill in the library, and it is often important that you should consult the latest copy, which incorporates all the

Example Page from the House of Commons Weekly Information Bulletin for March 27, 1993

REGISTRATION OF DOMICILIARY CARE AGENCIES   Mr D Hinchliffe
  Y)   Commons: (172)   1R: 24.3   (not printed)

REGULATION OF WHEEL-CLAMPING   Mr J Spellar
  Y)   Commons: (65)   1R: 20.10   (not printed)

REPRESENTATION OF THE PEOPLE (AMENDMENT)   Mr H Barnes
  W6) Commons: (17)   1R: 10.6   2R: 12.2 (deb adjourned)   *P2R: no day named*

RIGHT TO KNOW   Mr M Fisher
  W7) Commons: (18)   1R: 10.6   2R: 19.2   Comm (SC C): 24.3-

ROAD TRAFFIC (AMENDMENT)   Mr K Vaz
  X)   Commons: (137)   1R: 16.2

ROAD TRAFFIC (DRIVING INSTRUCTION BY DISABLED PERSONS)   Sir J Hannam
  W8) Commons: (19)   1R: 10.6   2R: 11.12   Comm (SC D): 3.2   *P Rep: 23.4(1st)*

➤ SEA FISH (CONSERVATION)   Mr J Gummer / Earl Howe   (Government)
  A)   Commons: (10,94)   1R: 22.5   2R: 8.6   Comm (SC D): 18.6-2.7   Remaining stages: 14.7
                 LA: 9.12
       Lords: (28,40,46)   1R: 15.7   2R: 26.10   Comm: 10.11   Rep: 24.11   3R: 3.12
       Royal Assent (cap 60, 1992): 17.12

SECRET SOCIETIES (DECLARATION)   Mr C Mullin
  Y)   Commons: (51)   1R: 1.7

SEXUAL OFFENCES   Mr J Hayes
  W11) Commons: (22)   1R: 10.6   2R: 29.1   Comm (SC F): 17.2   *P Rep: 30.4 (1st)*

SEXUAL OFFENCES (AMENDMENT) Etc.   Mr H Cohen
  Y)   Commons: (66)   1R: 28.10   (not printed)   Bill withdrawn 2.11

SEXUAL OFFENCES (AMENDMENT)   Mr H Cohen
  X)   Commons: (75)   1R: 2.11

SHOPS   Mr J Couchman
  W14) Commons: (25)   1R: 10.6   *P2R: no day named*

SHOPS (AMENDMENT)   Mr R Powell
  W3) Commons: (14, 165)   1R: 10.6   2R: 22.1   MR: 1.3*   Comm (SC C): 3-17.3   *P Rep: 14.5 (2nd)*

SLAUGHTERHOUSES   Dr L Fox
  Y)   Commons: (107)   1R: 16.12   (not printed)

SMALL AIRCRAFT (INSURANCE)   Mr A Coombs
  Y)   Commons: (116)   1R: 20.1   (not printed)

SOCIAL SECURITY   Mr P Lilley / Lord Henley   (Government)
  A)   Commons: (88)   1R: 19.11   2R: 30.11   Remaining stages: 7.12
       Lords: (53)   1R: 8.12   2R: 19.1   Remaining stages: 28.1
       Royal Assent (cap 3, 1993): 28.1

SPORTING EVENTS (CONTROL OF ALCOHOL ETC) (AMENDMENT) [HL]   Lord Dormand of Easington /
  Z)   Lords: (7)   1R: 14.5   2R: 8.6   OCD: 25.6   3R: 6.7*   Mr T Pendry
       Commons: (60)   1R: 14.7   All stages: 20.11*
       Royal Assent (cap 57, 1992): 3.12

TATTOOING (INSURANCE COVER)   Mrs T Gorman
  Y)   Commons: (49)   1R: 30.6   (not printed)

TELEPHONE ENTERTAINMENT SERVICES (SUPERVISION)   Mr T Lewis
  Y)   Commons: (115)   1R: 19.1   (not printed)

TERMINATION OF MEDICAL TREATMENT [HL]   Lord Alport
  Z)   Lords: (70)   1R: 25.2

TOBACCO ADVERTISING   Mr H Bayley
  Y)   Commons: (122)   1R: 27.1   (not printed)

TRADE BOYCOTTS   Mr S Batiste
  X)   Commons: (101)   1R: 9.12   (not printed)

TRADE UNION AND LABOUR RELATIONS (CONSOLIDATION) [HL]   Lord Chancellor / Sir N Lyell
                                            (Government)
  B)   Lords: (9)   1R: 19.5   2R: 2.6*   OCD: 3.6   3R: 11.6*
       Commons: (35)   1R: 11.6   All stages: 14.7*
       Royal Assent (cap 52, 1992): 16.7

amendments. The *House of Commons Weekly Information Bulletin* will indicate which is the latest copy of the Bill.

For instance, the entry on page 92 from the *House of Commons Weekly Information Bulletin* relates to a Government Bill, the Sea Fish (Conservation) Bill, which was introduced into the House of Commons by Mr. Gummer and Earl Howe. The Bill was printed twice during its passage through the Commons—H.C. Bill [10] and H.C. Bill [94], in Parliamentary Session 1992–93. The first version of the Bill to be considered by the House of Lords was H.L. Bill (28); there were later printings H.L. Bill (40) and H.L. Bill (46) incorporating subsequent amendments. The Bill received its First Reading in the House of Commons (1R) on May 22, 1992; after the Second Reading (2R), it was referred to Standing Committee D (Comm. (SC D)) which discussed it between mid-June and early July 1992. The Report stage and Third Reading took place on July 14. The Bill was then passed to the House of Lords, where it went through a similar procedure. After the Commons had considered the Lords' amendments (LA) on December 9, the Bill received the Royal Assent on December 17, 1992 and became law as the Sea Fish (Conservation) Act 1992 (c. 60). (A full list of the abbreviations used will be found in the *House of Commons Weekly Information Bulletin*.) The debates on the Bill will be found in *Hansard* (paras. 5–11, 5–17) on the appropriate dates. The reports of the Debates in Standing Committee are issued separately (para. 5–6).

At the end of each session, a House of Commons Paper entitled *Public Bills: Return of the Number of Public Bills* is published, showing which Bills considered during the session received the Royal Assent and which were dropped, postponed or rejected. The same information is more readily available in the last issue of the *House of Commons Weekly Information Bulletin* published during that parliamentary session, or in the *Sessional Information Digest* produced by the Public Information Office of the House of Commons Library.

Tracing recent Bills   5–8
The number(s) assigned to a recent Bill, and any amendments, can be found by using the latest copy of the *House of Commons Weekly Information Bulletin* (para. 5–7) or by looking through the *HMSO Daily Lists* (para. 5–14). The progress of a Bill can be checked in the latest *House of Commons Weekly Information Bulletin*. If this is unavailable, the *New Law Journal* follows the progress of Bills on the "In Parliament" page in the "The Practitioner" section of the journal. The *Current Law Monthly Digests* give similar information under the heading "Progress of Bills". Bills published a few months ago can be traced in the monthly and annual *HMSO*

Catalogues (para. 5–14), or in the last copy of the *House of Commons Weekly Information Bulletin* published during the appropriate session of Parliament.

The House of Commons Bills will be shelved together. In the case of House of Lords Bills, these may be interfiled with House of Lords papers, for both the papers and the Bills shared the same numerical sequence until session 1987/88, after which they are separately numbered.

Debates on the Bill which take place at the committee stage may be found in the *Official Reports of Standing Committees* (para. 5–6). Debates in the House are reported in *Hansard* (paras. 5–11 and 5–17). When a Bill receives the Royal Assent, this will be noted in publications such as the *House of Commons Weekly Information Bulletin*, the *New Law Journal* and *Current Law*. When the Royal Assent is given, a copy of the Act is printed, and an entry for the Act appears in the relevant *HMSO Daily List*.

5–9   Tracing older Bills

It is not often that you will need to refer to Bills from earlier sessions, for they will either have become law (in which case you should consult the resultant Act) or they will have lapsed. However, when you do need to consult older Bills, if your library has the bound sessional sets available, the text of all the versions of the Bill, together with all amendments, will be found in alphabetical order in the volumes entitled *Bills* at the beginning of the sessional set. If the bound sets are not available, details of all the published versions of the Bill will be found at the beginning of the *HMSO Annual Catalogue* and in the *House of Commons Weekly Information Bulletins* during that session.

5–10   Papers of the House of Lords and House of Commons

Until 1988, the House of Lords Papers and Bills were issued in a common numerical sequence, so the Papers and Bills were integrated. Since then, they have been issued in separate numerical sequences in the same way as the House of Commons Papers are numbered separately from the Commons Bills.

The number of each House of Lords Paper is printed in round brackets at the foot of the front cover. The citation is: H.L. session (paper number), *e.g.* H.L. 1993–94 (7) 1st Report [Session 1993–94]: Enforcement of Community Competition Rules: Report with Evidence—Select Committee on the European Communities.

The Papers of the House of Commons include reports of some committees, together with accounts, statistics and some annual reports which are required by Parliament for its work. The citation of a House of Commons Paper contains the initials H.C., the session and the paper number, *e.g.* H.C. 1992–93 371 is a report by the National Audit Office, *The Administration of Student Loans.*

Parliamentary Debates   5–11

The first semi-official reports of Parliament's debates were published in 1803 by William Cobbett. The man whose name is so closely linked with the publication, *Hansard,* was a subsequent printer of the reports. There have been six series of *Parliamentary Debates, i.e.* first series, 1803–20; second series, 1820–30; third series, 1830–91; fourth series, 1892–1908; fifth series, 1909–1981; sixth series, 1981–present. Since 1909, the *Official Reports of Parliamentary Debates* have been published by the House of Commons itself. The House of Lords Debates have been published separately since 1909; previously, both Lords and Commons Debates were published together.

The *Official Report of Debates (Hansard)* is published daily and the daily issues are later replaced by volumes containing reports of the debates during a parliamentary session, with a Sessional Index. There are also indexes at the back of each individual bound volume. A *Weekly Hansard* (containing all the daily reports, in one issue) is also published, and a fortnightly index to the debates is available.

In *Hansard* each column (rather than each page) is numbered, and references in the index are to column numbers, not page numbers. If, in the index, the column number is followed by a "w" (or, in a pre-1984 index, if the column number is in italics), this is a reference to the written answers which are in a separate sequence at the back of the volume, and not to the column in the Debates which bears that number. (See figures on pp. 97 and 98.) The index contains entries under the names of the Members of Parliament who have spoken, as well as under subjects. The first issue of *Hansard* for each session contains a list of all Members of the House of Commons. Members of the government are listed in each volume.

Hansard is also available on CD-ROM, updated three times during the year. Each disc contains the full text of the debates and oral and written questions during one session, with discs available from the 1988–89 session onwards (see para. 5–17). In addition to providing all the information found in the bound volumes, *Hansard* on CD-ROM also contains a database of Members of Parliament, detailing constituency, party, past and present portfolios and date of entering, and where applicable leaving, Parliament.

5–12   NON-PARLIAMENTARY PUBLICATIONS

These are publications which are not presented to Parliament. The term covers a vast range of government publications, including statutory instruments (para. 3–20). In many libraries, these publications (other than statutory instruments) are entered in the library catalogue. In card catalogues, they are normally indexed under the heading "Great Britain", followed by the name of the government department which produced the publications, *e.g.* Great Britain, Lord Chancellor's Department. Non-parliamentary publications are often scattered around the library according to the subject matter of their content, rather than being kept together as a separate collection.

A large number, but by no means all, of those non-parliamentary publications are published by HMSO. A microfiche collection of non-HMSO items published since 1980 is found in *British Official Publications Not Published by HMSO*, issued by Chadwyck-Healey. Chadwyck-Healey produce a bi-monthly and annual *Catalogue of British Official Publications*, which is also available on the UKOP CD-ROM (para. 5–18). The *Catalogue* covers the publications issued by over 400 bodies, financed or controlled partly or wholly by the government. Examples are the Child Poverty Action Group, the Commission for Racial Equality, the Civil Service, the Director of Public Prosecutions, the Equal Opportunities Commission and the National Consumer Council. The majority of the material found in the *Catalogue* is available in the microfiche collection. In addition, a Keyword Index to the microfiche collection is available on the microfiche, containing entries under all the key words in the title of the publications.

5–13   TRACING GOVERNMENT PUBLICATIONS

5–14   HMSO Catalogues

The *HMSO Daily Lists* (see page 99) are useful for tracing very recent copies of Acts and other recent government publications. The content is divided into parliamentary publications (House of Lords and Commons Papers and Bills, Command Papers, Acts and Debates) and non-parliamentary publications (arranged by the government department producing the report), including statutory instruments. There is also a list of publications by bodies such as the E.C., the U.N. and the WHO, whose publications are sold, but not published, by HMSO.

The *Daily Lists* are replaced (several months later) by the *HMSO Monthly Catalogue*. This contains lists of House of Lords and House

Example Page from the Fortnightly Index to the House of Commons Parliamentary Debates (Hansard)

24th September—30th October 1992

Example Page from the House of Commons Parliamentary Debates (Weekly Hansard)

Expenditure by overnight visitors to Wales[1]

Year	United Kingdom visitors[2] £ million	Overseas visitors £ million
1981	n/a	50
1982	n/a	55
1983	n/a	85
1984	n/a	90
1985	n/a	95
1986	n/a	100
1987	n/a	120
1988	n/a	100
1989	985	120
1990	900	130
1991	900	130

Sources: United Kingdom Travel Survey, International Passenger Survey.

[1] These estimates, derived from sample surveys and thus subject to potential random sampling errors, have been rounded to the nearest £5 million.

[2] Since 1989 information has been obtained from the United Kingdom Tourism Survey (UKTS), sponsored jointly by the statutory tourist boards from England, Scotland, Northern Ireland and Wales. It is not possible to make a direct comparison between the results of this latter survey and those of earlier surveys.

Alcohol Consumption

Mr. Llwyd: To ask the Secretary of State for Wales what assessment he has made of the percentage of young people between the age of 16 to 19 years who drink alcohol at least once a week in each health authority area in Wales.

Mr. Gwilym Jones: The latest available best estimates from the Health Promotion Authority for Wales are as follows:

Estimated percentage drinking alcohol at least weekly by District Health Authority, Wales 16 to 19 year olds, 1990

	Male	Female
Clwyd	58·0	51·5
Dyfed	57·6	53·7
Gwent	61·0	47·7
Gwynedd	66·3	49·7
Mid Glamorgan	66·1	49·2
Powys	58·5	47·7
South Glamorgan	59·8	47·7
West Glamorgan	61·9	57·1
Wales	61·1	50·6

Pregnant Girls

Mr. Llwyd: To ask the Secretary of State for Wales how many girls under 16 years became pregnant in each health authority area in Wales in each year since 1981.

Mr. Gwilym Jones: Data on conceptions are not available at district health authority level. However, the number of conceptions to girls aged under 16 usually resident in Wales, which led to a maternity or were terminated by abortion under the Abortion Act 1967, are presented in the table. Conceptions which led to an illegal or spontaneous abortion are excluded.

	Conceptions (aged under 16)
1981	455
1982	547
1983	558

	Conceptions (aged under 16)
1984	553
1985	577
1986	510
1987	545
1988	536
1989	460
1990	523

Source: Office of Population Censuses and Surveys

Road Safety

Mr. Wigley: To ask the Secretary of State for Wales when he last met representatives of local councils in Wales to discuss levels of provision for road safety measures; and if he will make a statement.

Mr. David Hunt: Local government finance issues are discussed at the Welsh Consultative Council on Local Government Finance, a meeting of which I chaired on 6 July.

Ecstasy

Mr. Llwyd: To ask the Secretary of State for Wales if he will make it his policy to undertake detailed research on the use of MDMA (ecstasy) in Wales.

Mr. Gwilym Jones: Data are currently collected on the incidence of drug misusers presenting for treatment in Wales. A specialist sub-committee of the Welsh Committee for Drug Misuse is already looking at methodologies for undertaking prevalence studies.

Children's Hospital

Mr. Morgan: To ask the Secretary of State for Wales what consultations he has had with the chairmen of Welsh health authorities concerning the provision of a specialist children's hospital for Wales; and if he will make a statement.

Mr. Gwilym Jones: None. I am aware, however, that South Glamorgan health authority has commissioned the King's Fund to assess the feasibility and viability of a proposal to establish a comprehensive child health service providing specialist services to children across Wales.

Bruce Report

Mr. Win Griffiths: To ask the Secretary of State for Wales if he will publish the Bruce report on careers guidance and education.

Sir Wyn Roberts: The review of careers guidance was an internal review carried out by the Employment Department. It is not customary to publish and release internal reviews. The review was taken into account in the consultation exercise which led to proposals for developing careers advice and guidance published in the White Paper "Education and Training for the 21st Century" (Cm. 156, Volume 1, Chapter 7).

Disability

Mr. Wigley: To ask the Secretary of State for Wales if he will publish the latest available figures for the number of disabled people in Wales between the ages of 16 years

Example front page from an HMSO Daily List

Books

DAILY LIST

List no. 12, Wednesday 19th January 1994

PARLIAMENTARY PUBLICATIONS

Issued on 18th January 1994

House of Lords bills - Session 1993-94

(5-II)   **Trade Marks Bill [H.L.]:** 2nd marshalled list of amendments to be moved in committee. – 12p.: 30 cm. – 0 10 872964 8 *£2.85*

(6a)   **British Nationality (Hong Kong) Bill [H.L.]:** amendment to be moved in committee. – 2p.: 30 cm. – 0 10 872994 X *£0.65*

(9-Ia)   **Local Government (Wales) Bill [H.L.]:** amendment to be moved in committee: [supplementary to the marshalled list]. – 2p.: 30 cm. – 0 10 873004 2 *£0.65*

(15a)   **Social Security (Contributions) Bill [H.L.]:** amendments to be moved in committee. – 2p.: 30 cm. – 0 10 873014 X *£0.65*

Parliamentary debates (Hansard)

House of Lords official report. – [5th series]. – ISSN 03098834. – Daily, unrevised
[Session 1993-94] Vol. 551. No. 23. 17 January 1994. – cols. 317-446, WA 37 - WA 42: 30 cm. – 0 10 702394 6 *£4.20 Available on subscription £615.00*

House of Commons papers - Session 1993-94

70-i   **The operation of pension funds:** minutes of evidence Wednesday 1 December 1993. – Social Security Committee. – Frank Field (chairman). – 17p.: tables: 30 cm. – About the estate of the late Robert Maxwell. – 0 10 275894 8 *£5.95*

Parliamentary debates (Hansard)

House of Commons official report. – [6th series]. – ISSN 03098826. – Daily, unrevised
[Session 1993-94] Vol. 235. No. 27. 17 January 1994. – cols. 511-640, 351-402: 30 cm. – 0 10 602794 8 *£7.50 Available on annual subscription £1275.00*

ISSN 0951-8843
HMSO Publications Centre
(Mail and telephone orders only)
PO Box 276, London, SW8 5DT
Telephone orders 071-873 9090
General enquiries 071-873 0011
Enquiries about previously placed orders 071-873 0022
(Queuing system in operation on all numbers)
Enquiries about agency publications 071-873 8372
Telex 297138
Fax (general enquiries) 071-873 8463
Fax (orders only) 071-873 8200
Fax (subscriptions/standing orders only) 071-873 8222
HMSO Prestel lead frame 50040 (orders accepted)
HMSO Bookshops
49 High Holborn, London, WC1V 6HB 071-873 0011
(Counter service only)
258 Broad Street, Birmingham B1 2HE 021-643 3740
Southey House, 33 Wine Street, Bristol, BS1 2BQ
(0272) 264306
9-12 Princess Street, Manchester, M60 8AS 061-834 7201
16 Arthur Street, Belfast, BT1 4GD (0232) 238451
71 Lothian Road, Edinburgh, EH3 9AZ 031-228 4181
Publications may also be ordered through HMSO's accredited agents (see Yellow Pages) or any good bookseller
Posted daily £85.00, posted weekly £50.00

NON PARLIAMENTARY PUBLICATIONS

Board of Inland Revenue

Tax cases reported under the direction of the Board of Inland Revenue: (with notes of argument supplied by the Incorporated Council of Law Reporting).ISSN 01419641. – Irregular
Vol. 63. Part 4. – p. 395-525: 25 cm. – 0 11 729978 2 *Available on subscription only £40.00*

CCTA - the government centre for information systems

Programme and project managment library. ISSN 0967957x.
PRINCE: an outline. – [6], 55p.: 26 cm: – 0 11 330599 0 *£10.00*

Central Statistical Office

Financial statistics.ISSN 0015203X. – Monthly
No. 381. January 1994. – 199p.: chiefly tables: 30 cm. – 0 11 620607 1 *£10.30 Annual subscription £124.00 (1994 rate)*

Prices are liable to change without notice   *Page 1*

of Commons Papers and Bills arranged in numerical order, a list of Command Papers in numerical order (which can be used to trace the title of publications, if you only have the Command Paper number) and a list of Acts published during that month. The second part of the *Catalogue* consists of a list of both parliamentary and non-parliamentary publication, excluding Bills, Acts and Debates, which appear only in the first part of the *Catalogue*. This list is arranged by government departments and includes all items published by each department during that month, with details of their prices and the Command Paper numbers or Lords or Commons Paper numbers (in the case of parliamentary papers). Where the name of the Ministry began with the word "Ministry" or "Department", the entry was formerly inverted, *e.g.* Environment, Department of. Entries now appear under the normal form of the name, *e.g.* Department of the Environment. An index gives entries under the key word of the titles. Statutory instruments are excluded—a separate monthly index is published (para. 3–22). The *Monthly Catalogues* are replaced by an *Annual Catalogue*. Formerly entitled *Government Publications 19 ....*, it is now referred to as the *HMSO Annual Catalogue 19 ....* Every five years, a Consolidated Index was published, *e.g.* 1961–65, 1966–70, 1971–75, 1976–80. In many libraries, the catalogues for these years are bound together. To allow for this, the pagination of the catalogues was continuous over the five-year period.

The annual and five-yearly *Catalogues* contain:

(1) lists of parliamentary publications, arranged by parliamentary session and then in numerical order (by Bill numbers, Commons or Lords Paper numbers and Command Paper numbers);

(2) a classified list of both parliamentary and non-parliamentary publications (excluding Bills, Acts and Debates, which appear only in the first list). The list is arranged by the name of the government department which produced the publication and full details of prices, Command Paper numbers, etc., are given (see figure on p. 102);

(3) a list of periodicals published by HMSO, with prices;

(4) an alphabetical index, with entries under the key words of titles and under the names of authors and chairmen of committees. Statutory instruments are not included; a separate *Annual Catalogue* is published for these. A quarterly microfiche lists *HMSO in Print*. It provides a complete list all HMSO publications, of whatever date, which are currently available in print.

The *HMSO Catalogues* since 1980 are available on the UKOP CD-ROM (para. 5–18). They can also be searched online from 1976 onwards, via DIALOG and BLAISE-LINE (para. 5–18).

Indexes covering longer periods are also available. There is a *General Alphabetical Index to the Bills, Reports and Papers printed by Order of the House of Commons and to the Reports and Papers presented by Command*, covering a 10-year period, *e.g.* 1950–59 (session 1962–63, H.C. 96) and a *General Index 1900–1949*. Indexes and breviates (summaries) of nineteenth century papers also exist.

Tracing Lords and Commons Papers   5–15

If you have the Paper number, the citation (para. 5–10) should include the session, the Paper number, and whether it relates to the Lords or the Commons. If the library has bound the papers into sessional sets the appropriate volume and page can be traced from the Sessional Index. In more recent sessions, the Papers have been arranged in the sessional sets in numerical order.

Tracing Reports if You Know the Chairman   5–16

If you know the name of the chairman of the report but lack further details (except possibly some idea of the subject matter), you should consult:

S. Richard, *British Government Publications: an Index to Chairmen of Committees and Commissions of Enquiry, Vol. I 1800–1899;*

S. Richard, *British Government Publications: an Index to Chairmen and Authors, Vol. II 1900–1940;*

S. Richard, *British Government Publications: an Index to Chairmen and Authors, Vol. III 1941–1978, Vol. IV 1979–1982.*

More recent reports can be traced in the *Index to Chairmen of Committees*, now renamed the *Committee Reports published by HMSO, Indexed by Chairman*. The *HMSO Catalogues* also include entries under chairmen in their indexes.

Tracing Parliamentary Debates   5–17

The last bound volume of the *Parliamentary Debates* for each session contains a Sessional Index. Discussions on a Bill are entered under the name of the Bill. The abbreviations 1R, 2R and 3R indicate the First, Second and Third Readings. There are entries under subject and under the names of Members of Parliament. Until 1984, entries give the volume number in square brackets and

Example Page from the HMSO Annual Catalogue 1991

Land Authority for Wales

Accounts 1990-91: accounts, prepared pursuant to paragraph 3 (1) of schedule 21 to the Local Government, Planning and Land Act 1980, of the Land Authority for Wales for the year ended 31 March 1991, together with the report of the Comptroller and Auditor General thereon. – 12p.: 30 cm. – House of Commons papers 612. – 0 10 261291 9 *£3.40*

Law Commission

5th programme of law reform. – Mr Justice Peter Gibson (chairman). – ii, 4p.: 30 cm. – Cm. 1556. – Law Com. No. 200. – 0 10 115562 x *£1.85*

25th annual report 1990. – Mr. Justice Peter Gibson (chairman). – iv, 35p.: 30 cm. – House of Commons papers 249. – Law Com. no. 195. – 0 10 224991 1 *£6.60*

Consultation paper.

    117. The hearsay rule in civil proceedings. – Mr. Justice Peter Gibson (chairman). – iv, 130p.: 21 cm. – Law Commission working papers have been retitled Consultation papers. – 0 11 730199 x *£6.20*

    118. The law of trusts: delegation by individual trustees. – Mr. Justice Peter Gibson (chairman). – vi, 90p.: 21 cm. – 0 11 730200 7 *£4.80*

    119. Mentally incapacitated adults and decision-making: an overview. – Mr. Justice Peter Gibson (chairman). – viii, 184p.: 21 cm. – 0 11 730201 5 *£6.90*

    120. Restitution of payments made under a mistake of law. – Mr. Justice Peter Gibson (chairman). – vi, 137p.: 21 cm. – 0 11 730202 3 *£5.60*

    121. Privity of contract: contracts for the benefit of third parties. – Mr. Justice Peter Gibson (chairman). – iv, 167p.: 21 cm. – 0 11 730203 1 *£6.50*

Criminal law: corroboration of evidence in criminal trials: report on a reference under section 3 (1) (e) of the Law Commissions Act 1965. – Mr. Justice Peter Gibson (chairman). – iv, 43p.: 30 cm. – Cm. 1620. – Law Com. No. 202. – 0 10 116202 2 *£6.60*

Deer Bill: report on the consolidation of certain enactments relating to deer. – Mr Justice Peter Gibson (chairman of Law Commission). – 7p.: 30 cm. – Cm. 1476. – Law Com. No. 197. – 0 10 114762 7 *£1.90*

Landlord and tenant: distress for rent. – Mr Justice Peter Gibson (chairman). – iv, 72p.: 30 cm. – House of Commons papers 138. – Law Com. No. 194. – 0 10 213891 5 *£9.65*

Rights of suit in respect of carriage of goods by sea. – Mr. Justice Peter Gibson (chairman, Law Commission), The Lord Davidson (chairman, Scottish Law Commission). – vi, 58p.: 30 cm. – House of Commons papers 250. – Scottish Law Com. No. 139. – Law Com. No. 196. – 0 10 225091 x *£8.85*

Social Security Contributions and Benefits Bill: Social Security Administration Bill: Social Security (Consequential Provisions) Bill: report on the consolidation of the legislation relating to social security. – Mr Justice Peter Gibson (chairman of Law Commission), The Lord Davidson (chairman of Scottish Law Commission). – 16p.: 30 cm. – Cm. 1726. – Law Com. No. 203. – Scot. Law Com. No. 132. – 0 10 117262 1 *£3.25*

Transfer of land: implied covenants for title. – Mr Justice Peter Gibson (chairman). – iv, 51p.: 30 cm. – House of Commons papers 437. – Law Com. no. 199. – 0 10 243791 2 *£8.20*

Transfer of land: land mortgages. – Mr Justice Peter Gibson (chairman). – vi, 159p.: 30 cm. – House of Commons papers 5. – 0 10 200592 3 *£15.90*

Transfer of land: obsolete restrictive covenants. – Mr Justice Peter Gibson (chairman). – iv, 40p.: 30 cm. – House of Commons papers 546. – Law Com. No. 201. – 0 10 254691 6 *£7.40*

The Water Resources Bill, the Water Industry Bill, the Statutory Water Companies Bill, the Land Drainage Bill, the Water Consolidation (Consequential Provisions) Bill: report on the consolidation of the legislation relating to water. – Mr Justice Peter Gibson (chairman). – 16p.: 30 cm. – Cm. 1483. – Dated April 1991. – 0 10 114832 1 *£3.60*

Law Society of Northern Ireland

Legal Aid Fund (Northern Ireland): account 1989-90: account prepared pursuant to article 20 (1) of the Legal Aid, Advice and Assistance (Northern Ireland) Order 1981 of the receipts and payments of The Law Society of Northern Ireland paid into and out of the Legal Aid Fund (Northern Ireland) in the year ended 31 March 1990. – [2], 10p.: 30 cm. – House of Commons papers 490. – 0 10 249091 0 *£2.85*

the column number (not the page number). Column numbers in *italic* type refer to the written answers, which are printed separately at the back of each volume.

Entries in more recent Indexes give the volume (in bold) and the column number. A "w" after the column number indicates a written answer. Thus a reference **145** 434–5w refers to Volume 145 of the sixth series, columns 434 and 435 of the written answers (which are found in the back of the volume).

Indexes to the House of Commons Debates are also published fortnightly as part of (but issued separate from) the daily and *Weekly Hansard*. Entries in the fortnightly Indexes (see figure on page 97) omit the volume number. The correct volume or weekly part can be traced through the dates covered by the Index. In addition, the issue numbers of the *Weekly Hansard* covered by the Index are indicated on the front cover of the Index.

The *House of Commons Weekly Information Bulletin* (para. 5–7) will refer you to the relevant dates when debates on a Bill took place. These can then be traced easily in *Hansard*. Remember that debates of Standing Committees are bound separately from *Hansard* (see para. 5–6).

Hansard is now also available on CD-ROM. Each disc contains one complete parliamentary session, the earliest being the 1988–89 session. Searching *Hansard* on CD-ROM is much quicker than using the volumes. You can search for any word or combination of words in any Commons debate, oral or written question or answer, simply by keying them in. If you prefer, you can search for words spoken by a particular Member of Parliament or on a particular day or debate, or any combination of these. The CD-ROM contains the full text of *Hansard*. For those who prefer to read the bound volumes, and also for citation purposes, the CD-ROM provides the volume and column number references to the printed work.

Tracing Publications on a Subject   5–18

Parliamentary and some non-parliamentary publications on a subject can be traced in the daily, monthly, annual and five-yearly *HMSO Catalogues* (see para. 5–14) and in the *General Indexes 1900–1949* and *1950–1959* (see para. 5–14). If the bound sessional sets are available, the Sessional Indexes may be used as an alternative, when searching for parliamentary publications.

Non-parliamentary publications have, in the past, been notoriously difficult to trace. If the item you wish to trace was published by HMSO, you should look in the *HMSO Catalogues*. If it was published elsewhere, look in the *Keyword Index to British Official Publications Not Published by HMSO* (on microfiche) or the annual *Catalogue of British Official Publications Not Published by HMSO*.

In the past few years, tracing government publications on a subject has become easier, with the introduction of new electronic sources of information. The most useful electronic source for finding information on non-parliamentary publications is UKOP, the *Catalogue of United Kingdom Official Publications on CD-ROM*. This CD-ROM, published quarterly, combines the *HMSO Catalogues* since 1980 with Chadwyck-Healey's *Catalogue of British Official Publications Not Published by HMSO*. UKOP allows you to trace both parliamentary and non-parliamentary government publications, whoever the publisher. You can search by subject or title, as well as by many other categories, *e.g.* author, chairman, publication year, session of Parliament, publisher or any combination of these.

HMSO publications from 1976 onwards can be traced online via the DIALOG and BLAISE-LINE services. The database provides more flexibility in searching than the printed *Catalogues*, but since the database is updated monthly, you will still need to use the *HMSO Daily Lists* to find the most recent publications.

Although the *HMSO Daily Lists* are published daily, many libraries choose to have them delivered on a weekly basis. If you need to trace an item which has been published since the latest *Daily List* available, you may be able to access it via the Prestel service. Prestel provides access to the *HMSO Daily Lists* for the current week and is updated daily.

Your library may also be able to access the POLIS database. POLIS the Parliamentary Online Information Service, is run by the House of Commons Library and is designed primarily for Members of Parliament. The database contains references to parliamentary publications and some non-parliamentary publications, with detailed indexing to help you locate information on a subject. The database is updated daily and is therefore one of the most current sources of information on government papers. POLIS was started in 1980 and as a result is excellent for tracing, for example, any Debates or Papers on a subject or a Bill over a number of years. Whereas *Hansard* on CD-ROM provides the full text of House of Commons Debates since 1988, POLIS is still the only electronic means of tracing debates in *Hansard* prior to 1988. POLIS is available as a series of CD-ROM disks. These Justis Parliament CD-ROMs are updated twice a year, and the daily updates can be accessed online.

For research on nineteenth-century material, Chadwyck-Healey have produced a *Subject Catalogue of the House of Commons Parliamentary Papers 1801–1900*. This indexes the microfiche *House of Commons Parliamentary Papers 1801–1900*, which reproduces the text of the documents.

Tracing Statutes, Statutory Instruments and Treaties   5–19

The *Chronological Table of the Statutes* (para. 3–14) and the *Index to the Statutes* (para. 6–18) can be used to trace Acts, and a separate annual *List of Statutes* is also published. Statutory instruments are traced through the monthly and annual *List of Statutory Instruments* (para. 3–22). Treaties are listed in the *HMSO Catalogues*. In addition there are the *Indexes to Treaty Series* (para. 12–8) and the *Index of British Treaties* (para. 12–14). There is also a *sectional list* giving all Treaty Series from 1919. The most recent statutes, statutory instruments and treaties can all be traced through the *HMSO Daily Lists*.

Tracing Law Commission Reports and Working Papers   5–20

Some of the Law Commission reports are published as Command Papers and others are House of Commons Papers, whilst many more are non-parliamentary papers. As a result you may find that in your library they are not all shelved as one collection. Every report and working paper has its own individual number. A complete list of all the reports and working papers which have been published is given in the latest copy of the *Law Commission's Annual Report* (issued as a House of Commons Paper). The list gives the Command Paper number or Paper numbers, where relevant, and indicates, for each report, whether the Commission's proposals for reform have been implemented. Law Commission papers can also be traced through the *HMSO Catalogues* (see figure on p. 102).

Tracing Press Releases   5–21

Government departments use press releases and information memos to inform the media of new developments and initiatives or to give a more detailed commentary on measures already announced. Your library or law firm may subscribe to the press releases of selected departments. Most press releases are single sheets of A4 paper, so are likely to be filed in a ring binder or box.

The HERMES database provides online access to the full text of press releases and announcements from most government departments. It is updated daily and 7,000 releases are added each year. The HERMES database can be accessed through several online computer systems and, in addition, is available as a CD-ROM. The Official Press Release CD-ROM from JUSTIS also includes RAPID, the database of press releases and information memos from the European Community.

Another computerised source of information on press releases is BADGER, created by the producers of the *Legal Journals Index*. BADGER abstracts and indexes selected official press releases and consultative documents, along with other official publications which can otherwise be difficult to trace.

5–22   Tracing Statistics

The government produces a wide range of official statistics. A useful short guide, *Government Statistics: a brief guide to sources*, is produced annually by the Central Statistical Office. Under the heading "Justice and Law", it lists such publications as *Criminal Statistics, England and Wales*, issued annually in the Command Papers series; *Prison Statistics; Offences of Drunkenness; Offences relating to motor vehicles; Statistics on the misuse of drugs; Statistics on the operation of certain police powers under the Police and Criminal Evidence Act*; etc. The Central Statistical Office also issues a more comprehensive *Guide to Official Statistics*. Both are published by HMSO.

CHAPTER 6

How to Find Information on a Subject

INTRODUCTION

It is probable that you will frequently be asked to discover the law relating to a particular topic. Your essays, moots and seminar preparation will often require you to know not simply the present state of the law but also its development and such criticisms and suggestions for reform as have been made.

To find information on a subject you will need to consult some or all of the following sources:

Acts of Parliament;
Delegated legislation;
European Communities legislation, and international Treaties and Conventions;
Cases;
Textbooks;
Journal articles;
Relevant government publications, including Law Commission Reports (especially those which have made suggestions for reform of the law);
Reports and comments in newspapers;
Bills and Parliamentary Debates.

In order to tackle a legal problem, you may need to ask yourself the following questions:

QUESTION: Where can I find a general statement of the law on this subject?
ANSWER: In encyclopedias, such as *Halsbury's Laws* (para. 6–3) and in textbooks (para. 6–25).

QUESTION: What books are there on this subject?
ANSWER: Consult the library catalogue (para. 1–4) and bibliographies (para. 6–26).

QUESTION: What journal articles have been written on this subject?
ANSWER: Consult indexes to journals (para. 4–2).

QUESTION: What cases have there been on this topic?
ANSWER: Use the indexes to the law reports (para. 6–7).

QUESTION: What judicial interpretation has been placed on particular words?
ANSWER: Look in *Words and Phrases Legally Defined* and similar works (para. 6–15).

QUESTION: Which Acts of Parliament deal with this subject and are in force?
ANSWER: Use *Halsbury's Statutes* (para. 6–19) or the *Index to the Statutes* (para. 6–18).

QUESTION: Are there any relevant statutory instruments?
ANSWER: Use the *Index to Government Orders* (para. 6–23) and the *Lists of Statutory Instruments* (para. 6–24) or *Halsbury's Statutory Instruments* (para. 6–22).

QUESTION: Have there been any government reports or Law Commission reports on this topic?
ANSWER: Use the HMSO indexes (para. 5–18) and the *Annual Reports* of the Law Commission (para. 5–20).

QUESTION: Are there any Bills before Parliament which would change the law on this subject? Has the issue been discussed in Parliament?
ANSWER: Consult the *House of Commons Weekly Information Bulletin* (para. 5–7) and *Parliamentary Debates* (paras. 5–11, 5–17).

Having mapped out the ground, you can now proceed to tackle these questions. If you encounter any difficulties in carrying out a search on a legal subject, never be afraid to ask the library staff or your lecturer for help. Remember that other students may also be working on the same subject—start work well within the time limits set, otherwise you may discover that the material is unavailable because of high demand.

LEGAL ENCYCLOPEDIAS   6–2

These contain a detailed up-to-date statement of the law on a particular subject. The major general legal encyclopedia is *Halsbury's Laws of England*, which is now in its fourth edition. It is a most useful source of information on a wide variety of topics. In addition, there are a number of more specialised encyclopedias, many of them issued in looseleaf form, so that the information can be kept up to date.

Halsbury's Laws of England   6–3

This is the major legal encyclopedia. It covers all areas of English law and is a useful starting point for research on any legal topic. Because it is kept up to date, it has the advantage over textbooks of including recent information.

The main body of the work consists of approximately 60 text volumes. The fourth edition was completed in 1987, but there is an ongoing reissue programme to update and reissue those volumes which have been most affected by changes in the law.

Halsbury's Laws provides a straightforward statement of the whole of the law of England and Wales. The volumes are arranged alphabetically by subject, from "Administrative Law" to "Wills", with each volume covering between one and seven subjects. The subjects are divided into numbered paragraphs. Each paragraph gives a description of the law relating to a particular topic, together with copious footnote references to relevant statutes and cases. Remember that *Halsbury's Laws* gives a useful summary of the law: you will need to go to other works to find the actual text of an Act of Parliament or law report.

How to use Halsbury's Laws   6–4
Start by looking up the subject that interests you in the *Consolidated Index* (Volumes 55 and 56). The entry refers you to the appropriate *volume* number (in **bold** type) and *paragraph* number (not page number). The presence of "n" followed by a small number indicates that you are being referred to one of the footnotes at the end of the appropriate paragraph number. Thus the entry for "Body corporate—*meaning*" reproduced on page 111, refers you to Volume 7(1), paragraph 772, footnote 5 for details of the meaning of the term "body corporate". For information on the law related to bomb hoaxes, you would turn to Volume 11(1), paragraph 484.

The relevant page from Volume 11(1) is reproduced on page 112. Paragraph 484 gives a statement of the law relating to bomb hoaxes, together with footnotes which refer you to relevant statutes. *Halsbury's Laws* also refers you to cases and other sources of information, as appropriate.

Remember that it is possible that the information in the volumes is out of date. New legislation, or other changes in the law, could have made the information incomplete or inaccurate. The encyclopedia provides for this possibility. To find out if there have been any changes in the law since the volumes were published, make a note of the relevant volume and paragraph numbers, and turn to the *Cumulative Supplement*. For example, the information on bomb hoaxes was contained in Volume 11(1), paragraph 484. If you turn to the latest *Cumulative Supplement* (only the latest Supplement should be used) and look up the entry for Volume 11(1), paragraph 484, you will find that there have been changes in the law since Volume 11(1) was written. (See figure on p. 113.) It is therefore important to read the information in the *Cumulative Supplement* in conjunction with that found in the main volume.

These two volumes bring the information up to date to the end of last year. But have there been changes in the law since then? To find out, turn to the looseleaf *Noter-up* in Binder 2. The *Noter-up* is arranged in the same way as the *Cumulative Supplement*, in volume and paragraph number.

SUMMARY: HOW TO USE HALSBURY'S LAWS, 4TH ED.

1. Look up the subject in the *Consolidated Index*. This tells you the number of the *volume* and *paragraph* which contains the information.
2. Find the relevant volume and paragraph number in the main work.
3. To make sure the information is up to date, consult:
    (a) the *Cumulative Supplement*, and
    (b) the *Noter-up* in Binder 2, under the relevant volume and paragraph number.

Remember there are four steps in using *Halsbury's Laws*:

Consolidated Index;
Main Work;
Cumulative Supplement;
Noter-up.

At the back of each volume of the main work, there are separate indexes to each of the subject areas dealt with in the volume.

Example Page from Halsbury's Laws, Volume 55 Consolidated Index

Example Page from Halsbury's Laws Volume 11(1) Reissue

2 For the meaning of 'grievous bodily harm' see para 470 text and note 7 ante.
3 Offences against the Person Act 1861 s 31; Penal Servitude Act 1891 s 1 (1); Criminal Justice Act 1948 s 1 (1); Criminal Law Act 1967 s 1.
4 Offences against the Person Act 1861 s 31. As to defence of property see para 457 ante.
5 *Jordin v Crump* (1841) 8 M & W 782 at 786. See also *Wootton v Dawkins* (1857) CBNS 412. Where death is caused by setting such an instrument, the setter is guilty of manslaughter: *R v Heaton* (1896) 60 JP 508.

484. Bomb hoaxes. Any person who (1) places any article[1] in any place whatever, or dispatches any article by post, rail or any other means whatever of sending things from one place to another, with the intention, in either case, of inducing in some other person a belief that it is likely to explode or ignite and thereby cause personal injury or damage to property[2]; or (2) communicates any information which he knows or believes to be false to another person with the intention of inducing in him or any other person a false belief that a bomb or other thing liable to explode or ignite is present in any place or location whatever[3], is guilty of an offence and liable on conviction on indictment to imprisonment for a term not exceeding five years, or on summary conviction to imprisonment for a term not exceeding three months or a fine not exceeding the prescribed sum, or to both[4].

For a person to be guilty of an offence under heads (1) or (2) above, it is not necessary for him to have any particular person in mind as the person in whom he intends to induce the belief there mentioned[5].

1 For these purposes, 'article' includes substance: Criminal Law Act 1977 s 51 (1).
2 Ibid s 51 (1).
3 Ibid s 51 (2).
4 Ibid s 51 (4) (amended by the Magistrates' Courts Act 1980 s 32 (2)). For the meaning of 'the prescribed sum' see para 807 post.
5 Criminal Law Act 1977 s 51 (3). As to threatening to contaminate or interfere with goods see para 193 ante; and as to threatening to destroy or damage property see para 595 post.

(viii) Endangering Railway Passengers

485. Placing wood etc on railway, taking up rails, turning points, showing or hiding signals etc with intent to endanger passengers. Any person who unlawfully and maliciously[1]:

(1) puts or throws upon or across any railway any wood, stone or other matter or thing; or

(2) takes up, removes or displaces any rail, sleeper or other matter or thing belonging to any railway; or

(3) turns, moves or diverts any points or other machinery belonging to any railway; or

(4) makes or shows, hides or removes, any signal or light upon or near to any railway; or

(5) does or causes to be done any other matter or thing,

with intent to endanger the safety of any person travelling or being upon such railway, is guilty of an offence and liable on conviction on indictment to imprisonment for life or for any shorter term[2].

1 For the meaning of 'maliciously' see para 470 text to note 8 ante.
2 Offences against the Person Act 1861 s 32 (amended by the Criminal Justice Act 1948 s 83 (1), Sch 10 Pt I); Criminal Justice Act 1948 s 1 (1). An acquittal on indictment under the Offences against the

Example Page from Halsbury's Laws Cumulative Supplement

471 Unlawful wounding
NOTES—For extended territorial scope of unlawful wounding in connection with acts in relation to or by means of Nuclear Material, see Nuclear Material (Offences) Act 1983, Vol 16, Supp para 415A post.
NOTE 1—As to the direction to be given, see also *R v Rushworth* (1992) 95 Cr App Rep 252, CA.
NOTE 6—*R v Durkin*, cited, reported at (1989) 11 Cr App Rep (S) 313.

475 Administering poison etc
NOTE 4—As to appropriate sentence, see *R v Jones* (1990) 12 Cr App Rep (S) 233, CA (equation of offence with either offence under s 20 (para 471) or serious assault occasioning actual bodily harm (para 490)).

479 Attempting to cause explosion
NOTE 7—See *R v Ellis* (1992) 95 Cr App Rep 52 ("who in the United Kingdom" in the Explosive Substances Act 1883, s 3(1) governs the acts rather than the person and in doing so it creates a geographical limitation on the place where the relevant acts complained of take place).

▶ **484 Bomb hoaxes**
TEXT and NOTE 4—Maximum terms of imprisonment increased to seven years and six months respectively: Criminal Justice Act 1991, s 26(4).

488 Assault and battery
NOTE 6—See *DPP v Taylor; DPP v Little* [1992] 1 ALL ER 299, DC (assault and battery separate statutory offences; information alleging assault and battery contrary to Criminal Justice Act 1988, s 39 therefore bad for duplicity).
NOTE 10—*DPP v K (a minor)*, cited, overruled in *R v Spratt* [1990] 1 WLR 1073, CA, itself disapproved in *R v Savage; R v Parmenter* [1991] 4 All ER 698, HL, para 490 post.

490 Assault occasioning actual bodily harm
NOTE 1—In order to establish the offence of assault occasioning actual bodily harm, it is sufficient to prove that the defendant committed an assault and that actual bodily harm was occasioned by the assault; it is not necessary to prove that the defendant intended to cause some actual bodily harm or was reckless as to whether such harm would be caused: *R v Savage; R v Parmenter* [1991] 4 All ER 698, HL.

493 Kidnapping
TEXT and NOTES 9, 10—Where a count alleging abduction contrary to 1984 Act, s 1 encompasses the allegation against the defendant, inclusion on the indictment of a count alleging kidnapping is to be deprecated: *R v C (Kidnapping: Abduction)* [1991] 2 FLR 252, CA.

494 Consent to assault
NOTES 2, 3—See also *R v Brown* [1992] 2 All ER 552, CA (consent no defence to charge of assault occasioning actual bodily harm where defendants participating in sado-masochistic acts of violence against each other).

495 Marital rights
TEXT and NOTE 2—Marital exemption in respect of rape no longer applies: *R v R (rape: marital exemption)* [1991] 4 All ER 481, HL.

501 Alternative verdicts
NOTE 1—See also *R v Savage; R v Parmenter* [1991] 4 All ER 698, HL (offence of assault occasioning actual bodily harm may be substituted for offence of wounding or causing grievous bodily harm).

502 Effect of summary conviction or dismissal of information
NOTE 5—1973 Act, s 13(4)(a) now ibid, s 1C(1); Criminal Justice Act 1991, Sch 1.

513 Guardianship of victim of incest
TEXT and NOTES—Repealed: Children Act 1989, Sch 12, para 15, Sch 15.

514 Rape
NOTE 4—*R v Khan, R v Dhokia, R v Banga, R v Faiz*, cited, reported: [1990] 2 All ER 783, CA.

515 Husband and wife
TEXT and NOTES 1–4—A husband can now be convicted of raping his wife: *R v R (rape: marital exemption)* [1991] 4 All ER 481, HL.

520 Restrictions on reporting; anonymity of victim of a rape offence
TEXT and NOTES 2–10—In heads (1)(b), (2)(b) for "broadcast or included in a cable programme" read "included in a relevant programme for reception" and for "broadcasting or inclusion in a cable programme" read "inclusion in a relevant programme": 1976 Act, s 4(1); Broadcasting Act 1990, Sch 20, para 26(1)(a). "Relevant programme" means a programme included in a programme service (within the meaning of the 1990 Act; see s 201 and TELECOMMUNICATIONS AND BROADCASTING): 1976 Act, s 4(6); 1990 Act, Sch 20, para 26(1)(d).
As to anonymity of victim of other sexual offences, see paras 520A, 520B post.
NOTE 10—Head (1) omitted: Criminal Justice Act 1988, Sch 16. In head (2) for "broadcast or inclusion in

The last two volumes of *Halsbury's Laws* (Volumes 51–52) are devoted to the law of the European Communities, and its effect upon United Kingdom law. A similar but more sophisticated system of paragraph numbers is used in these two volumes and footnote references refer you to the relevant Directives, Decisions and Regulations of the European Communities. Volume 52 contains a useful glossary of technical terms, as well as a detailed index to both volumes. The information is kept up to date by the information in the *Cumulative Supplement* and *Noter-up*.

The *Monthly Reviews* (published as booklets and filed in Binder 1) can be used as a general means of keeping up with new developments in subjects you are studying since they give, under subject headings, recent changes in the law with summaries of cases, statutes, statutory instruments and other materials. The *Monthly Reviews* are not arranged in the same volume and paragraph order as the main volumes, so in order to find relevant information you will need to look up the subject again in the Cumulative Index to the Reviews at the back of the Binder. The *Monthly Reviews* are replaced by an *Annual Abridgment*, which summarises all the changes in the law during a particular year (commencing in 1974 when the first *Abridgment* appeared). At the beginning of the volume, a section headed "In brief" summarises the major development in the law of each subject during the year. At the beginning of each subject, there is a reference to the main volume of *Halsbury's Laws* which deals with that subject and there is a highly selective list of journal articles written on the subject during the year.

6–5   Specialised Encyclopedias

There are a number of specialised encyclopedias which can provide you with an up-to-date statement of the law in particular subject areas. Many of these are issued in looseleaf format, so that the information can be updated by the insertion of replacement pages whenever there is a change in the law. The looseleaf *Encyclopedia of Planning Law and Practice*, published by Sweet & Maxwell, is an example. It is part of the series called "The Local Government Library," which also includes works on topics such as housing, environmental law and health and safety at work. A number of other publishers have issued similar works covering, for example, social welfare law (Longmans), landlord and tenant (Butterworths) and company law (CCH). Looseleaf encyclopedias are particularly useful in subjects such as taxation, where the law changes very rapidly. Before using a looseleaf encyclopedia, you should check the pages near the beginning of the volume which tell you how recent the information is. This will enable you to be certain that the latest supplementary pages have all been inserted. Looseleaf encyclopedias usually contain an explanation of the law, together with the up-to-date versions of the relevant statutes, statutory instruments and government circulars, and notes of relevant cases. Publishers are now issuing some practitioners' books, such as *Ruoff and Roper on Registered Conveyancing*, in looseleaf format, so that the text can be kept up to date. This is a development of the long-established practice of issuing cumulative supplements in between editions, to update the last edition.

Precedent Books and Rule Books   6–6

These are principally intended for the practitioner. The basic object of precedent books is to provide specimens of wills, conveyances, tenancy agreements or other forms of legal documents which solicitors are called upon to draw up. In addition, there are some precedent books which provide specimens of the types of forms which will be required whenever a case is taken to court. Rule books contain the rules which govern procedure in court, and specimen copies of the various orders and forms used by the courts and by the parties to litigation.

The multi-volume *Encyclopaedia of Forms and Precedents* aims to provide a form for every transaction likely to be encountered by practitioners, except for court forms. The entries are arranged by subject, *e.g.* "Animals", "Mortgages". Some idea of the wide scope of the work can be obtained by glancing through the subject headings. For instance, the section on animals covers such diverse topics as the sale and leasing of animals, applications for a licence to keep mink or to keep an animals' boarding establishment, a veterinary surgeon's certificate for the destruction of an animal and the relevant documents prohibiting movement of animals during an outbreak of disease. The looseleaf service volume keeps the information up to date. The *Cumulative Index* refers you to the *volume* (in **bold** type) and *paragraph* number which you require. Each individual volume also has its own index. References in the index to paragraph numbers in square brackets refer to precedents: paragraph numbers not enclosed in brackets refer to the preliminary notes. Checklists of procedures to be followed are provided under some subject headings.

Atkins' Encyclopaedia of Court Forms in Civil Proceedings is a complementary publication, covering the procedure in civil courts and tribunals. The volume on divorce, for instance, contains all the necessary documents needed during the court action, together with a detailed list of the steps to be taken and the forms required at each stage. The volumes are reissued from time to time to incorporate new material. An annual supplement keeps the information up to date. The *Consolidated Index* is also published yearly.

There are many precedent books dealing with specific areas of the law, *e.g.* the looseleaf *Precedents for the Conveyancer* (issued as a supplement to the journal *The Conveyancer*). In addition, some textbooks designed for practitioners will include precedents.

The rules and procedures governing various courts are set out in a number of places. The *County Court Practice* (often referred to as the *Green Book*) and *The Supreme Court Practice* (the *White Book*) set out the documents required for those appearing in those courts. *Archbold's Criminal Pleading, Evidence and Practice* is used by those engaged in criminal work.

The coloured pages in each issue of the *Law Society Gazette* are of particular interest to practitioners. These often include specimen forms and precedents, and details of Home Office circulars and practice directions. Practice directions are also published in the major series of law reports, *e.g.* the *All England Law Reports* and the *Weekly Law Reports*.

6–7 TRACING CASES ON A SUBJECT

Cases on a particular subject can be traced by consulting:

> *Current Law* (paras. 6–8 and 6–9);
> *The Digest* (paras. 6–10 and 6–11);
> *Halsbury's Laws of England* (para. 6–4);
> *The Daily Law Reports Index* and *Legal Journals Index* (para. 6–12);
> Indexes to individual series of law reports (para. 6–13);
> Relevant textbooks (para. 6–25);
> Electronic sources, *e.g.* LEXIS, Lawtel, etc. (Chapter 7).

6–8 How to Use the Current Law Monthly Digests

Current Law is published monthly under the title *Current Law Monthly Digest*. It is an important publication and it is essential that you should learn how to use it.

The main part of each *Monthly Digest* is arranged by subject and under each subject heading is given a summary of recent cases on the subject, new statutes and statutory instruments, government reports and recent books and journal articles on that subject. Full details are given to enable you to trace the cases and other materials mentioned in your own library. A page from the *Monthly*

Example Page from Current Law Monthly Digest

CONTRACT
_____

CONTRACT

76. Hire-purchase or conditional sale agreement—transaction supported by documents dealing with default—nature of the transaction—whether transferee entitled to protection. See DODDS *v.* YORKSHIRE BANK FINANCE, §74.

77. Jurisdiction—restitution—bank's claim against Scottish authority brought in England—motion by Scottish authority to strike out for want of jurisdiction—whether special jurisdiction in English court—whether matter "relating to a contract". See BARCLAYS BANK *v.* GLASGOW CITY COUNCIL; KLEINWORT BENSON *v.* SAME, *sub nom.* KLEINWORT BENSON *v.* CITY OF GLASGOW DISTRICT COUNCIL; BARCLAYS BANK *v.* SAME, §72.

78. Service out of jurisdiction—reinsurance-led pool—derivative claims— issues raised on contract and tort—whether good arguable case— whether claims time-barred—whether leave to serve to be set aside. See SOCIETE COMMERCIALE DE REASSURANCE *v.* ERAS INTERNATIONAL (FORMERLY ERAS (U.K.)); ERAS EIL ACTIONS, THE, §406.

79. Articles

Exclusion clauses: the ambit of s.13(1) of the Unfair Contract Terms Act 1977 *(E. Macdonald)*: [1992] 12 L.S. 277.

Franchising and distribution under the Restrictive Trade Practices Act 1976 *(S. Singleton)*: [1992] 9 Tr.L. 194.

New Dutch Civil Code—developments in contract law *(M. Whincup)*: [1992] 142 New L.J. 1208.

Rome Convention on Contracts—its relevance to arbitration *(A. Quinn)*: [1992] 10 I.L.T. 244.

Strategic use of contracts in a competitive environment *(M. O'Ceidigh)*: [1992] 10 I.L.T. 251.

CONVEYANCING AND REAL PROPERTY

80. Completion—time of the essence—purchaser indicating inability to complete—subsequently willing to complete—vendor unable to give vacant possession—whether time still of the essence—Australia

[Aus.] Where a vendor elects to keep the contract, of which time is of the essence, on foot despite the purchaser's intimation that performance by the vendor will be nugatory, then although the vendor remains bound to perform its obligations under the contract, it will not, if it has acted upon the intimation to its detriment, be bound to perform those obligations at the appointed time. Consequently, any failure by it to do so will not amount to a breach of obligation entitling the other party to rescind.

AUSTRAL STANDARD CABLES PTY. *v.* WALKER NOMINEES PTY. [1992] ALMD 5513, Sup.Ct., NSW.

81. Consumer protection—property misdescriptions

PROPERTY MISDESCRIPTIONS (SPECIFIED MATTERS) ORDER 1992 (No. 2834) [£1·05], made under the Property Misdescriptions Act 1991 (c.29), s.1; operative on April 4, 1993; specifies matters for the purposes of s.1. of the 1991 Act.

Digest is shown on page 117. On this page alone, several articles are mentioned (item 79), a case is summarised (item 80) and a statutory instrument is outlined (item 81). In items 76 to 78, three cases of relevance to contract law are mentioned, although the summaries of the cases are to be found elsewhere in the issue (at items 74, 72 and 406).

At the back of each issue is a Table of Cases which contains a list of all the cases which have been reported during the current year. It is therefore only necessary to look at the Table of Cases in the *latest* issue of the *Current Law Monthly Digest* to trace a case reported at any time during the year. (This list of cases brings the information in the *Current Law Case Citators* up to date (para. 2–12).)

The *Current Law Monthly Digests* also contain a subject index. Again it is cumulative, so it is only necessary to consult the index in the latest month's issue. This enables you to trace any development in the law during the current year. The reference given, *e.g.* Feb 80, is to the appropriate monthly issue (in this example, the February issue) and the item number in the issue *i.e.* item 80. If the reference is followed by an S (*e.g.* Jan 821S), the item contains Scottish material.

The Table of Cases provides a list of reports of cases. Suppose, however, that you know that there has been a recent case on the subject but you do not know the name of the parties. In this instance, you can trace the cases on the subject during the current year by looking in the cumulative Subject Index in the latest issue of the *Current Law Monthly Digest*. The Subject Index can also help when you have spelt the name of the parties incorrectly or have an incomplete reference.

6–9 How to Use the Current Law Year Books

The issues of the *Current Law Monthly Digest* are replaced by an annual volume, the *Current Law Year Book*.

The *Year Book* is arranged by subject, in the same way as the *Monthly Digest*, and contains a summary of all the cases, legislation and other developments in that subject during the year. Lists of journal articles and books written on a subject during the year are printed at the back of the volume. (The 1956 *Year Book* contains a list of journal articles published between 1947 and 1956.)

The *Current Law Year Books* from 1986 to 1990 are also available on a CD-ROM. The CD-ROM will search for words anywhere in the summaries. It is therefore more flexible, as well as quicker to search for cases on a subject using the CD-ROM than using the printed *Current Law Year Books*.

Since 1991, the *Current Law Year Book* contains Scottish material as well as that from England. Before then, there was a separate Scottish version, called the *Scottish Current Law Year Book*. Despite the name, this included all the English material, plus a separate section at the back of the volume containing Scottish developments during the year. The Scottish section remains separate from the English material in the *Current Law Year Book* and there are separate indexes to the two sections.

At the back of the 1976 *Year Book*, there is a Subject Index to all the entries in all the *Year Books* from 1947–1976. Entries give the last two digits of the year, and a reference to the individual item number within that year's volume, *e.g.* 69/3260 is a reference to item 3260 in the 1969 *Year Book*. Entries which have no year in front of them will be found in the *Current Law Consolidation 1947–1951*. A second Cumulative Index is found in the 1986 *Year Book* for the years 1972–1986. The 1989 *Year Book* contains a Cumulative Index for 1987–1989. These three sources, together with the *Year Books* since 1989 and the latest *Current Law Monthly Digest*, provide complete coverage of any developments in the law of that subject since 1947.

Master Volumes were published in the 1956, 1961, 1966 and 1971 *Year Books*. These volumes contain, under the usual subject headings, detailed entries for all developments during the year in which they were published, together with a summary of the developments during the previous four years. References are given to enable you to trace the full details in the appropriate *Current Law Year Book*. Thus it is possible, by using the *Master Volumes* and the *Current Law Consolidation 1947–1951*, to see at a glance a summary of every entry which has appeared in *Current Law* on a particular subject over a five-year period.

SUMMARY: HOW TO USE CURRENT LAW

(1) If you know the name of a case and want to find out where it has been reported and whether the case has subsequently been judicially considered, consult:

   Current Law Case Citator 1947–1976;

   Current Law Case Citator 1977–1988;

   the *Current Law Case Citator* from 1989 to the end of last year; and

   the Table of Cases in the latest *Current Law Monthly Digest*.

(2) To trace any developments (cases, statutes, etc.) on a particular subject, consult:

   The Cumulative Index covering 1947–1976 at the back of the 1976 *Current Law Year Book*;

the Cumulative Index at the back of the 1986 *Year Book* covering the years 1972–1986;
the Cumulative Index at the back of the 1989 *Year Book* covering the years 1987–1989;
the Indexes in the back of the *Year Books* since 1989; and
the Subject Index in the latest issue of the *Current Law Monthly Digest*.

(3) To obtain a general view of developments in a topic over a number of years, consult:
the *Current Law Consolidation 1947–1951*:
the *Master Volumes* (1956, 1961, 1966, 1971 *Year Books*);
all the *Year Books* published since the last *Master Volume* was issued; and
all the issues of the *Current Law Monthly Digest* for this year.

(4) To trace books and journal articles on a subject, look in the back of the 1956 *Year Book* and each subsequent *Year Book* and in the *Current Law Monthly Digests* under the appropriate subject heading. There are, however, quicker and more comprehensive sources for tracing journals (para. 4–2) and books (paras. 6–25 *et seq.*).

Remember that *Current Law* only contains information on cases reported or mentioned in court since 1947 and other developments in the law since 1947. To trace earlier cases, use *The Digest*.

6–10   The Digest

The Digest (formerly known as the *English and Empire Digest*) contains summaries of cases which have appeared in law reports from the thirteenth century to the present day, arranged in subject order. It enables you to trace cases of any date which deal with your particular subject. In addition to English cases, reports of Irish, Scottish and many Commonwealth cases are included, together with cases on European Communities law. These are printed in smaller type to enable them to be easily distinguishable from English cases.

For each case, a summary of the decision is given, followed by the name of the case, and a list of places where the case is reported. The subsequent judicial history of the case is also shown, in the annotations section. A list of the abbreviations used for law reports will be found in the front of Volume 1 and also in the front of the *Cumulative Supplement*.

Example Page from The Digest Consolidated Index

LOCAL AUTHORITY—*cont*
compensation, assessment of **11** *Comp Pche* 2118
compulsory acquisition **11** *Comp Pche* 2120
contributing to nuisance **36(2)** *Nuis* 1282
conveyance to **36(2)** *Open Sp* 1380
county hall
  use as court **28(1)** *Inc T* 63
defence of act authorised by **36(2)** *Nuis* 1071, 1072
definition by, by bye-law **36(2)** *Nuis* 86, 97
delegation by Metropolitan **1(2)** *Agcy* 86
development by **47(1)** *T&CP* 550, 28, 54
discretion of, in widening extra-Metropolitan streets
  26 *Hghys* 5001
dismissing proceedings against **30** *Jdgmts* 12, 13
disposal of housing land
  sale of house by local authority **26** *Housg* 5361, 5362
  sale of land **26** *Housg* 5363
disqualification of member of **1(1)** *Action* 288, 305
duty of, as to statutory works **26** *Hghys* 4953
duty to supply water for ships and town **13** *Corpns* 2674
educational purposes
  injurious affection
    remedy **11** *Comp Pche* 2115
  power of acquiring land compulsorily **11** *Comp Pche*
    2114
  power to build **11** *Comp Pche* 2113
entertainments committee
  whether for charitable purposes **28(2)** *Inc T* 3176
establishment expenses
  whether deductible from income **28(1)** *Inc T* 950, 1612
executed contract by municipal corporation *See* EXECUTED
  CONTRACTS
execution of work of rendering unfit houses fit by
  conditions precedent **26** *Housg* 5367
  expenses, recovery of **26** *Housg* 5378–5386
  order for payment of full sum **26** *Housg* 5377
execution of work rendering unfit houses fit by order for
  payment of full sum **26** *Housg* 5383
expropriation by town **11** *Comp Pche* *1084
failure to carry out order to abate an owner's default
  36(2) *Nuis* 1316
free library
  whether exempt **28(1)** *Inc T* 47, 48, 53
gas undertakers
  whether expenses deductible from income **28(1)** *Inc T*
  951
gasworks
  expenses of public supply **28(1)** *Inc T* 951, 1604
housing accommodation powers
  homeless persons **26** *Housg* 5325–5338
  rehousing displaced persons **26** *Housg* 5324
Housing Acts *See* HOUSING ACTS
inadequacy of summary proceedings **36(2)** *Nuis* 1058
injunction against
  application to Parliament to sell common land
    28(4) *Injon* 5788
  carrying water mains through private land **28(4)** *Injon*
    5791
  discharge of road water into private ground **28(4)** *Injon*
    5790
  excess of statutory powers **28(4)** *Injon* 5785
  generally **28(4)** *Injon* 5773
  interference with watercourse **28(4)** *Injon* 5787
  irregular appointment of teachers **28(4)** *Injon* 5808
  misapplication of poor rate **28(4)** *Injon* 5783, 5784
  removal of electric standard **28(4)** *Injon* 5799

LOCAL AUTHORITY—*cont*
injunction against—*cont*
  resignation of members **28(4)** *Injon* 5774
  to compel exercise of powers **28(4)** *Injon* 5780, 5781
  to open schools closed as result of industrial action
    28(4) *Injon* 5782
  to restrain board from enforcing order **28(4)** *Injon* 5789
  to restrain closing of streets **28(4)** *Injon* 5805
  to restrain commission of statutory nuisance **28(4)** *Injon*
    5794
  to restrain construction of tramway **28(4)** *Injon* 5797
  to restrain continuation of publicity campaign
    28(4) *Injon* 5792
  to restrain council pulling down new buildings
    28(4) *Injon* 5801
  to restrain entry on land **28(4)** *Injon* 5786
  to restrain erection of works **28(4)** *Injon* 5804
  to restrain execution of contract **28(4)** *Injon* 5803
  to restrain exercise of powers **28(4)** *Injon* 5775–5779
  to restrain holding council meetings **28(4)** *Injon* 5802
  to restrain holding election **28(4)** *Injon* 5795
  to restrain making illegal rate **28(4)** *Injon* 5800
  to restrain payment of unsanctioned loan **28(4)** *Injon*
    5798
  to restrain proceedings with notice to treat **28(4)** *Injon*
    5796
  to restrain proposed expenditure **28(4)** *Injon* 5806
  to restrain ultra vires act **28(4)** *Injon* 5807
  to restrain use of land as caravan site **28(4)** *Injon* 5793
interest on loans
  charged on rates and assessments **28(1)** *Inc T* 2019
  payable from rates **28(1)** *Inc T* 1944
joinder of claim for declaration **36(2)** *Nuis* 1057
letter in newspaper commenting on proceedings at meeting
  of **32** *Libel* 2142
liabilty to repair bridges in case of alteration of boundaries
  extension of boundary **26** *Hghys* 4581
mandamus against refusal of, to enter **36(2)** *Nuis* 1322
Metropolis *See* METROPOLIS
moneys of consolidated loan fund **13** *Corpns* 2682
municipal buildings
  assessability **28(1)** *Inc T* 62, 63, 62
necessity for compulsory acquisition **11** *Comp Pche* 2057,
  2058
notice by, to do work **12(2)** *Contr* 8045
outgoing tenant **11** *Comp Pche* 2117
outgoing tenant, right of **11** *Comp Pche* 2119
ownership of property **13** *Corpns* 2713, 2714
payment out of corporate funds
  costs of application to Parliament for Act **13** *Corpns* 2671
  costs of opposing *mandamus* proceedings **13** *Corpns* 2670
  costs of opposing rule **13** *Corpns* 2663, 2664
  costs of petitioning court **13** *Corpns* 2668
  costs of town clerk acting as solicitor for corporation
    13 *Corpns* 2669
  excess of statutory powers, in **13** *Corpns* 2660
  expenses of running omnibuses **13** *Corpns* 2673
  improvements within borough, for **13** *Corpns* 2665–
    2667, *485
  making up salaries of employees **13** *Corpns* 2672
  purposes not included in local Act **13** *Corpns* 2661
  power to acquire land for public park **13** *Corpns* *488
  power to borrow specific sum for construction **13** *Corpns*
    *489
  power to change rates charged for public utilities **13** *Corpns*
    *487

Example Page from The Digest, Volume 26

Housing obligations; provision and management of houses   Cases **5325–27**

available. Applicant brought proceedings against the authority for an order of mandamus compelling them to fulfil the duty imposed on them by s 39 of Land Compensation Act 1973 to secure that he was provided with "suitable alternative residential accommodation on reasonable terms". Applicant contended that s 39 required the authority to provide him with permanent accommodation on terms which gave him security of tenure equivalent to that which he had enjoyed by virtue of Rent Acts under his previous tenancy: *Held* applicant was not entitled to an order of mandamus. The duty imposed on the local authority to provide applicant with suitable accommodation on reasonable terms did not require them to give priority to applicant over other persons on the housing list; their duty was to act reasonably and do their best, as soon as practicable, to provide him with other accommodation. By providing for applicant until a council house was available and then offering the house to him on the terms normally offered to prospective tenants, the local authority were doing all that was required of them by s 39.

Per *Scarman LJ*: if there is evidence that a local authority is doing all it can to comply with its statutory obligation but has failed to do so because of circumstances over which it has no control, it would be improper for the court to make an order of mandamus compelling it to do that which it cannot do, or which it can only do at the expense of other persons not before the court.

R v Bristol Corporation, ex p Hendy [1974] 1 All ER 1047, [1974] 1 WLR 498, 72 LGR 405, 27 P&CR 180, sub nom *Hendy v Bristol Corporation* (1973) 117 Sol Jo 912, CA

➤ **iv Accommodation for homeless persons**

LAW See Halsbury's Laws (4th edn) vol 22 paras 509–523
STATUTE See Housing (Homeless Persons) Act 1977; 47 Halsbury's Statutes (3rd edn) 314

5325 Homeless persons—Duties of local authorities—Time at which duties arise The applicant, having been classified by the housing authority as homeless and having a priority need according to the Housing (Homeless Persons) Act 1977 s 1, sought an order of mandamus requiring the authority to carry out its duties under s 4 of that Act to secure available accommodation. The authority contended that such a duty did not arise until the applicant had been notified of its decision as to her status. It further submitted that notification of its decision to another authority under s 5 of the Act had not constituted constructive notice of its decision to the applicant: *Held* the authority's duties under s 4 arose as soon as it was satisfied that the applicant was homeless: the existence of such duties was not dependent on notification of the decision

under s 8 of the Act. Further, s 5 (6) provided that notification by the authority of its decision to a second housing authority requiring the latter to take the responsibility of providing housing accommodation did not absolve the notifying authority from performing its duties under s 4 of the Act until the issue of responsibility was finally determined. However, it was unnecessary to grant the order sought, and the application would be refused.

R v Beverley Borough Council, ex p McPhee (1978) *Times*, 27 October, [1979] JPL 94, DC

5326 —— —— Whether duty complied with by giving advice and assistance A woman left her matrimonial home in Eire due to her husband's violence and was sent to a women's aid hostel in Bristol with her children. Although she had no local connection with Bristol, the council accepted her as a homeless person with a priority need. However, a community welfare officer for the woman's home town assured the council that accommodation would be provided there if she returned to Eire. The council therefore decided that it could properly fulfil its duty under the Housing (Homeless Persons) Act 1977 by advising the woman to return to Eire, paying her fares and contacting the appropriate authorities there. The woman refused to return to her home town on the ground that she had suffered violence there and applied for an order of mandamus compelling the Bristol council to house her: *Held* (i) the woman had only suffered violence in the matrimonial home itself and the welfare officer, with full knowledge of her circumstances, had guaranteed her accommodation elsewhere; (ii) under the 1977 Act s 6 (1) (c) the council could comply with its duty to provide accommodation by giving the woman any advice and assistance necessary for obtaining accommodation from another person. As the welfare officer was a person who could provide accommodation without risk of violence to the woman or her children, the council had properly fulfilled its statutory duty. The application would be refused.

R v Bristol City Council, ex p Browne [1979] 3 All ER 344, [1979] 1 WLR 1437, 123 Sol Jo 489
ANNOTATION **Consd** R v Hillingdon BC, ex p Streeting [1980] 3 All ER 413

5327 —— —— Intentional homelessness— Cohabitee's conduct A woman lived with a farm labourer who had been provided with a house on the farm. Both lived there until he voluntarily terminated his employment and his employer, the farm owner, took possession of the house. The labourer applied under the Housing (Homeless Persons) Act 1977 for accommodation but the local housing authority considered that both were intentionally homeless as he had voluntarily given up his job. The woman subsequently unsuccessfully applied for accommodation under the Act making it clear that the labourer would share any accommodation given to her. In an application by the woman for judicial review of the decision of the local

How to use The Digest to trace cases on a subject 6–11
To find cases on a particular subject, you start by looking in the three-volume *Consolidated Index*. The *Index*, however, is not always as simple as you might expect. To find cases on local authorities' duties to house the homeless, for example, you would need to look in the *Index* under "Local authority—housing accommodation powers—homeless persons", as shown on page 121. You would not have found the entry under "Homelessness", "Homeless persons", "Housing" or "Accommodation". The reference in the *Index* refers you to the volume number, the subject heading ("Housing") and the relevant case numbers (see page 122). Cases with an asterisk in front of the number refer to Scottish, Irish and Commonwealth cases.

Scottish, Irish and Commonwealth cases in the main volumes are always printed in smaller type than English cases on the same subject. In most volumes of *The Digest* all the case numbers, of whatever jurisdiction, are numbered consecutively: case 2040 may be an English case, while case 2041 is a Canadian case on the same subject. However, in some older volumes of *The Digest*, the non-English cases have a separate sequence of case numbers, preceded by an asterisk. There are thus two *separate* sequences of case numbers on the same page. A glance at the top of the page shows the case numbers, both unasterisked (English cases) and asterisked (other jurisdictions) which appear on that page.

In the back of each volume of *The Digest* is a Reference Adaptor. When a volume is reissued, the case numbers change as additional cases are inserted. Wherever you find a cross-reference to a volume which has been reissued more recently than the *Consolidated Index* or volume from which you have been referred, you will need to look in the volume's Reference Adaptor to convert the reference. The Reference Adaptor consists of a long list of all the case numbers from the old volume, alongside the number which replaces it in the new 2nd reissue volume.

After finding the relevant cases on your subject in the main volumes, you should check to see if there have been more recent cases on the subject since the volume was written. To do this update, you must consult the *Cumulative Supplement*. Make a note of the volume number, subject heading and case number(s) in the main volumes which contain relevant information. Now turn to the *Cumulative Supplement* and look to see if there is an entry for that volume, subject heading and case number. If there is an entry, this will provide information on a later case, in which the case you were consulting in the main works has been referred to, considered, overruled, etc. (A full list of the abbreviations used and their meanings appears at the front of the *Cumulative*

Supplement, under the heading "Meaning of the terms used in classifying annotating cases.") For example, the entry:

> *5321 Consd.* (dictum Upjohn J.) *Collin* v. *Duke of Westminster* [1985] 1 All E.R. 463

in the *Cumulative Supplement* means that case 5321 in the main volumes has subsequently been considered in the 1985 case of *Collin* v. *Duke of Westminster* (see p. 125).

The *Cumulative Supplement* also includes references to new cases on the same subject matter. These new cases *either* provide a summary, followed by the name of the case (and a reference to where the case will be found in various series of law reports) *or* they refer you to one of the *Continuation Volumes* where further details of the case, including a full-length summary, will be found. The system of numbering the new cases in the *Cumulative Supplement* corresponds to that in the main volumes. The small letter after the number shows that the case follows on naturally from the similarly numbered case in the volumes.

The *Cumulative Supplement* is revised annually; the front cover tells you how recent the information is. If you are looking for new cases on a particular subject, within the last few months, then *The Digest* is not sufficiently up to date and you should consult other publications, such as *Current Law*, the latest *Pink Index* to the *Law Reports* or the *Monthly Reviews* in *Halsbury's Laws of England*.

SUMMARY: TRACING CASES ON A SUBJECT IN THE DIGEST

1. Look up the subject in the *Consolidated Index*. This will refer you to the volume, subject heading and case numbers where cases on that subject can be found.
2. To see if there have been any more recent cases on the same subject, look in the *Cumulative Supplement* under the relevant volume, subject heading and case number. This will provide you with up to date information. You may be referred to one of the *Continuation Volumes* for further details. If so, look under the volume number, subject heading and case number in the *Continuation Volume*.

6–12 Daily Law Reports Index and Legal Journals Index

These two sources are very useful for finding recent cases which have not been reported by the major series of law reports but have been reported in the newspapers or discussed in journal articles. They are both published by Legal Information Resources Ltd. and therefore use the same indexing terms.

Example Page from The Digest Cumulative Supplement

363   **Vol 26—Housing**

5180 Distd Chubb Cash Ltd v John Crilley & Son (a firm) [1983] 2 All ER 294

5189a Mortgage—Deferred sale agreement—High interest—Whether extortionate credit bargain *Davies v Directloans Ltd* (1986) See Continuation Vol H

5189b Advertisements—Secured loans— Statutory warning to borrowers Regulations made under the Consumer Credit Act 1974 required advertisements offering loans secured by a mortgage or charge on the debtor's home to contain the warning that the debtor's home was at risk if he did not keep up repayments on a mortgage or other loan secured on it. The defendant bank sought a declaration that this requirement was ultra vires the 1974 Act because it was unreasonable and misleading as it implied that an unsecured loan carried no such risk. *Held,* even if the requirement in question was not expressly provided for by the relevant provision of the 1974 Act, it was reasonably necessary for the protection of consumers and was not in conflict with the express requirements of that provision. While there was a more immediate risk of a debtor losing his home in the case of a loan secured by a mortgage, there was no danger of people taking up unsecured loans at higher rates merely because there was a warning in the one case but not in

the other. The regulations in question were not ultra vires, and were not unreasonable. Accordingly, the application would fail.

R v Secretary of State for Trade and Industry, Ex p First National Bank plc (1990) Times, 7 March, CA

Part 2—EXISTING LAW OF HIRE PURCHASE

5202 Consd Spiro v Glencrown Properties Ltd and another [1991] 1 All ER 600

5206 Consd Clough Mill Ltd v Martin [1984] 1 All ER 721

5236 Apld Rover International Ltd and others v Cannon Film Sales Ltd (No 3) [1989] 3 All ER 423

5247a Punctual payment of the essence of contract— Alleged repudiation—Damages *Lombard North Central plc v Butterworth* (1987) See Continuation Vol H

5254a Sale of goods—Conditional sale agreement— Statutory right to terminate agreement—Effect of clause entitling seller to elect for accelerated payment on buyer's default *Wadham Stringer Finance Ltd v Meaney* (1980) See Continuation Vol F

5274 Apld Neumann v Bakeaway Ltd [1983] 2 All ER 935

5297 Apld Lombard North Central plc v Butterworth [1987] 1 All ER 267; [1987] 2 WLR 7

5302 Folld Lawlor v Gray [1984] 3 All ER 345

HOUSING

Part 2—HOUSING OBLIGATIONS

5312a Abuse of powers—Allocation of council house based on irrelevant considerations *R v Port Talbot Borough Council and others* Ex p *Jones* (1988) See Continuation Vol H

5320 Apld R v Cornwall County Council, Ex p Huntington and another [1992] 2 All ER 566

➤**5321 Consd** (dictum Upjohn J) Collin v Duke of Westminster [1985] 1 All ER 463

5322 Apld (dictum Megaw J) R v Rochdale MBC, Ex p Cromer Ring Mill Ltd [1982] 3 All ER 761 **Apld** R v Inner London Education Authority, Ex p Westminster City Council [1986] 1 All ER 19

5323 Apld (dictum Forbes J) Green & Secretaries of State for Environment and Transport (1984) 271 EG 550

5325a Homeless person—Duties of local authority— Priority needs—Test of vulnerability *R v Waveney District Council,* Ex p *Bowers* (1982) See Continuation Vol F

5325a(i) —— —— —— *R v Wandsworth Borough Council,* Ex p *Banbury* (1986) See Continuation Vol H

5325a(ii) —— —— **Residence of dependent child** The Housing Act 1985, s 59(1)(*b*), provides that a person, with whom dependent children reside or might reasonably be expected to reside, has a priority need for accommodation.

The unmarried parents of a 5-year-old child had never lived at the same address. They had always shared equally the care and control of the child. The mother claimed social security benefits in respect of the child. The appellant father worked. For three years, up to September 1989, the appellant lived in a

house owned by a housing co-operative. The child lived there with him for half of every week. The appellant was evicted and made an application to the respondent local authority because he was homeless. The appellant unsuccessfully applied for judicial review of the respondent's refusal to accord him priority for accommodation. On appeal, *held,* the section required the appellant to show that a dependent child resided with him. It did not require, as the respondent had contended, the appellant to show either that the child was wholly and exclusively dependent on, or residing with, him. The judge had not decided whether the respondent had applied the correct test. Accordingly, the appeal would be allowed and the case remitted to the local authority for reconsideration.

R v London Borough of Lambeth, Ex p *Vagliviello* (1990) 22 HLR 392, CA

5325a(iii) —— —— —— —— The Housing Act 1985, s 59(1)(*b*) provides that a person with whom dependent children reside or might reasonably be expected to reside, has a priority need for accommodation.

A couple were divorced and were awarded joint custody of their children with care and control vesting in the mother. The couple made an informal agreement, subject to the father finding suitable accommodation, whereby the children would live half the week with each parent. The father applied to the local council for accommodation, asserting a priority need under s 59(1)(*b*). The council refused the application,

The *Daily Law Reports Index* is published fortnightly and indexes the law reports from the daily newspapers. To find a case on a particular subject, look in the Keyword Index. Each case has an entry under several keywords (*i.e.* subject headings) to help make sure you find all the relevant cases. The entry in the Keyword Index gives the name of the case, as well as a full reference to the newspapers in which it was reported. A summary of each case is found in the Case Index. The quarterly and annual cumulations also contain a Case Report Index, which lists, with further citations, those newspaper law reports which have since been reported in one of the major law reports series.

The *Legal Journals Index* will enable you to find case notes, case summaries and other articles discussing cases on a particular subject published in British legal journals. A full explanation of searching the *Legal Journals Index* can be found at para. 4–3 and the benefits of searching the electronic versions of these indexes are described in para. 7–1. Any cases discussed are clearly indicated after the title of the article. If there is no title other than the case name, the item will be a case note.

The *Daily Law Reports Index* and the *Legal Journals Index* are very useful for finding the most recent decisions, since they index the newspapers and journals, which are usually the first to report new cases. However, as the *Daily Law Reports Index* began publication in 1988 and the *Legal Journals Index* in 1986, you will need to use other sources to find older cases.

6–13   How to Use Individual Indexes to Series of Law Reports to Trace Cases on a Subject

If the facilities in your library are limited, you may need to use the indexes to individual series of law reports to trace relevant cases on a subject. The most useful is the *Law Reports Index* (para. 2–14) because it covers a number of other important series in addition to the *Law Reports*. Indexes are available covering each 10-year period since 1951 and supplementary indexes (an annual *Red Index* and the latest *Pink Index*: para. 2–14) bring the information up to date to within a few weeks. The *Law Reports Index* is easier to use than *The Digest*, but remember that it covers fewer series of English law reports and no foreign cases.

In addition to the *Law Reports Index* (and the series of *Digests*, which preceded them, going back to 1865) there are indexes to other series, such as the *All England Law Reports*, which have a *Consolidated Tables and Index* in three volumes, covering 1936–1992.

This is kept up to date by supplements (para. 2–14). In addition, there is an *Index* volume to the *All England Law Reports Reprint*, which includes a subject index to selected cases from 1558–1935. Electronic databases excel at searching by subject. LEXIS, for example, contains the full text of many series of law reports and unlike paper indexes, can search for a word anywhere in the law report. Some series of law reports are being published on CD-ROM. Justis Weekly Law CD-ROM, for example, contains the full text of all the law reports published in the Weekly Law Reports since the early 1980s, along with the *Law Reports Index* since 1981.

TRACING THE SUBSEQUENT JUDICIAL HISTORY OF A CASE   6–14

Judges often rely upon earlier cases to support the reasons which they have given for their decision, and from time to time a judge will review the case law in an attempt to explain the principles stated in earlier cases, or to use them as a spring-board to create a new application of the principles. Occasionally a case will be distinguished in order that the judge will not feel obliged to follow it. Less frequently, a superior court will state that an earlier case was wrongly decided, and will overrule it, so that the principles laid down in the case will not be followed thereafter.

The treatment that a case receives when it is subsequently judicially considered has a direct bearing on its importance and reliability. For example, if in a moot or essay you cited as an authority the common law rules relating to compensation for war damage which were laid down in *Burmah Oil Co.* v. *Lord Advocate* [1965] A.C. 75, you would be embarrassed to discover that it was abolished by statute, the War Damages Act 1965. Similarly, you should be aware that the case of *Gillick* v. *West Norfolk Area Health Authority* [1985] 1 All E.R. 533 was reversed on appeal to the House of Lords. Consequently, you must be alert to the need to trace the full judicial history of a particular case.

The simplest way to do this is to use the *Current Law Case Citator* (para. 2–12). This will give the citation of any English case which has been judicially considered since 1947 and show its treatment. For instance, the well-known old case *Carlill* v. *Carbolic Smoke Ball Co.*, which was reported in 1892, appears in the *Current Law Case Citator 1947–1976*, because it was considered in court several times since 1947. After giving the name of the case, and a reference to where the case is to be found in the *Law Reports*, the following entry appears:

Dicta applied, 67/1745: *Applied*, 73/1529: *Distinguished*, 73/3095

This means that if you turn to the *Current Law Year Book* for 1967, item 1745 will be found to be a summary of a case in which the *Carlill* case was applied. Similarly, the 1973 *Year Book* contains two reports of cases (items 1529 and 3095) in which the case was considered. The entries in more recent *Citators* show that the *Carlill* case has been considered subsequently; in 1980, in 1984, in 1988 and again in 1991.

The *Law Reports Index* contains a list of cases judicially considered and the *Index* to the *All England Law Reports* also includes a list of cases reported and considered. *The Digest* (para. 6–11) contains annotations to entries, showing the subsequent judicial history of a case. This is kept up to date by the information in the *Cumulative Supplement*.

6–15   HOW TO FIND WORDS AND PHRASES JUDICIALLY CONSIDERED

The meaning of words is of great importance to lawyers. The interpretation of statutes and documents may hinge upon the meaning of a single word. For example, does "day" in banking terms mean 24 hours, or does it end at the close of working hours? Can a mistress be considered part of a "family"?

Two specialised dictionaries record the courts' decisions on problems such as these. *Stroud's Judicial Dictionary* provides the meaning of words as defined in the case law and in statutes. *Words and Phrases Legally Defined* is a similar publication; both are kept up to date by supplements.

The *Law Reports Index* includes a heading "Words and Phrases", in which full details of cases defining a particular word or phrase are given (see the figure on p. 129).

The *Current Law Monthly Digests* and *Year Books* also include an entry "Words and Phrases" and the *Index* to the *All England Law Reports* and the *Consolidated Index* to *Halsbury's Laws* have a similar heading.

6–16   HOW TO TRACE STATUTES ON A SUBJECT

Legislation on a particular subject can be traced by consulting:

Statutes in Force (para. 6–17);
Index to the Statutes (para. 6–18);

Example First Page of the Entry under "Words and Phrases" in the Law Reports Cumulative Index—the "Pink Index"

The Weekly Law Reports 17 December 1993

Subject Matter 93

➡ WORDS AND PHRASES

"*Act complained of*"—Race Relations Act 1976, s. 68(1)
Adekeye v. The Post Office, E.A.T. [1993] I.C.R. 464
"*Action . . . brought*"—Solicitors Act 1974, s. 69(1)
In re A Debtor (No. 88 of 1991), Sir Donald Nicholls V.-C. [1993] Ch. 286;
[1992] 3 W.L.R. 1026
"*Aggravating factor*"—Criminal Justice Act 1991, s. 29(2)
Reg. v. Hayton, C.A. [1993] R.T.R. 310
"*Annuity or other annual payment*"—Income and Corporation Taxes Act 1970, s. 52(1)
Moodie v. Inland Revenue Comrs., H.L.(E.) [1993] 1 W.L.R. 266
"*Any liability . . . under the terms of any policy*"—Policyholders Protection Act 1975, s. 8(2)
Scher v. Policyholders Protection Board, C.A. [1993] 2 W.L.R. 479
"*Any proceedings*"—Children and Young Persons Act 1933, s. 39(1)
Reg. v. Lee, C.A. [1993] 1 W.L.R. 103
"*Arrangements*"—Sex Discrimination Act 1975, s. 6(1)(*a*)
Ealing Hammersmith and Hounslow Family Health Services Authority v. Shukla,
E.A.T. [1993] I.C.R. 710
"*As a result of*"—Costs in Criminal Cases (General) Regulations 1986, reg. 3(1)
Reg. v. Wood Green Crown Court, Ex parte Director of Public Prosecutions,
D.C. [1993] 1 W.L.R. 723
"*Beginning with*"—Employment Protection (Consolidation) Act 1978, s. 67(2)
University of Cambridge v. Murray, E.A.T. [1993] I.C.R. 460
"*Civil proceedings*"—Antigua and Barbuda Constitution Order 1981, s. 122(1)(*a*)
Sundry Workers v. Antigua Hotel and Tourist Association,
P.C. [1993] 1 W.L.R. 1250
"*Commensurate with the seriousness of the offence*"—Criminal Justice Act 1991, s. 2(2)(*a*)
"*Company*"—Insolvency Act 1986, s. 40
In re Devon and Somerset Farmers Ltd., Judge Hague Q.C. [1993] 3 W.L.R. 866
Reg. v. Cunningham, C.A. [1993] 1 W.L.R. 183
"*Conviction*"—Road Traffic Offenders Act 1988, s. 29(1)(*b*)
Reg. v. Brentwood Justices, Ex parte Richardson, D.C. [1993] R.T.R. 374
"*Disclose*"—Contempt of Court Act 1981, s. 8(1)
Attorney-General v. Associated Newspapers Ltd., D.C. [1993] 3 W.L.R. 74
"*Disposal*"—Income and Corporation Taxes Act 1970, s. 273
N.A.P. Holdings U.K. Ltd. v. Whittles, C.A. (1993) T.C. Leaflet No. 3374
"*Disposition of property*"—Insolvency Act 1986, s. 284(1)
In re Flint (A Bankrupt), Nicholas Stewart Q.C. [1993] Ch. 319; [1993] 2 W.L.R. 537
"*Driving*"—Road Traffic Act 1988, s. 16(3)(1)
Leach v. Director of Public Prosecutions, D.C. [1993] R.T.R. 161
"*Duly made*"—Wildlife and Countryside Act 1981, Sch. 15, para. 7(1)
Lasham Parish Meeting v. Hampshire County Council, Potts J. (1992) 91 L.G.R. 209
"*Duty of assured*"—Institute Cargo clauses (A), cl. 16
Noble Resources Ltd. v. Greenwood, Hobhouse J. [1993] 2 Lloyd's Rep. 309
"*Employment*"—Sex Discrimination Act 1975, s. 82(1)
Ealing Hammersmith and Hounslow Family Health Services Authority v. Shukla,
E.A.T. [1993] I.C.R. 710
"*Equipment*"—Employer's Liability (Defective Equipment) Act, s. 1(1)(*a*)(3)
Knowles v. Liverpool City Council, C.A. [1993] I.C.R. 21
H.L.(E.) [1993] 1 W.L.R. 1428
"*Equivalent effect*"—E.E.C. Treaty, art. 30
Stoke-on-Trent City Council v. B. & Q. Plc. (Case C 169/91),
E.C.J. and H.L.(E.) [1993] A.C. 900; [1993] 2 W.L.R. 730
"*Exceptional circumstances*"—Powers of Criminal Courts Act 1973, s. 22(2) (as substituted)
Reg. v. Okinikan, C.A. [1993] 1 W.L.R. 173
"*Excessive*"—Courts and Legal Services Act 1990, s. 8(1)
Rantzen v. Mirror Group Newspapers (1986) Ltd., C.A. [1993] 3 W.L.R. 953
"*Exposed to risks to their health*"—Health and Safety at Work etc. Act 1974, s. 3(1)
Reg. v. Board of Trustees of the Science Museum,
C.A. [1993] 1 W.L.R. 1171; [1993] I.C.R. 876
"*First seised*"—Civil Jurisdiction and Judgments Act 1982, Sch. 1, art. 21
Neste Chemicals S.A. v. D. K. Line S.A., Sheen J. [1993] 1 Lloyd's Rep. 424
"*Folding pocketknife*"—Criminal Justice Act 1988, s. 139
Harris v. Director of Public Prosecutions, D.C. [1993] 1 W.L.R. 82
"*Garden*"—Common Land (Rectification of Registers) Act 1989, s. 1(3)
In re Land at Freshfields, Warner J. (1993) 91 L.G.R. 502
"*Good and sufficient cause*"—Prosecution of Offences Act 1985, s. 22(3)(*a*)
Reg. v. Nowich Crown Court, Ex parte Cox, D.C. (1992) 97 Cr.App.R. 145
"*Goods*"—Transport Act 1968, s. 60(1)
Booth v. Director of Public Prosecutions, D.C. [1993] R.T.R. 379

Example Page from the Index to the Statutes 1235–1990

LONDON CITY

1297 *(Mag.Car.)* c.9 [Confirmation of liberties] **(a) (106:1)**
1662 c.3   City of London Militia **(b) (7:2)**
1751 c.30   Calendar **(121)**
1820 c.100   Militia (City of London) **(7:2)**
1824 c.74   Weights and Measures
1884 c.70   Municipal Elections (Corrupt and Illegal Practices) **(c)**
1888 c.41   Local Govt. **(81:1)**
1897 c.30   Police (Property) **(95)**
1898 c.16   Canals Protection (London) **(102)**
1907 c.cxl   City of London (Union of Parishes) **(103:1)**
1921 c.37   Territorial Army and Militia
1925 c.49   Supreme Ct. of Judicature (Consolidation) **(37)**
1929 c.17   Local Govt. **(81:1)**
1936 c.49   Public Health **(100:1)**
1945 c.42   Water **(130)**
1957 c.x   City of London (Various Powers)
1960 c.67   Public Bodies (Admission to Meetings) **(81:4)**
1963 c.33   London Govt. **(81:1)**
1963 c.37   Children and Young Persons **(20)**
1964 c.42   Admin. of Justice **(82)**
1964 c.48   Police **(95)**
1965 c.45   Backing of Warrants (Republic of Ireland) **(48)**
1969 c.12   Genocide **(39:4)**

1969 c.19   Decimal Currency **(10)**
1969 c.57   Employers' Liability (Compulsory Insurance) **(43:3)**
1971 c.23   Courts **(37)**
1971 c.48   Criminal Damage **(39:6)**
1972 c.70   Local Govt. **(81:1)**
1972 c.71   Criminal Justice **(39:1)**
1979 c.55   Justices of the Peace **(82)**
1980 c.9   Reserve Forces **(7:2)**
1980 c.43   Magistrates' Courts
1982 c.32   Local Govt. Finance **(81:1)**
1984 c.46   Cable and Broadcasting **(96)**
1984 c.60   Police and Criminal Evidence
1985 c.43   Local Govt. (Access to Information) **(81:1,2)**
1985 c.51   Local Govt. **(81:1)**
1985 c.61   Admin. of Justice **(76:1)**
1985 c.68   Housing **(61)**
1985 c.72   Weights and Measures **(131)**
1988 c.4   Norfolk and Suffolk Broads **(81:1)**
1988 c.13   Coroners **(33)**
1988 c.19   Employment **(43:5)**
1988 c.40   Education Reform **(41:1,2)**
1988 c.41   Local Govt. Finance **(81)(103:2)**
1989 c.15   Water **(130)**
1989 c.33   Extradition **(48)**
1989 c.43   Statute Law (Repeals)
1990 c.42   Broadcasting **(96)**

1 *Constitution, etc.*
2 *Authorities*
3 *Administration of Justice*

4 *Finance*
5 *Miscellaneous*

1 Constitution, etc.

(a) POSITION OF CITY WITH REGARD TO GREATER LONDON OR OTHER AREAS
Inclusion in—
    Greater London: 1963 c.33 s.2(1)
    Metropolitan Traffic Area *See* ROAD TRAFFIC AND VEHICLES, 1*(b)*
Exclusion from—
    Metrop. Police District *See* METROP. POLICE DISTRICT, 1
    Tithe Commutation Acts *See* TITHES, E&W, 2*(l)*
A county borough for licensing purposes *See* LICENSING, E&W, 1
Separate county for purposes of lieutenancies and the militia: 1980 c.9 s.138(2)

(b) LIBERTIES, CUSTOMS, ETC.
City of London to have all its old liberties and customs: 1297 *(Mag. Car.)* c.9
Coroners for the City: 1988 c.13 s.1
Saving of privileges of Lord Mayor, etc., as to—
    gauging of wines, oil, honey, and other liquors: 1824 c.74 s.25

(c) UNION OF PARISHES
Union of parishes in city of London into one parish: 1907 c.cxl s.5(1)–(3)
Common Council to be overseers: 1907 c.cxl s.11
                1988 c.41 s.149,sch.13,Pt.I
Common Council to be overseers: 1907 c.cxl s.11
Precepts to Common Council: 1907 c.cxl s.12
Transfer of powers of vestry: 1907 c.cxl s.13
Savings for wards and wardmotes: 1907 c.cxl s.27

(a) 9 H. 3 in Ruffhead
(b) 13–14 C. 2 in Ruffhead
(c) Made permanent by Representation of the People Act 1948 (7–8 G. 5) c.64 s.35

Halsbury's Statutes of England (para. 6–19);
Current Law (para. 6–20);
Electronic sources, *e.g.* LEXIS (para. 7–8).

Statutes in Force   6–17

Statutes in Force contains the text of all Public General Acts which are at present in force in the United Kingdom, arranged in subject groups. Each subject is given a number; large subjects are subdivided. The work is issued in looseleaf form, so that alterations and amendments to Acts can easily be incorporated, and new legislation inserted at the appropriate point. *Cumulative Supplements* are issued for each subject group, to keep the information up to date. *Statutes in Force* is issued by HMSO, and is intended to be the definitive edition of the statutes of the realm; unfortunately, inadequate subject indexes and a failure to keep the work completely up to date, make it less useful than *Halsbury's Statutes*. There are alphabetical and chronological indexes of all the Acts included in the work, indicating the group number (and subgroup) where the Act is to be found. Within each group or subgroup, Acts are arranged in date order. The *Index to the Statutes* (para. 6–18) serves as a subject index to *Statutes in Force*. Following the name of each statute in the *Index to the Statutes*, the group number in *Statutes in Force* is given in **bold** type. For instance, under the heading "Dangerous Drugs" in the *Index to the Statutes*, there appear the following entries:

Dangerous Drugs
1971 c. 38 Misuse of Drugs (84)
1977 c. 45 Criminal Law (39:1)

This indicates that information on dangerous drugs will be found in *Statutes in Force* in the Misuse of Drugs Act 1971, which is printed in group 84 of the work; there is also information on dangerous drugs in the Criminal Law Act 1977, which is printed in group 39, subgroup 1 of *Statutes in Force*.

Index to the Statutes   6–18

A detailed alphabetical index to the statute law on a particular subject will be found in the *Index to the Statutes*. This is unfortunately several years behind in publication, so it will be necessary to consult *Halsbury's Statutes* (para. 6–19) or similar works to ensure that there have not been any recent changes.

The *Index to the Statutes* is comprehensive. It gives a complete list in subject order of all the statutes still in force. The number which appears in **bold** type after each Act refers you to the appropriate group or subgroup in *Statutes in Force* (para. 6–17) where the Act will be found printed. Following this, there is a detailed analysis of each subject, showing the section and subsections of all statutes which are relevant to that topic. Cross-references are given from one entry to another. (See the figure on p. 130.)

Where the law relating to England, Scotland and Northern Ireland is different, under some subject headings the topics are subdivided according to area. For instance, the law relating to agricultural holdings in England and Scotland is different, and there are therefore two main subject headings: "Agricultural holdings, England and Wales" and "Agricultural holdings, Scotland" (denoted by the abbreviations E & W, and S, respectively).

6–19   Halsbury's Statutes of England

Halsbury's Statutes provides the amended text of legislation which is still in force, along with annotations detailing, for example, statutory instruments made under the Act, case law, judicial interpretation of words and phrases and references to relevant sections of *Halsbury's Laws*.

The 50 volumes of the main work are arranged alphabetically by broad subject areas. Acts dealing with agriculture, for example, are found in Volume 1, whereas statutes on the subject of wills are found in Volume 50.

The annual *Table of Statutes and General Index* provides a comprehensive subject index to the volumes to enable you to find statutes on a particular topic. The Index will refer you to the appropriate *volume* and *page* number. In the *Table of Statutes and General Index* volume there is a separate subject index to the *Current Statutes Service*, which contains those Acts which were passed after the main volumes were issued. If you are looking for the latest Acts on a particular subject, look also in the subject index at the front of the looseleaf Volume 1 of the *Current Statutes Service*. This indexes the material which has been added to the *Service* since the annual *Table of Statutes and General Index* was published.

Once you have identified those Acts which are of relevance to you, it is essential to consult both the *Cumulative Supplement* and the *Noter-up* to see if there have been any changes in the law. An explanation of how to do this, along with further details of *Halsbury's Statutes*, can be found at para. 3–11.

Other Sources for Tracing Legislation on a Subject 6–20

Halsbury's Laws (para. 6–3) contains references to relevant statutes, although the text of the Acts is not printed. The *Current Law Monthly Digests* and *Year Books* (paras. 6–8, 6–9) are arranged by subject and include entries for new statutes and statutory instruments as well as for cases on a subject. A brief summary appears under the appropriate subject heading.

The full text of statutes still in force on a particular subject will be found in *Statutes in Force*, *Halsbury's Statutes* and on LEXIS. The text of statutes will also be found printed in *Public General Acts* (para. 3–6), *Law Reports: Statutes* (para. 3–8) and *Current Law Statutes Annotated* (para. 3–9).

HOW TO TRACE STATUTORY INSTRUMENTS ON A SUBJECT 6–21

Statutory instruments on a particular subject can be traced by consulting:

Halsbury's Statutory Instruments (para. 6–22);
The *Index to Government Orders* (para. 6–23);
Electronic sources, *e.g.*: LEXIS, Lawtel, SI-CD (para. 7–8).

For an explanation of the nature and purpose of statutory instruments, refer back to para. 3–20.

Halsbury's Statutory Instruments 6–22

Halsbury's Statutory Instruments is a series which covers every statutory instrument of general application in force in England and Wales. It reproduces the text of a selected number and provides summaries of others. The series is arranged alphabetically by subject and is kept up to date by looseleaf *Service* binders containing, in Binder 1, notes of changes in the law and, in Binder 2, the text of selected new instruments. A full description of the work can be found in para. 3–23.

If you are looking for statutory instruments dealing with a particular subject, you should start by looking up your subject in the *Consolidated Index and Alphabetical List of Statutory Instruments*. This paper-covered volume is issued annually and indexes the contents of all the main volumes, along with the information in the *Annual Supplement* in Binder 1. The entries give you the volume number (in **bold** type) and page number in the main work and the number of the statutory instrument (in brackets). Where "S" appears instead of a volume and page number, you should refer to the *Chronological List* in Binder 1, which will direct you to the appropriate title in the *Annual Supplement*.

Occasionally you will find that the volume to which you are referred has been reissued since the latest *Consolidated Index* was published. The references from the *Consolidated Index* will no longer be correct and in this case you will need to refer to the subject index at the back of the new volume.

Once you have traced the relevant statutory instruments on your subject in the main volumes, it is important to turn to Binder 1 to find out if the information you have traced is still up to date. To do this, turn first to the *Annual Supplement* in Binder 1 and look up the relevant subject title. This shows new statutory instruments which have appeared since the main volume was compiled. It tells you which statutory instruments printed in the main volumes are no longer law and provides you with a page-by-page guide to changes made since the main volume was published.

For the most recent changes in the law, you should consult the *Monthly Survey—Key* in Binder 1. Under the appropriate subject titles, this lists new statutory instruments and any amendments or revocations of earlier instruments. Summaries of the new instruments are given in numerical order in the *Monthly Survey— Summaries*.

SUMMARY: HOW TO USE HALSBURY'S STATUTORY INSTRUMENTS TO FIND INFORMATION ON A SUBJECT

1. Consult the *Consolidated Index*. This tells you the volume, page number and statutory instrument numbers you require. Where "S" appears instead of a volume number, the instrument appears in the *Annual Supplement* in Binder 1.
2. To check if there have been any changes in the law, look in:
    the *Annual Supplement* and
    the *Monthly Survey—Key*
   under the appropriate title.

6–23   **Index to Government Orders**

The *Index to Government Orders* is published every two years. It is arranged alphabetically by subject and enables you to trace statutory instruments which were in force at the time the *Index* was issued and which deal with a particular subject. Where there are a large number of entries under a subject heading, the subject is divided into a number of subsections. For instance, under the heading "Legal Aid and Advice", there are a number of subdivisions—"Legal Aid Board and legal aid, Advice and assistance, Civil legal aid, Criminal legal aid", etc.

Every entry gives the statute under which a power to make statutory instruments was conferred and the instruments which have been made under the provisions of that statute. If the power conferred by the Act has not yet been exercised (*i.e.* if no statutory instruments have been made under a particular Act), this is stated. Suppose, for instance, that you were interested in locating the law relating to the use of poisons for killing animals regarded as pests. Under the heading "Animals" there are a large number of entries, which have been subdivided. A relevant entry is found under "Animals—prevention of cruelty" in the subsection "Use of poisons." (See the figure on p. 136.) This indicates that the powers conferred under section 2 of the Animals (Cruel Poisons) Act 1962 were exercised by Statutory Instrument 1278 passed in 1963. This will be found in the 1963 volumes of *Statutory Instruments*.

Tracing Recent Statutory Instruments on a Subject   6–24

Statutory instruments which have been passed since the latest *Index to Government Orders* was published may be traced by consulting the subject indexes in the bound volumes of *Statutory Instruments*, and, for more recent changes, the monthly and annual *Lists of Statutory Instruments*, which contain entries in subject order. If you suspect that there has been a very recent change, it may be necessary to go through the *HMSO Daily Lists* (para. 5–14) for the past few weeks, to bring the information in the latest monthly *List* up to date. Recent instruments can also be traced by looking in the *Current Law Monthly Digests*, or in the *Monthly Reviews* in *Halsbury's Laws* or by looking in *Halsbury's Statutory Instruments* (para. 6–22). New instruments are also noted weekly in the *Solicitors' Journal* and the *New Law Journal*. Lawtel will also give information on amendments to statutory instruments and is updated daily (para. 7–10).

If you suspect that the text of an instrument has been changed or amended, *Halsbury's Statutory Instruments*, or one of the specialist looseleaf encyclopedias (if there is one available covering your subject field), is probably the easiest place to trace the updated version of the instrument. Amendments to the text can be traced in the *Table of Government Orders* (para. 3–24). The *Current Law Legislation Citator* contains a numerical list of statutory instruments passed since 1947, showing, for each one, whether it has been amended or revoked.

Example Page from the Index to Government Orders in Force on December 31, 1989

ANIMALS—*cont.*

1 Prevention of cruelty—*cont.*

➤(5) USE OF POISONS—*cont.*

(5) USE OF POISONS

Power

1962   Secy. of State, if satisfied that a poison cannot be used for destroying animals without causing undue suffering, and that other, adequate, methods of destroying them exist, may by regs. made by S.I. prohibit or restrict use of that poison for destroying animals, or animals of any description S.I. to be subject to annulment on resolution of either House

Animals (Cruel Poisons) Act 1962 (c. 26) s. 2

Exercise

1963/1278   Animals (Cruel Poisons) Regs.

Power

1972   Relevant Min. (*see* below) may by O. as to whole or part of G.B. specify poison for destroying grey squirrels or coypus, and manner of its use. Min. not to make O. except after consulting with organisations representing interests concerned; draft O. to be approved by resolution of each House O. may make different provn. as to grey squirrels and coypus, to be by S.I., may be varied or rev. "Relevant Min." means, in O. as to

E., Min. of Agric., Fisheries and Food
S., Secy of State for S.
E. and S., Min. and Secy. of State for S. jointly
W., Secy. of State
E., S. and W., Min., Secy. of State for S. and Secy. of State jointly

Agric (Misc. Provns.) Act 1972 (c. 62) s. 19
S.I. 1978/272

Exercise

1973/744   Grey Squirrels (Warfarin) O.

(6) WELFARE OF LIVESTOCK

Power

1968   Mins. (*see* AGRICULTURE, **1** (1) (*a*)) may, after consultation with representatives of interests concerned, by regs. provide as to welfare of livestock on agric. land. Regs. may provide (*a*) as to accommodation for livestock, (*b*) for ensuring balanced diets, prohibiting or regulating use of any substance as food for livestock and importation, etc., of substances intended for such food; (*c*) for prohibiting or regulating bleeding, mutilation, marking, etc., of livestock. Regs. may (*a*) provide that persons who contravene or fail to comply with regs. to be guilty of an offence; (*b*) provide for exemptions; (*c*) contain incidental, etc., provisions. Regs. to be by S.I., to be approved in draft by resolution of each House

Regs. may be made as to E. and W. only, by Min. of Agric., Fisheries and Food; as to S. only, by Secy. of State ..   ..   ..   Agric. (Misc. Provisions) Act 1968 (c. 34) ss. 2, 8 (4) ,51 (1)

Exercise

1978/1800   Welfare of Livestock (Intensive Units) Regs.
1980/593   Welfare of Livestock (Deer) O.
1982/1884   Welfare of Livestock (Prohibited Operations) Regs.
1987/114   Welfare of Livestock (Prohibited Operations) (Amdt.) Regs.
1987/2020   Welfare of Battery Hens Regs.
1987/2021   Welfare of Calves Regs.

(7) RIDING ESTABLISHMENTS

Power

1964 (inserted 1970)   Secy. of State may by O. prescribe "approved certificates" (other than those issued by British Horse Society, or the Fellowship of the Institute of the Horse) as to suitability of applicants for licences to keep riding establishments

O. to be by S.I., may be varied or rev.

Riding Establishments Act 1964 (c. 70) ss. 1 (4) (*a*), 6 (4), 6A
Riding Establishments Act 1970 (c. 32) ss. 5, 6

Exercise

Power not yet exercised

(8) PROTECTION OF ANIMALS

Commct. of *Animals (Scientific Procedures) Act 1986 (c.14) See* S.I. 1986/2088, 1989/2306 made under s. 30(3), the last apptg. 1.1.1990 for those provns. not already in force.

Power

1986   Secy. of State may by O. by S.I. (*a*) extend defn. of protected animal, (*b*) alter the stage of development specified in s. 1 (2) of Act of 1986 [stage of development of vertebrate], (*c*) make provn. in lieu of s. 1 (2) as to protected animals included in extended defn.

O. subject to annulment on resolution of either House

Animals (Scientific Procedures) Act 1986 (c. 14) ss. 1, 28

FINDING BOOKS ON A SUBJECT 6–25

Your first task should be to find out what suitable books are available in your own library. Most computerised library catalogues will offer the facility to search for books by subject (sometimes called "keyword"). If you do not find your desired subject, try some alternative headings or look under a more general, or a more specific, subject. For instance, suppose that you require information on negligence, which is part of the law of torts. There will be a chapter on negligence in any general textbook on the law of torts but, in addition, there may be books specifically on negligence, or even on one specialised aspect of negligence, *e.g.* professional negligence.

As an alternative to searching by keyword, you can look for books on a subject using the classification scheme. Paragraph 1–3 explains that the classification scheme is intended to bring together on the shelves all books dealing with the same subject. Computerised library catalogues usually allow you to identify the appropriate classification number (or "classmark") for your subject. You will then be able to search the catalogue for all books with that classification number, or you can go to the shelves at the classification number to see what is available. If you do not have a computer catalogue in your library, there will be a card index to the classification scheme.

Footnotes and bibliographies (lists of books) in textbooks and journal articles will refer you to other books, journals and cases on the subject. You can check in the library catalogue to find out if these are available in your library. Remember that government reports on the subject may not be entered in the library catalogues. You may need to consult the separate indexes to government publications (para. 5–18) to trace these in the library.

You may be able to access the computer catalogues of other libraries from your library. This is a quick way to find out what other books are available on the topic and where they can be found. Ask the library staff for details on how to access and search other libraries' catalogues.

Legal Bibliographies 6–26

Bibliographies list books which have been published on a subject, both in this country and abroad. A number of possible sources of information are given below. Not all of them may be available in your library, and you will probably only need to use one or two of them in order to trace relevant books.

6–27   D. Raistrick—Lawyers' Law Books
Lawyers' Law Books (published by Professional Books in 1987; new edition expected to be published by Bowker-Saur in 1996) is probably the quickest and easiest way for students to find out what has been written on a particular subject. It is alphabetically arranged by subject (see the figure on p. 139). Under each subject heading, it gives a list of textbooks written on that topic. There are also references to relevant government publications, such as reports issued by the Law Commission. At the beginning of each subject heading, there are references to alternative headings, and a list of the major legal reference works and journals which contain information on that topic. Full details of the authors, titles, publishers and dates of books are provided. This information enables you to look in your own library catalogue to see if the books mentioned are available in the library.

6–28   Information Sources in Law
Information Sources in Law, edited by R. G. Logan (published by Butterworths in 1986) provides a detailed guide to sources of legal information, although it is now in need of updating. There are chapters, written by leading experts, on sources of information for each of the major areas of law, *e.g.* revenue, criminal, social and welfare law, etc. The work covers sources of information on the law of the United States of America, the Commonwealth, international law and European Communities law, as well as English, Scottish and Irish law. There are useful references to historical sources of information. The book is particularly helpful for anyone starting research on an unfamiliar subject.

6–29   International Legal Books in Print
First published in 1990, this two-volume bibliography is published every two years. It contains references to over 15,000 books published in the English language in the United Kingdom, Western Europe and the Commonwealth countries of the past and present, excluding, for the most part, the United States. Only those books in print at the time the bibliography is published, are included. Entries are arranged in subject order in Volume 2, and contain comments on the book, as well as price and publisher details. Author and title indexes are printed in Volume 1.

6–30   Current Law
At the back of each *Current Law Monthly Digest* is a list of new books published during that month (mainly British, with a few foreign works in English). When the *Monthly Digests* are replaced by the *Current Law Year Book*, a list of books published during the

Page from D. Raistrick, Lawyers' Law Books

BUSINESS NAMES
See also Trade Marks.

Encyclopaedias

Statutes in Force. Group: Partnerships and Business Names.
Halsbury's Laws of England. 4ed. see index vol.
Halsbury's Statutes of England. 3ed. vol.

37.
Encyclopaedia of Court Forms in Civil Proceedings (Atkin). 2ed. vols. 30,38.
Encyclopaedia of Forms and Precedents. 4ed. vol. 5.

Texts

CHOWLES, V.G., WEBSTER, G.C. & PAGE, N.S.
South African law of trademarks, company names and trading styles. 2ed. Butterworths (S.Africa), 1973.

JOSLING, J.F.
Registration of business names. 3ed. Oyez, 1955 (Practice notes no.2).

KERLY, Sir D.M.
The law of trade marks and trade names. 11ed. Sweet & Maxwell, 1983.

STONE's Justices' manual. Butterworths. 3 vols. Annual.

BUSINESS TENANCIES
See also Landlord and Tenant.

Encyclopaedias and periodicals

Statutes in Force. Group: Landlord and Tenant.
Halsbury's Laws of England. 4ed. vol. 27.
Halsbury's Statutes of England. 3ed. vol. 18.
Encyclopaedia of Court Forms in Civil

Proceedings (Atkin). 2ed. vol. 24.
Encyclopaedia of Forms and Precedents. 4ed. vol. 11.

Estates Gazette. 1858–

Texts

ALDRIDGE, T.M.
Letting business premises. 4ed. Oyez, 1981.

ALDRIDGE, T.M. & JOHNSON, T.A.
Managing business property: a legal handbook. Oyez, 1978.

ENVIRONMENT, DEPARTMENT OF THE
Security of tenure of business premises: how landlord and tenant are affected. 5ed. HMSO, 1977.

FOX-ANDREWS, J.
Business tenancies. 3ed. Estates Gazette, 1978.

MAGNUS, S.W.
Business tenancies. Butterworths, 1970.

RUSSELL-DAVIES, M.
Letting and managing residential or business premises: a legal and practical outline. R.I.C.S., 1978.

BY-LAWS
See also Delegated Legislation; Local Government.

Encyclopaedias

Halsbury's Laws of England. 4ed. see index vol. 4ed.
Encyclopaedia of Forms and Precedents. 4ed. see index vol.

year is printed at the back of the *Year Book*, arranged in subject order.

6–31   Law Books Published
Law Books Published is issued in several parts during the year and these parts are then replaced by an annual volume, giving details of all books on law and allied topics published during a particular year. It covers British and American books and some foreign books written in English. There are entries under authors and under titles, in a single alphabetical sequence. The second half of each volume is a list of books published on particular subjects during the year. The subject headings are American, as is the spelling, *e.g.* railroads, labor.

6–32   Law Books in Print
Law Books in Print is published at intervals and gives a list of all law books which are still in print at the time of publication. Entries are arranged in the same way as in the companion *Law Books Published* (*i.e.* under authors, titles and subjects).

6–33   Current Publications in Legal and Related Fields
Current Publications in Legal and Related Fields is published in looseleaf parts which are replaced by annual volumes. There are entries under authors and titles in the looseleaf volume.

In the annual volume, a detailed subject index at the front of the volume guides you to relevant entries in the main (alphabetically arranged) part of the work. Each item has its own individual number.

6–34   Law Books 1876–1981
The first three volumes of this work are arranged by subject and cover books published in English mainly in the United States, although some British and other countries' publications are also included. The fourth volume contains entries under authors, titles and serials and a list of the names and addresses of legal publishers in the United States. The work was updated by *Law Books and Serials in Print 1988: a Multimedia Sourcebook*, which continues annually with quarterly *Cumulative Supplements*.

6–35   Bibliographical Guide to the Law
This is based on international, foreign and English language publications received by the American Library of Congress. It appears annually, and has entries for authors, titles and subjects in one single alphabetical sequence. It is particularly useful for tracing books on law written in languages other than English.

Other legal bibliographies   6–36

Raistrick's *Lawyers' Law Books* (para. 6–27) contains a useful list of more specialised legal bibliographies (under the heading "Bibliographies") and Logan's *Information Sources in Law* (para. 6–28) is likewise very helpful. The catalogues of specialised law libraries, such as the Squire Law Library (at the University of Cambridge), the Institute of Advanced Legal Studies Library (London University), the Radzinowicz Library of Criminology (University of Cambridge) and the Harvard Law School Library (on microfiche) are valuable sources of information.

Two detailed bibliographies are Sweet & Maxwell's *Legal Bibliography of the British Commonwealth* (especially useful for tracing older British books) and C. Szladits, *Bibliography on Foreign and Comparative Law* (which covers books and articles in English only).

Many other specialist legal bibliographies have been published, *e.g.* P. O'Higgins and M. Partington, *Social Security Law in Britain and Ireland: a Bibliography*; E. Beyerly, *Public International Law: a Guide to Information Sources*; and R. W. M. Dias, *Bibliography of Jurisprudence*.

The library staff will help you to trace relevant bibliographies. Remember that many textbooks will also contain a bibliography on their subject.

Non-Legal Bibliographies   6–37

If your library does not possess the specialised legal bibliographies, or if you are trying to trace information on a non-legal topic, you can use a number of more general bibliographies, which cover law in addition to other topics.

General Bibliographies and Guides to Books in Print   6–38

The main source of information for British books which have been published since 1950 is the *British National Bibliography*. This is published weekly. The last issue of each month has a green cover, and this issue contains an index to all the books published that month. Every few months, the information is cumulated. At the end of the year, an annual volume is produced containing details of all British books published during that year. Entries are arranged by subject in a classification scheme. You will first need to look up your subject in the Subject Index, which will refer you to the classification number under which you will find the books on your subject. Entries for law books will be found at the numbers

340–349. There is also an alphabetical list of all authors and titles of books included. The *British National Bibliography* is available on three CD-ROM discs and can also be searched online via BLAISE-LINE. These electronic versions are much quicker and less cumbersome to use.

Whitaker's Books in Print, formerly called *British Books in Print*, is printed annually and lists all books published in Britain and still in print. Entries appear under author and title but not under subject area. This has been partly rectified by the CD-ROM (called Bookbank), which will search for words anywhere in the title. Bookbank will also search under the author, publisher and date of publication, or any combination of these. The CD-ROM is more current than the printed version, with monthly updates.

Books in Print is an American publication listing all books published or distributed in the United States and still in print. There are entries under authors and under titles (in separate volumes). There is also a *Subject Guide to Books in Print*. Similar guides to books in print in other countries are available. Ask a member of the library staff to help you locate them.

The catalogues of large general libraries can also provide very useful lists of books on a subject. The catalogues of some major law libraries are available (para. 6–36) in printed form, or on microfiche. The American Library of Congress published a *National Union Catalog* giving details of books published in the United States and foreign books, on all subjects, in both author and subject orders. The British Library has published a *General Catalogue of Printed Books* listing, in author order, all the books in the British Library. This is kept up to date by supplements and by the *British National Bibliography*. The national libraries in several other countries have produced similar catalogues. Your librarian can tell you which of these are available locally.

6–39   THESES

If you are undertaking a comprehensive piece of research, you may need to find out if any theses have already been written on that subject. The Institute of Advanced Legal Studies (University of London) has published a complete list of all theses on legal topics—*Legal Research in the United Kingdom 1905–1984*. Until 1988, this was kept up to date by an annual *List of Current Legal Research Topics*, which showed research in progress in universities and polytechnics in the United Kingdom.

Other sources of information cover theses in all subject areas. The *Index to Theses* covers all British theses, while *Dissertation Abstracts* contains references to theses from North America. The library staff can help you to find out what theses have been written on subjects of interest to you.

Theses which have been completed at your own institution are normally available for consultation in the library. It may be possible for the library staff to borrow, on inter-library loan, copies of theses completed in other universities in this country and abroad.

CHAPTER 7

Using Computers to Find the Law

7–1 INTRODUCTION

Most law firms now use computers for various office tasks such as word processing, drafting legal documents and accounting. Much of the law of the United Kingdom and other countries is available in computer databases. It is now possible to instruct a computer to find, for example, all cases and all legislation dealing with a particular legal problem. Eventually, this may be the normal way in which solicitors and barristers will research legal problems—by turning, not to the printed book, but to their computer screen. It is important, therefore, that you should know something about "information technology" as it affects the law. Law schools and law libraries have access to computer databases and instruction in their use is usually available.

Computers can search a vast amount of information very quickly. Whereas it would take you many hours, for example, to search for a name or a subject in the contents of a newspaper over a year, a computer can undertake such a search almost instantaneously. Computers, then, are ideal for what is called *full-text* searching, where the computer stores the whole of the text of a document or collection of documents and can search for a word anywhere in the text. LEXIS is an example of a *full-text database*, as it can look for a word anywhere in a law report or statute. You can then read the text on the computer screen or print it out.

Some databases are not full-text. Rather than storing the whole text, they contain references to documents. These are called *bibliographic databases*. The *Legal Journals Index* database (para. 4–3) is an example of a bibliographic database. It contains the information found in the printed *Legal Journals Index* and other indexes of articles and law reports. Unlike a full-text database, you only receive a reference, rather than the full article itself. You will need to use the reference to find the journal article in your own library.

Electronic versions of databases are quicker to search and give more flexibility in finding the information. In both the electronic and printed versions of the *Legal Journals Index*, you can search for a journal article by author, subject, case name or legislation. The electronic version gives you additional options for searching, such as by any word in the title. The electronic database is also much quicker to use. Whereas in the printed version you need to look in each annual volume of the index and the latest few monthly issues, then write out the references, the electronic version will search all years simultaneously (unless you specify particular dates) and will print out relevant references.

Electronic databases may allow the searcher to find information not otherwise practically possible using printed sources. LEXIS, for example, contains the full text of a vast number of British cases, some of which are not readily available in printed form. In addition, since LEXIS is able to search for words or names anywhere in the law report, it can retrieve relevant cases which could not be identified simply by searching under the main subject headings used in printed indexes.

The growth of electronic legal databases has given lawyers access to a vast array of information they would not otherwise be able to access through their own library.

ACCESSING LEGAL DATABASES   7–2

The computer database you wish to search may be physically located on a computer in your institution, or may be many miles away, even in another country.

Remote Online Databases   7–3

These are databases which are accessed through a telecommunications network to a "remote" site (*i.e.* to somewhere outside your own institution). The first commercial electronic legal databases were all online databases, since only very large, expensive computers were able to store such vast amounts of data.

There are many thousands of online databases available throughout the world. Many of these databases are available through *online hosts*. These are organisations which store databases on large computers in order to make them accessible to searchers. The DIALOG service, for example, stores more than 400 databases on its computer in California, while Data-Star offers access to 250 databases from its computer in Berne.

In order to undertake an online search, you normally need a computer and modem linked to a telecommunications line. The modem (Modulator Demodulator) converts messages from the computer into a form which can be transmitted. If your computer is linked to JANET (see para. 7–5) you may be able to access the database you require without a modem. Whether you use a direct telecommunications link or JANET, you will first dial the number for the service you require. Once you have linked up with the host or database provider, you will be asked for your password. A password is given to each institution when it subscribes to the service. When the *log-in* procedure has been successfully completed, the computer will wait for you to enter your search.

There are several costs involved with online searching. Many hosts or database providers charge an annual subscription fee for a password to access the databases. In addition, the database provider may charge every time you use the database. The cost is often calculated in terms of the amount of time spent logged in to the service, although some providers also charge for the number of lines of information shown on the screen or the number of pages you print out. The telecommunications provider (*e.g.* British Telecom) will charge your institution for the telecommunications link (the telephone call).

Since both the host and the telecommunications providers charge for the amount of time you spend logged in to the database, it is important that you have planned your search beforehand (see Appendix IV). Many online databases are command-driven (para. 7–7) and require some training, so the library staff may offer to search the databases for you. You may find that they will ask you to check the paper sources first, in order to define your search objectives more clearly and find suitable search terms.

7–4   CD-ROMs

The introduction of CD-ROMs (*Compact Discs—Read Only Memory*) in 1985 meant that databases could now be stored locally without the need for a large computer. CD-ROMs look like audio CDs but rather than containing music, they contain data. CD-ROMs are able to store vast amounts of information, with each disc able to store the equivalent of about 250,000 sheets of A4 copy. In the same way that you would change your CD if you wish to hear different music, you only need to change the CD-ROM to search a different database. To search a CD-ROM, you may need to borrow a disc and insert it in the CD-ROM player attached to the computer. Alternatively, the CD-ROMs in your library may be *networked*. If so, rather than handling the CD-ROM, you need only to choose the appropriate database from the selection given on the computer screen.

Unlike online searching, there are no costs attached to the time spent searching a CD-ROM database. CD-ROMs are designed to be used by the researcher or student rather than by library staff and the search software (para. 7–7) has become much easier to use. You are unlikely to need much training before you feel confident searching the database.

Although the data on the disc can be read as many times as wished, it cannot be erased or written over (hence CD-*ROM* or *Read Only Memory*). The database can only be updated by the publisher reissuing a new disc. Most publishers only update CD-ROM databases three or four times each year, whereas most online databases are updated weekly or even daily. It is important, therefore, to check the date of the CD-ROM and, if necessary, up-date the information by using printed current awareness services or searching online. Some publishers, *e.g.* Context, are trying to overcome this problem. It is possible, for example, when searching Justis Weekly Law, the CD-ROM of the *Weekly Law Reports*, to log in to the online database simply by pressing one key. Once in the online database, the user can quickly update the search using the same search strategy as on the CD-ROM.

Internet Resources   7–5

Computers in universities throughout Britain are linked together by the Joint Academic Network (JANET). Universities have negotiated jointly to load commercial databases onto the network at much reduced prices. As a result, your institution may have access over JANET to electronic versions of *The Times* and the *Social Sciences Citation Index*, along with other databases useful for your studies. The university will pay a subscription for the databases but there will be no charges for searching.

JANET is just part of a 'worldwide computer network called the Internet. Computer databases in thousands of institutions can be accessed free of charge. To help you track down relevant databases and search them, several software packages, such as Gopher and World Wide Web, have been developed, providing a standard way to access many of the databases. You may find the library has produced a leaflet explaining some of the most useful databases to search.

7–6   Locally Stored Databases

Many databases are not stored on CD-ROMs; nor do they need to be accessed via telecommunications links or networks to remote computers. Instead, the data is held on a computer in your own institution. The library computer catalogue is an example of a locally stored database, created by staff working within your institution. Similarly, your department may hold information on students in a database. It is also possible to buy databases from commercial database providers for installation on local machines. The *Legal Journals Index*, for example, is available on CD-ROM, issued three times a year, but is also available on magnetic tape to be loaded onto the purchaser's own computer. The magnetic tapes are issued fortnightly and so are more current than both the printed index and the CD-ROM. Locally stored databases often have the advantage of allowing more people to search the database at the same time and can take less time in calculating the answers to search requests than networked CD-ROMs.

Many law firms use locally stored databases. In addition to many of the commercial law databases found in educational institutions, law firms use commercially prepared precedent databases and create their own "know-how" databases of useful information, *e.g.* conference papers, collections of recent research on a topic, helpful precedents, etc. As the number of law-related databases increases, you will be expected to know how to use electronic "libraries", as well as the more traditional paper-based law libraries.

7–7   Search Software

The search software enables you to communicate with the computer so that it can find the information you need from the database. Until fairly recently, most search software was *command-driven*. The computer expected you to type in a command in a format it could understand. There were few hints on the screen as to what you should do next and it was necessary to know the *command language* of the software. Since training was necessary, only frequent researchers and librarians tended to search the databases. Many online databases still offer command-driven software for experienced searchers who can do quicker (and therefore less expensive) searches this way. Most online services now also offer a more "user friendly" service as an alternative to command-driven searching.

Although most online hosts use their own search software with their own language, all search software use the same principles for searching. You will need to master these principles if you wish to search databases effectively. Appendix IV gives an explanation of the principles of searching LEXIS.

With the introduction of CD-ROMs and locally stored databases, researchers and students have been given the opportunity to search electronic databases themselves. Search software requiring little or no instruction has been designed. This *menu-driven* software offers you a list of options on the screen (in the same way as the restaurant menu gives you a choice of dishes). Follow the instructions on the screen to choose the appropriate menu option for your search. Further menus and instructions will appear until your search is completed. You will frequently find the menu options in a line at either the very bottom or along the top of the screen. Many CD-ROMs use the same search software. If you find yourself in any difficulty, the software can give you helpful hints and instructions. Look for the *help* facility on the menu.

Some CD-ROMs and locally stored databases use search software called *hypertext*. As with more traditional search software, hypertext will search for the desired word or words in the full text of the documents. However, hypertext also allows you to jump between related screens to explore the information. Let's suppose you have asked Hypertax (a hypertext CD-ROM of U.K. tax legislation) to search for a particular section of an Act. The full text of that section will be displayed and many of the words will be highlighted. Whilst reading the full text, you may come across a highlighted word for which you would like clarification (*e.g.* you do not understand the meaning of the word, or you would like to see the full text of the document mentioned). When you select the highlighted word or phrase, a new screen comes up with the details. You can then return to the original page once you have read the details, or again select a highlighted phrase from the new page. In this way, hypertext databases are designed as learning tools, by which you can browse the information in the database. Using hypertext as a *computer-assisted learning* tool is very different from searching online databases such as LEXIS, where you need a clearly defined search strategy and must keep the time spent logged in to the database to a minimum.

7–8   LEGAL DATABASES

There is now a wide range of databases dealing with aspects of law and new titles are constantly becoming available. Paragraphs 7–9 and 7–10 give details of LEXIS and Lawtel. These two databases give the broadest range of legal information, including both statute and case law on every area of the law.

7–9   LEXIS

LEXIS is the most well-known legal database. The database is situated in Ohio, USA, although in Britain the call is made to a London telephone number which then links to the computer. The cost is that of a telephone call to London coupled with a charge for the use of LEXIS.

LEXIS has traditionally been searched using a special terminal, which was usually situated in the library. More recently, it has become possible to search LEXIS on standard PCs. Instead of there being only one LEXIS terminal, situated in the library, you may find that your lecturers are now accessing LEXIS from a wide range of locations within the institution.

LEXIS includes the full text of many thousands of cases, statutes and statutory instruments. Briefly, LEXIS covers:

1. all the cases reported in the major general series of English law reports (the *All England Law Reports*, the *Law Reports*, the *Weekly Law Reports*, etc.) plus all cases reported in many more specialised series (the *Building Law Reports*, the *Family Law Reports*, the *Criminal Appeal Reports*, the *Estates Gazette*, the *Insurance Law Reports*, the *Lloyd's Reports* and many others). The case is reported in its entirety;
2. many unreported cases from superior courts (excluding the Court of Appeal Criminal Division) and from some tribunals since 1980. Cases which have only been reported briefly in *The Times*, the *Solicitors' Journal* and other publications can usually be read in full by using LEXIS;
3. all Public General Acts which are currently law in England and Wales. If an Act has been amended, the latest version of the Act is given;
4. all statutory instruments currently in force;
5. tax material, including double taxation agreements, Inland Revenue documents, and the text of the latest Finance Bill;
6. a file giving details of damages awarded for all forms of personal injuries;

7. the full text of all articles from the *New Law Journal* and the *Law Society Gazette* since 1986 and the *Estates Gazette* since January 1991;
8. European law: cases heard in the European Court of Justice, European commercial cases and cases on the European Convention on Human Rights;
9. Commonwealth materials: Australian and New Zealand cases;
10. American law reports (both Federal and State) and the full text of some legal journals published in the United States;
11. French cases and legislation (in the French language);
12. Scottish and Irish cases.

In addition to the above, new material covering new areas of law is being added. When you log in to LEXIS, you are presented with a full list of available material. Similar information is found in the red looseleaf LEXIS folder, which should be available in the library.

Since LEXIS is such a large database, it is divided into *libraries*. All English statute and case law, for instance, is found in the English General Library (ENGGEN). Similarly, the European Communities Library (EURCOM) contains the full text of European cases and Commission decisions. Each library is subdivided into *files*. The ENGGEN library includes the CASES file in which you can search for case law, the STAT file with all Public General Acts still in force and the SI file with current statutory instruments. There is also a file called STATIS, which combines the information in the STAT and the SI files. Before you can undertake a search in LEXIS, you need to specify which library and which file you wish to search. You can only search one file at a time, although it is easy to change files and repeat the search without rekeying.

New cases and legislation are added on a weekly basis. It takes on average about six to eight weeks from the date of the court hearing until the time that LEXIS carries a full report. LEXIS is therefore not as up to date as Lawtel, but is good for finding the full text of recent developments in statute or case law.

Further information about LEXIS, together with hints on good searching techniques, are found in Appendix IV.

Lawtel   7–10

Lawtel is a cumulative and continuously updated digest of legal information. It includes summaries of leading cases, statutes, Bills in progress, statutory instruments, significant subsidiary legislation, practice directions, white and green papers, commencement dates, DSS Commissioners' decisions, damages awards and references to legal articles.

The database is updated every working day. Lawtel summarises the most significant material added to the database during the previous 24 hours in the Daily Update.

Lawtel contains summaries of cases since January 1980 and references to the law reports and newspapers in which they are printed are added as soon as the report becomes available. Lawtel is therefore a useful way to find the latest reports of a case.

Lawtel is also very useful in identifying the current status of a piece of legislation. For every Act passed since January 1984, Lawtel provides details of any commencement orders, amendments or repeals. Similarly, you can discover whether any statutory instruments have been made since 1984 under a section of an Act and whether they have since been repealed.

7–11   Other Legal Databases

There are many other legal databases. Most of these databases contain one type of information such as case law (*e.g.* the *Weekly Law Reports* database (para. 2–6)) or references to journal articles (*e.g.* the *Legal Journals Index* database (para. 4–3)), while others deal with one area of the law (*e.g.* Hypertax (para. 7–7); Eurocat CD-ROM (para. 11–7)).

Increasing numbers of legal publications are becoming available in electronic format. Examples of relevant databases are outlined in other chapters, but you may find that your library has other databases which also would be useful to your studies. Ask your librarian for information on databases available from your library. Remember that electronic sources are not necessarily more comprehensive nor more up to date than conventional printed sources. You will still need to know how to find information from paper-based research tools and be able to find law reports and statutes in their printed versions.

7–12   DATABASES OF LAW-RELATED INFORMATION

There are many databases which, although not dealing specifically with the law, are of use to legal researchers. Many electronic indexes of literature in the social sciences, for example, contain law-related articles (para. 4–9). Newspapers, also, are useful, not only for their law reports but for news and comment on proposed legislation, the impact of new statutes and background information on cases going through the courts. The quality newspapers are all available on CD-ROM as well as via several online hosts and through the Internet.

CHAPTER 8

Scots Law

8–1 INTRODUCTION

Several legal systems flourish in the British Isles, including the three to be found in the United Kingdom. The law of England and Wales and Northern Ireland is similar but that of Scotland can be markedly different. This fact must be borne in mind when considering questions of law and where you look to find the answers. Throughout the United Kingdom, the law is uniform in a number of respects, as regards taxation and company law for example; broadly speaking, it is within criminal law and the area called private law that the differences are greatest.

An overview of the history and development of Scots law is included in most general textbooks. A classic account is Lord Cooper, *The Scottish Legal Tradition*, first published in 1949. The 1991 reprint is accompanied and enhanced by two essays by other hands which survey the present position of Scots law and place it in historical perspective. Cooper's book should be read by anyone interested in Scots law or in Scottish history.

The rest of this chapter outlines the main categories of printed information which will be of help to you: law reports, legislation, institutional writings, reference books, textbooks, journals and official and other publications. Further detail may be found in a sister publication by D. D. Mackey, *How to Use a Scottish Law Library* (1992).

LAW REPORTS   8–2

Chapter 2 contains detailed information on English law reports
and how to use them; it should be noted that these are often cited
in Scotland, so that it is necessary to be familiar with them.

Civil cases are heard in the Sheriff Courts, the Court of Session
and, as a final court of appeal, in the House of Lords. The Outer
House of the Court of Session determines cases at first instance,
while the Inner House is mainly a court of appeal. Criminal cases
are heard in the District Courts, the Sheriff Courts and the High
Court of Justiciary. The High Court is both a court of first instance
and the court of appeal. Courts of special jurisdiction include the
Court of the Lord Lyon and the Scottish Land Court, while the
Crofters Commission, the Lands Tribunal for Scotland and
the Children's Hearings are among the statutory tribunals.

The most important series of Scottish reports is *Session Cases*.
Five series appeared between 1821–1906 and these are known by
the names of five respective editors.

First Series	Shaw (S.)	1821–1838, 16 vols.
Second Series	Dunlop (D.)	1838–1862, 24 vols.
Third Series	Macpherson (M. or Macph.)	1862–1873, 11 vols.
Fourth Series	Rettie (R.)	1873–1898, 25 vols.
Fifth Series	Fraser (F.)	1898–1906, 8 vols.

These are cited by the volume number, the initial letter of the
editor's name, and the page number. If your reference is 6 M. 321,
this indicates that you need to consult volume 6 of the third series
of *Session Cases*, edited by Macpherson, at page 321. The year is
occasionally included and certainly helps to avoid confusion, *e.g.*
(1868) 6 M. 321.

After 1906, the editor's name was no longer used and the
citation became S.C. It is important to note that there are three
separate sets of page numbers within each bound volume of *Session
Cases*. The first deals with cases which have gone to appeal in the
House of Lords; these are cited, *e.g.* 1990 S.C.(H.L.) 63. The second
series of page numbers in each volume covers criminal cases,
decided in the High Court of Justiciary; these are cited, *e.g.* 1990
J.C. 62. The third sequence consists of cases decided in the Court of
Session itself, *i.e.* civil cases; these are cited, *e.g.* 1990 S.C. 61.

The House of Lords series was first issued with separate
pagination as far back as 1850, so that an 1852 case is cited, *e.g.* 15
D.(H.L.) 28. Similarly, High Court of Justiciary cases are separately
paged from 1874, *e.g.* 2 R.(J.) 22 *or* 1916 S.C.(J.) 18.

Session Cases is slow to appear, so the other major series of Scottish law reports is the *Scots Law Times*. This has been published weekly during session since 1893 and is divided into two chief sections:

(a) *News*, which includes articles; and
(b) *Reports*.

The weekly parts are cumulated into annual volumes. The *Reports*, which form the major part of each volume, include cases heard in the Court of Session, the High Court of Justiciary and the House of Lords. Unlike their counterparts in *Session Cases*, these cases do *not* appear in separately paged sections. The citation is straightforward, *e.g.* 1992 S.L.T. 182. However, the *Reports* section also contains the following which *are* paged separately.

(1) *Sheriff Court Reports*;
(2) *Reports of Cases decided in the Scottish Land Court and the Lands Tribunal for Scotland*; and
(3) *Reports of Cases decided in the Lyon Court*.

These are cited as, *e.g.* 1992 S.L.T. (Sh.Ct.) 33, 1992 S.L.T. (Land Ct.) 45, 1992 S.L.T. (Lands Tr.) 89 and 1992 S.L.T. (Lyon Ct.) 2. Before 1982, there was also a section entitled *Notes of Recent Decisions*, to which reference may still be made, *e.g.* 1981 S.L.T. (Notes) 5. Care should be taken when using either the thin weekly parts or the bulky annual volumes to ensure that you are looking in the right portion. Each volume has its own indexes and cumulative indexes cover cases reported 1961–1990 and 1991–1994.

The Law Society of Scotland is the moving force behind two other modern law reports. *Scottish Criminal Case Reports* (from 1981), cited, *e.g.* 1993 S.C.C.R. 493, includes brief commentaries on most cases. Hitherto unreported cases from 1950–1980 have been published as a supplement and there is a cumulative index 1981–1990. *Scottish Civil Law Reports* (from 1987), cited, *e.g.* 1993 S.C.L.R. 64, also includes brief commentaries. *Greens Weekly Digest* (from 1986), arranged by subject, summarises all decisions brought to the attention of the publishers, with judgments of legal significance reported subsequently in the *Scots Law Times*. As there are no cumulations, citation is by issue and paragraph number, *e.g.* 1993 G.W.D. 32–2024. A cumulative index covers 1986–1991. The *Scotsman* newspaper publishes law reports, which may be traced through the *Daily Law Reports Index* (from 1988) (para. 2–15).

There is a Scottish library on LEXIS, covering cases reported in *Session Cases* and the *Scots Law Times* from 1944, the *Scottish*

Criminal Case Reports, the *Scottish Civil Law Reports* and unreported decisions from the Court of Session (Outer House from 1985, Inner House from 1982). Most unreported decisions benefit from the inclusion of searchable catchwords.

Older Cases   8–3

Session Cases covers cases from 1821 onwards. The most important collection of cases from the mid-sixteenth to the early nineteenth centuries is *Morison's Dictionary of Decisions*. In 38 volumes, it is arranged by subject and the pages throughout the volumes are numbered continuously, from pages 1 to 17074. Thus a typical citation might be (1743) M. (*or* Mor.) 11274. Various appendices, supplements and synopses were added and, most importantly, an index (*Tait's Index*) was issued in 1823.

Two other sets of older reports are often consulted. The *Scottish Law Reporter* was issued in 61 volumes from 1865–1924 and is cited, *e.g.* 22 S.L.R. 116 (do not confuse with the *Scottish Law Review*, also S.L.R.). The *Sheriff Court Reports* appeared in 79 volumes from 1885–1963, being cited, *e.g.* 1951 Sh.Ct.R. 196; note that these were published as part of the *Scottish Law Review* and may be bound with that set.

House of Lords decisions in Scottish appeals for the period 1707–1873 are reported in 10 series of private reports, again cited by the editors, *e.g.* 7 W. & Sh. 19 (Wilson and Shaw). A further 10 series by private reporters cover early criminal cases, *e.g.* 4 Irv. 58 (Irvine).

A helpful summary of Scottish law reports, old and modern, is to be found in D. M. Walker, *The Scottish Legal System* (6th ed., 1992), pp. 470–475.

Indexes to Law Reports   8–4

There is no comprehensive index to the older law reports. This means that if you do not know the exact date of a case you have to look through the indexes to as many individual volumes as is necessary, a laborious task. However, there are short cuts for the more important cases in digests such as the *Scots Digest*, which covers 1800–1873 with subsequent volumes and parts for 1873–1947, and the *Faculty Digest*, covering 1868–1922, with six further volumes from 1922–1980. The indexes to these will often reveal the case you are seeking and, in the case of the *Faculty Digest*, inform you if it has been judicially referred to in subsequent decisions. Scottish cases are also included in *The Digest* (para. 2–13). For more recent cases, the appropriate sections of the *Scottish Current Law*

Case Citators 1948–1976 and *1977–1988* and the latest *Current Law Case Citator* (para. 2–12) can be consulted if you know the name of a case and want to find a citation for it. D. Raistrick, *Index to Legal Citations and Abbreviations* (2nd ed., 1993) is invaluable for checking both Scottish and English abbreviations.

The *Current Law Monthly Digest*, the *Scottish Current Law Year Book* (1948–1990), and the *Current Law Year Book* (from 1991) (paras. 6–8 and 6–9) enable you to see, at a glance, all recent developments in the law of a particular subject; new cases, legislation and official publications are summarised under appropriate subject headings and journal articles relating to Scots law are noted. Whereas the *Scottish Current Law Year Book* had a separate Scottish subject index, *Current Law* has a single index covering all jurisdictions.

The *Legal Journals Index* (from 1986) (para. 2–16) and the tables of cases which appear in textbooks can also be used to trace decisions.

8–5   LEGISLATION

Statutes and statutory instruments are dealt with in Chapter 3 and other parliamentary publications in Chapter 5. There are special procedures governing the consideration of Bills relating exclusively or mainly to Scotland: see Erskine May, *Parliamentary Practice* (21st ed., 1989), p. 478.

Before 1707, Scotland had its own Parliament and enacted its own laws. The standard edition of the *Acts of the Parliaments of Scotland*, known as the *"Record Edition"*, was published in the nineteenth century in 12 volumes. Some of these Acts are still in force and are to be found in *Statutes in Force* (para. 3–7). Since 1707, many Acts have applied to Britain or the United Kingdom, but there are a number each year pertaining to Scotland only. These are included in the standard collections of older statutes and were also collected together by the Edinburgh publishing firm of Blackwood, which issued three volumes covering 1707–1847, then produced annual volumes from 1848–1947. These are known as *"Blackwood's Acts"*. In modern times, Scottish Acts are published by HMSO as part of the *Public General Acts* (para 3–6), and appear in *Scottish Current Law Statutes* (1948–1990) and *Current Law Statutes Annotated* (from 1948) (para. 3–9). The HMSO publications *Index to the Statutes* (para. 6–18) and the *Chronological Table of the Statutes* (para. 3–14), and Butterworths' annual *Is It In Force?* (para. 3–12) cover Scottish Acts. Amendments and repeals can be traced through the *Scottish Current Law Statute Citator 1948–71*, the *Scottish Current Law Legislation Citator 1972–88*, the latest *Current Law Legislation Citator* (para. 3–13) and *Current Law* itself.

LEXIS is of little use, since it only includes those provisions of Scottish Acts which affect British or United Kingdom legislation. Provisions relating to Scotland in Acts of general application are only present from 1980.

From 1752 until after the Second World War, Local Acts formed the bulk of legislation reaching the Statute Book. The proliferation of measures on railways, harbours, lighting and water supply reflects the development of a modern urban society. In Scotland, the private Bill procedure has been almost completely superseded by the system introduced by the Private Legislation Procedure (Scotland) Act 1936, which involves application to the Secretary of State, an inquiry by commissioners if required, and an expedited passage in Parliament: see Erskine May, *Parliamentary Practice* (21st ed., 1989), pp. 965–975. Proposals are notified through the *Edinburgh Gazette* and the *London Gazette*, while further information can be gleaned from the very irregular *Private Legislation (Scotland) Procedure: Journal of Proceedings*. Published as Local and Personal Acts, from 1992 they also appear in *Current Law Statutes Annotated*.

The situation regarding personal Bills is not so clear cut: see Erskine May, *Parliamentary Practice* (21st ed., 1989), p. 944.

Scotland has its own statutory instruments too, forming part of the HMSO publication programme but additionally numbered and available as a subseries, *e.g.* S.I. 1993/2227 (S.237). They can be found through the *Index to Government Orders* (para. 3–25), the *Table of Government Orders* (para. 3–24), and the monthly *List of Statutory Instruments* (para. 3–22), while amendments and repeals can be traced through the *Current Law Statute, Legislation* or *Statutory Instrument Citators*. However, Scottish statutory instruments do not appear in publications such as *Halsbury's Statutory Instruments* or *Knight's Local Government Legislation*. Acts of Adjournal and Acts of Sederunt, which regulate court procedure, appear as statutory instruments and are reproduced in the *Scots Law Times*. Prior to 1991, they were published in *Scottish Current Law Statutes*. Those currently in force are included in the *Parliament House Book* (see below).

Once more, LEXIS is of little use but Scottish measures *are* included on the statutory instruments CD-ROM, SI-CD (para. 3–22).

INSTITUTIONAL WRITINGS   8–6

The formal sources of Scots law include certain authoritative writings dating from the mid-seventeenth to the early nineteenth centuries. These include Viscount Stair, *Institutions of the Law of*

Scotland (6th ed., 1981), which was first published in 1681; J. Erskine, *Institute of the Law of Scotland* (8th ed., 1871), which was first published in 1773; D. Hume, *Commentaries on the Law of Scotland Respecting Crimes* (4th ed., 1844), which was first published in 1797; and G. J. Bell, *Commentaries on the Mercantile Law of Scotland* (7th ed., 1870), which was first published in 1800. These may be regarded as potentially decisive in the absence of legislation or clear precedent, but only in those areas of law where social change over the intervening period has not diminished their persuasiveness (see, for example, *S.* v. *H.M. Advocate* 1989 S.L.T. 469 on marital rape). A comprehensive listing of institutional writings will be found in R. M. White and I. D. Willock, *The Scottish Legal System* (1993), with a succinct appraisal of their current standing at pp. 86–88.

8–7 REFERENCE BOOKS

Reference books, such as dictionaries and encyclopedias, can be of assistance when you begin the search for information on a subject. D. M. Walker, *Oxford Companion to Law* (1980), though dated, is a useful source, referring to all manner of legal topics including persons and institutions. As it was written by a professor of law in Glasgow, there is much Scottish material which would not be found in a similar work compiled south of the border.

There is a tradition of Scottish legal encyclopedias and a landmark in the renaissance of Scottish legal publishing was the appearance, in 1987, of the first of the 25 volumes of the *The Laws of Scotland: Stair Memorial Encyclopaedia*. Fully indexed and updated by a looseleaf service, and with reissue volumes projected, this is now an essential component of legal research. There have been many spinoffs, including several textbooks. *Greens Litigation Styles* and *Greens Practice Styles* will replace the venerable *Encyclopaedia of Scottish Legal Styles*. The *Parliament House Book* is a four-volume looseleaf compendium of primary and delegated legislation, covering private law and court procedure. It includes practice notes, solicitors' rules, guidance notes, and other information which can be hard to find. Sections are often reprinted and issued separately, *e.g. Greens Sheriff Court Rules* (6th ed., 1993). Some of the looseleaf subject encyclopedias, *e.g. Palmer's Company Law*, have Scottish editors and take account of any differences in the law, but it is always advisable to check.

The newcomer to law will be aided by J. A. Beaton, *Scots Law Terms and Expressions* (1982); *Green's Glossary of Scottish Legal Terms* (3rd ed., 1992) or the *Glossary: Scottish Legal Terms and Latin Maxims and European Community Legal Terms* which forms part of *The Laws of Scotland* and was published separately in 1988. The *Scottish Law Directory* (annual, often known as the *White Book*) and the Law Society of Scotland's own directory, the *Blue Book* (also annual), contain useful addresses and other information and will help you trace an individual or firm. In addition, the larger Scottish practices are now included in the *Legal 500*. The Faculty of Advocates, the Scottish Bar, produced its first *Directory* in 1992, although advocates are listed in other guides.

TEXTBOOKS   8–8

W. Green (Sweet & Maxwell) and Butterworths are the main players in Scottish legal textbook publishing, though important books are still produced by the smaller independents such as T. & T. Clark.

H. L. MacQueen, *Studying Scots Law* (1993) is primarily aimed at those contemplating entry into the legal profession. R. M. White and I. D. Willock, *The Scottish Legal System* (1993) is a useful alternative to D. M. Walker's established work with the same title (6th ed., 1992). W. M. Gloag and R. C. Henderson, *Introduction to the Law of Scotland* (10th ed., 1995) has long been a standard in universities, while E. A. Marshall, *General Principles of Scots Law* (6th ed., 1995) is much favoured by those pursuing non-law degree courses. A. A. Paterson and T. St. J. N. Bates, *The Legal System of Scotland: Cases and Materials* (3rd ed., 1993) is an important adjunct to any of the above. Scottish legal publishing is in a healthy state, with up-to-date textbooks in most subject areas. Due to the restricted size of the market, many older books tried to serve student, academic and practitioner, but there is now a better mix of introductory works, professional publications, and scholarly tomes.

The Scottish Universities Law Institute (SULI) has promoted a distinguished series of texts on modern Scots law, *e.g.* A. B. Wilkinson and K. McK. Norrie, *Parent and Child* (1993). These are generally regarded as the standard works in their respective areas. The Stair Society, founded in 1934 to encourage the study and advance the knowledge of the history of Scots law, makes valuable material available through its publications. *An Introductory Survey of the Sources and Literature of Scots Law* (1936) and *Introduction to Scottish Legal History* (1958) are still convenient for information on older sources.

8–9 JOURNALS

As previously noted, the *Scots Law Times* includes articles, news items, and book reviews. The *Journal of the Law Society of Scotland* and the *Scottish Law Gazette* combine articles with professional news while *SCOLAG*, published by the Scottish Legal Action Group, has a crusading streak. The more academic *Juridical Review* is the long-established law journal of the universities of Scotland and there is a cumulative index covering 1889–1988. *Scottish Planning and Environmental Law, Greens Business Law Bulletin,* and its *Criminal Law, Employment Law, Environmental Law, Family Law, Property Law, Civil Practice* and *Reparation* stablemates provide surveys of current law and procedure. All the above are covered by the *Legal Journals Index* (para. 4–3).

The *Journal of the Law Society of Scotland* from 1990 may be searched in full-text on LEXIS.

8–10 OFFICIAL AND OTHER PUBLICATIONS

8–11 Statistics

Criminal statistics are made available through the "Criminal Justice Series" of the Scottish Office *Statistical Bulletin*. Another series covers juvenile justice and the Children's Hearings system. Statistics relating to the business of the civil courts and legal and public departments, compiled by the Scottish Courts Administration, are published as *Civil Judicial Statistics, Scotland*. Statistics often form part of Annual Reports (see below).

8–12 Annual Reports

The Law Society of Scotland, the Scottish Legal Aid Board, the Scottish Legal Services Ombudsman, the Scottish Law Commission, the Scottish Committee of the Council on Tribunals, the Commissioner for Local Administration in Scotland (the Local Government Ombudsman), the Crown Office and Procurator Fiscal Service and the Police Authorities all publish Annual Reports.

8–13 Research and Law Reform

The Scottish Office publishes *Central Research Unit Papers*, reporting the results of research into a broad spectrum of socio-legal and other issues. The Scottish Law Commission publishes *Discussion Papers, Publications* (covering Annual Reports and other reports) and occasional research papers. Some of the reports appear as Command Papers and some are produced jointly with the Law Commission in London. The annual report contains a cumulative list of documents both published and with restricted circulation.

Continuing Education   8–14

The papers from all the seminars and conferences organised as part of the Law Society of Scotland's Update programme (formerly Post-Qualifying Legal Education) are published and represent a useful source of information, particularly for practitioners.

CHAPTER 9

Northern Ireland Law

9–1 INTRODUCTION

The student of Northern Ireland law, having read a statement of the law on a particular topic in a standard English textbook, has to determine the extent to which this law applies in Northern Ireland. As regards statute law, it may be that a particular Westminster Act applies completely, *e.g.* the Radioactive Substances Act 1993 (c. 12); or only certain sections may apply, *e.g.* the Clean Air Act 1993 (c. 11); or the Act may not apply at all, *e.g.* the Sexual Offences Act 1993 (c. 30). Usually the last or penultimate section of a recent Act will tell you whether, or to what extent, the Act applies in Northern Ireland. If a Westminster Act does not apply to Northern Ireland, and there is a Northern Ireland equivalent, then the Northern Ireland legislation may be similar, but with significant differences, or it may be virtually the same. In either case, the point is that if there is a separate piece of Northern Ireland legislation, it constitutes a different source, and the Westminster Act cannot be quoted as being the relevant legislation.

For a general introduction to Northern Ireland law, read Brice Dickson's book, *The Legal System of Northern Ireland* (3rd ed., 1993). At a more advanced level read his article in the Winter 1992 issue of *Northern Ireland Legal Quarterly* entitled "Northern Ireland's legal system—an evaluation" (1992) 43 *N.I.L.Q.* 315–329.

9–2 THE CONSTITUTIONAL BACKGROUND

For a full account of the constitutional position of Northern Ireland up to 1989, read Brigid Hadfield's book, *The Constitution of Northern Ireland* (1989), and for an update to 1991, her chapter in *Northern Ireland: Politics and the Constitution* (1992), of which she is the editor.

Briefly, the Northern Ireland jurisdiction came into existence in 1921, established by the Government of Ireland Act 1920 (10 & 11 Geo. 5, c. 67), which set up a parliament for Northern Ireland with power to legislate on many aspects of civil and criminal law, *e.g.* law and order, local government, health and social services, education, planning and agriculture. For some 50 years, the Parliament of Northern Ireland legislated on these transferred matters, taking a line independent of Westminster in some fields and following "step by step" in others, until the system of government was suspended on March 30, 1972, by virtue of section 1(3) of the Northern Ireland (Temporary Provisions) Act 1972 (c. 22). The last Act of the Northern Ireland Parliament received the Royal Assent on March 28, 1972.

During the first phase of "direct rule", *i.e.* from the end of March 1972 to the end of 1973, the Queen in Council legislated on transferred matters by means of Orders in Council (which were statutory instruments), while Executive powers were vested in a Westminster Secretary of State.

The Northern Ireland Constitution Act 1973 (c. 36) abolished the Northern Ireland Parliament on June 18, 1973, and established the Northern Ireland Assembly with a power-sharing Executive from January 1, 1974. The Assembly was given authority to legislate by Measure on a wide range of matters of Northern Ireland concern. Four Measures were passed before the Assembly, as a result of the collapse of the power-sharing Executive, was prorogued by Order in Council and its legislative power returned to Westminster in May 1974.

After a brief interim period, the second phase of "direct rule" was introduced in July 1974 by the Northern Ireland Act 1974 (c. 28). Under the present system, laws may be made for Northern Ireland by Order in Council on all matters which had fallen within the legislative competence of the Assembly.

A second Assembly was set up in 1982, under the Northern Ireland Act 1982 (c. 38), with "scrutiny, consultative and deliberative powers," not with legislative powers. It was dissolved in June 1986 by virtue of the Northern Ireland Assembly (Dissolution) Order 1986 (S.I. 1986 No. 1036).

LEGISLATION   9–3

The statute law which affects, or has affected, Northern Ireland comes from more than one source and in more than one form, comprising:

(a) Acts passed by the Irish Parliament in Dublin from 1310 to 1800;
(b) Acts passed by the Parliaments of England (1226 to 1707) and Great Britain (1707 to 1800) and by the United Kingdom Parliament thereafter;
(c) Acts passed by the Parliament of Northern Ireland from 1921 to March 1972;
(d) Orders in Council made in 1972 and 1973 under section 1(3) of the Northern Ireland (Temporary Provisions) Act 1972 (c. 22);
(e) Measures passed by the Northern Ireland Assembly in 1974; and
(f) Orders in Council made from 1974 onwards under paragraph 1 of Schedule 1 to the Northern Ireland Act 1974 (c. 28).

While the Northern Ireland Orders in Council, being Statutory Instruments, are delegated legislation in form, they are not so in substance.

This body of statute law is indexed, in four separate sequences, in the *Chronological Table of the Statutes, Northern Ireland*, which is published triennially by HMSO, Belfast. There is a companion volume, arranged by subject, the *Index to the Statutes, Northern Ireland*, which is also published triennially. At the time of writing, the current *Chronological Table*, covering the Statutes and Northern Ireland Orders in Council affecting Northern Ireland on December 31, 1992, was published in 1993. The current edition of the *Index to the Statutes*, covering the Statutes and Northern Ireland Orders in Council in force on December 31, 1993, was published in 1995.

9–4   Editions of Statutes

As regards the editions of the statutes affecting Northern Ireland, the most comprehensive edition of the statutes of the Dublin Parliament 1310 to 1800 is *The Statutes at Large Passed in the Parliaments Held in Ireland from AD 1310 to 1786 inclusive* (13 volumes), continued to 1800 in seven additional volumes, printed in Dublin by George Grierson, 1786 to 1810.

The Statutes, Measures and Orders in Council of Northern Ireland were published by HMSO, Belfast, singly at first and later in annual bound volumes from 1921 to 1981.

The first edition of *The Statutes Revised Northern Ireland* was published in 1956 in 16 volumes, covering all the legislation in force at 1950, revised to 1954. This included both Dublin and Westminster legislation. The second edition of *The Statutes Revised Northern Ireland* was published in 1982 in 13 looseleaf binders for convenience in updating. The Dublin Acts (up to 1800) are included, but the Westminster Acts after 1920 are omitted, as these are supposed to be available in their revised version in *Statutes in Force* (para. 3–7). So far this second edition (originally revised to 1981) has been updated annually by a looseleaf cumulative supplement which covers not only the 13 volumes of *Statutes Revised (2nd ed.)* but also subsequent Northern Ireland Orders in Council, *i.e.* from 1982 onwards, up to the end of the precurrent year. The cumulative supplement lists the sources of amendments, repeals, etc., which have occurred since 1981. You then have to check these at source.

From 1982, HMSO, Belfast, ceased to produce annual bound volumes of Orders in Council. Instead they have supplied looseleaf binders matching those of the 1981 revision. You may find that your library, while filing the majority of sets in the looseleaf binders, will have had one or more sets bound. This is because, although readers will usually be looking for updated versions of legislation, some readers will sometimes require a piece of legislation in its original version.

Identifying the Source of Legislation   9–5

Sometimes it is possible to tell by the date whether an Act was passed at Westminster, Dublin or in Northern Ireland (Belfast to 1932 and Stormont thereafter), since the all-Ireland Parliament was abolished in 1800, and the Northern Ireland Parliament was prorogued in 1972 and abolished the following year.

However, the indicator of source is generally the position of the words "Ireland" or "Northern Ireland" in relation to the word "Act." If "Ireland" or "Northern Ireland" in the title comes *before* "Act," the source is Westminster, *e.g.* the Bills of Exchange (Ireland) Act 1828; the Social Security Administration (Northern Ireland) Act 1992. If "Ireland" appears *after* "Act," and directly *before* the date, the source is Dublin, *e.g.* The Landlord and Tenant Act (Ireland) 1741. If "Northern Ireland" appears *between* "Act" and the date, the source is the Northern Ireland Parliament, *e.g.* the Factories Act (Northern Ireland) 1949.

Delegated Legislation   9–6

The rules, regulations and orders made by Northern Ireland

Example of Index to Statutory Rules and Orders in Force

132   INDEX TO STATUTORY RULES AND ORDERS IN FORCE

EDUCATION—*Contd.*

2. Statutory System of Education—*Contd.*

(b) PROVISION OF EDUCATION—*Contd.*

(i) *Primary and Secondary Education*—Contd.

Exercise

1973, Sept. 28	Heating, Lighting, Cleaning and Maintenance Regs. (N.I.) 1973 (No. 376)		1973, II, p. 2139
1973, Sept. 28	Maintained Schools (Equipment and Maintenance) Regs. (N.I.) 1973 (No. 378)		1973, II, p. 2146
1976, Jan. 16	Heating, Lighting, Cleaning and Maintenance (Amdt.) Regs. (N.I.) 1976 (No. 14)		1976, I, p. 45

Power

1986.   Dept. may by regs. make provn. as to the carrying on of grant-aided schools and may prescribe the purposes for which such schools may not be used

Education and Libraries (N.I.) Order, S.I. 1986/594 (N.I. 3) art. 17A

Education (N.I.) Order, S.I. 1987/167 (N.I. 2) art. 5

Exercise

1987, Sept. 28   Teachers' Salaries Regs. (N.I.) 1987 (No. 384)

1988, Aug. 18   Teachers' Salaries (Amdt.) Regs. (N.I.) 1988 (No. 304)

Power (replacing previous power)

1986.   Dept. shall by regs., subject to negative resolution, prescribe the standards to which premises of grant-aided schools shall conform

Education and Libraries (N.I.) Order, S.I. 1986/594 (N.I. 3) arts. 18, 134

Exercise

1973, Dec. 10   School Premises (Standards) Regs. (N.I.) 1973 (No. 491) 1973, II, p. 2852

(ii) *Religious Education in Schools*

Power (replacing previous power)

1986.   Dept. shall by regs., subject to negative resolution, secure that the provns. of art. 16 relating to religious education are complied with

Education and Libraries (N.I.) Order, S.I. 1986/594 (N.I. 3) arts. 21, 134

Exercise

1973, Sept. 26   Primary Schools (General) Regs. (N.I.) 1973 (No. 402)   1973, II, p. 2316

1973, Sept. 28   Secondary Schools (Grant Conditions) Regs. (N.I.) 1973 (No. 403)   1973, II, p. 2327

(iii) *Reservation of Places in Grammar Schools*

Power (replacing previous power)

1986.   Dept. may make regs., subject to negative resolution, in accordance with which the managers of each grammar school are to make available, for pupils having the prescribed qualifications, such number of places as are prescribed

Education and Libraries (N.I.) Order, S.I. 1986/594 (N.I. 3) arts. 25, 134

Exercise

1978, Aug. 1   Grammar School Pupils (Admissions, Grants and Allowances) Regs. (N.I.) 1978 (No. 217)

1984, July 31   Grammar School Pupils (Admissions, Grants and Allowances) (Amdt.) Regs. (N.I.) 1984 (No. 269)

Power (replacing previous power)

1986.   Dept. may make regs., subject to negative resolution, prescribing the types of fee which may be charged to prescribed pupils admitted to grammar schools. Dept. may also prescribe the maximum fee which may be charged by the Bd. of Governors of a voluntary grammar school of a prescribed description

Education and Libraries (N.I.) Order S.I. 1986/594 (N.I. 3) arts. 26, 134

Exercise

1984, July 31   Grammar Schools (Fees) Regs. (N.I.) 1984 (No. 268)

1986, July 3   Grammar Schools (Fees) (Amdt.) Regs. (N.I.) 1986 (No. 205)

EDUCATION—*Contd.*

2 Statutory System of Education—*Contd.*

(b) PROVISION OF EDUCATION—Contd.

(iv) *Assessments and Statement of Special Educational Needs*

Power (replacing previous power)
>1986.   Dept. may by regs., subject to negative resolution, make provn. as to the advice which a Bd. is to seek in making assessments. Regs. may also make provn. as to the manner in which assessments are to be conducted and to such other matters as the Dept. considers appropriate
>>Education and Libraries (N.I.) Order, S.I. 1986/594 (N.I. 3) arts. 29(3), 31(1), 134, sch. 11 pt. I para. (2)

Exercise
>1985, Dec. 30   Education (Special Educational Needs) Regs. (N.I.) 1985 (No. 365)

Power (replacing previous power)
>1986.   Dept. may by regs., subject to negative resolution, prescribe the form of a statement to be made by the Bd. with regard to a child's special educational needs
>>Education and Libraries (N.I.) Order, S.I. 1986/594 (N.I. 3) arts. 29(3), 31(1), 134, sch. 11 pt. II para. 6(1)

Exercise
>1985, Dec. 30   Education (Special Educational Needs) Regs. (N.I.) 1985 (No. 365)

Power (replacing previous power)
>1986.   Dept. may by regs. make provn. with respect to the keeping, disclosure and transfer of statements and may prescribe the frequency with which assessments are to be repeated
>>Education and Libraries (N.I.) Order, S.I. 1986/594 (N.I. 3) arts. 29(3), 31(1), 134, sch. 11 pt. II para. 6(2)

Exercise
>1985, Dec. 30   Education (Special Educational Needs) Regs. (N.I.) 1985 (No. 365)

(v) *Special Education*

Power (replacing previous power)
>1986.   Dept. may by regs., subject to negative resolution, prescribe requirements to be complied with by a school as a condition of approval of the school as a special school
>>Education and Libraries (N.I.) Order S.I. 1986/594 (N.I. 3) arts. 34, 134

Exercise
>1973, Sept. 28   Handicapped Pupils and Special Schools Regs. (N.I.) 1973 (No. 390)   1973, II, p. 2175
>1987, Sept. 28   Teachers' Salaries Regs. (N.I.) 1987 (No. 384)

(vi) *Compulsory Attendance*

Power (not exercised)
>1968.   Dept. may make regs. as to issue of certificates of attendance for purpose of proving that child or young person has attended school as regularly as trade or business of parent or guardian permits
>>Children and Young Persons Act (N.I.) 1968 (c. 34) ss. 28(2), 179

Cleanliness and Inspection of School-Children *See* HEALTH AND PERSONAL SOCIAL SERVICES, 3(*a*)

3 Independent Schools

Power (replacing previous power)
>1986.   Dept. may make regs., subject to negative resolution, with respect to the registration of independent schools
>>Education and Libraries (N.I.) Order, S.I. 1986/594 (N.I. 3) arts. 38, 134

Exercise
>1974, June   6   Independent Schools (Registration) Regs. (N.I.) 1974 (No. 106)   1974, I, p. 348

rule-making authorities are called *statutory rules and orders* (S.R. & O.s) up to the end of 1973 and *statutory rules* (S.R.s) thereafter. From 1973 onwards, they occupy two or more bound volumes per year, the annual indexes being available only upon publication of the final volume. Recently published *statutory rules* (S.R.s) are listed in the London *HMSO Daily Lists* (para. 5–14). Later they appear in the monthly and annual editions of the *List of Statutory Instruments together with the List of Statutory Rules of Northern Ireland for* . . . .

The triennial *Index to the Statutory Rules and Orders of Northern Ireland in force on 31st December 1991* (published 1993), like its counterpart the *Index to Government Orders* (para. 3–25), indicates the statutory powers under which the S.R. and O.s or S.R.s are made. (See figures on pp. 168–169.)

9–7   Identifying the Source of Delegated Legislation

In order to distinguish between a Westminster statutory instrument applying solely to Northern Ireland (which may or may not be a Northern Ireland Order in Council), on the one hand, and a Northern Ireland statutory rule, whether an "order," "rule" or "regulation," on the other, one is generally guided by the relative positions of "Northern Ireland" and "Order." The same principle applies as in the case of Acts, *e.g.* The Animals (Post-Import Control) Order (Northern Ireland) 1993 is a statutory rule, its citation being S.R. 1993 No. 307. The Local Elections (Variation of Limits of Candidates' Election Expenses) (Northern Ireland) Order is a statutory instrument, its citation being S.I. 1993 No. 941. The Family Law (Northern Ireland) Order 1993 is a statutory instrument which is also a Northern Ireland Order in Council and, therefore, has a double citation, *i.e.* S.I. 1993 No. 1576 (N.I. 6). The difference in the two numbers is accounted for by the fact that only about one statutory instrument in one or two hundred is a Northern Ireland Order in Council.

For further information, I strongly recommend George Woodman's article "Legislation in Northern Ireland" (1987) *The Law Librarian* 45–49.

9–8   LAW REPORTS

Although the Northern Ireland jurisdiction came into existence in 1921, the Incorporated Council of Law Reporting for Northern Ireland only started publishing the *Northern Ireland Law Reports* in

1925. Reports of cases in the Northern Ireland courts between 1921 and 1924 can be found in the *Irish Reports* and the *Irish Law Times Reports*.

Because of the inconvenience caused by the time lag before publication of the official law reports, the *Northern Ireland Law Reports Bulletin of Judgments* (which has had several minor changes of title over the years) has been produced from 1970 onwards. The bulletins consist of collections of recent judgments within blue paper covers. They are cited as: [year] number N.I.J.B.

Indexes to Law Reports   9–9

The *Index to Cases Decided in the Courts of Northern Ireland and Reported during the period 1921 to 1970*, edited by Desmond Greer and Brian Childs (ICLRNI, 1975), covers Northern Ireland cases reported in the *Northern Ireland Law Reports*, the *Irish Law Times Reports*, the *Irish Jurist Reports*, the *Irish Reports*, the *Law Reports: Appeal Cases*, the *Criminal Appeal Reports* and *Tax Cases*. The sections consist of:

(a) Alphabetical Table of Cases Reported;
(b) Subject matter titles;
(c) Subject Index;
(d) Statutes Judicially Considered (in four separate sequences: Public and General Acts of the Parliaments of England, Great Britain and the United Kingdom, 1215–1970; Parliament of Ireland to 1800; Parliament of Northern Ireland; Parliaments outside the United Kingdom);
(e) Private and Local Acts Judicially Considered (again four sequences);
(f) Statutory Rules and Orders Judicially Considered;
(g) Rules of the Supreme Court Judicially Considered;
(h) Cases Judicially Considered; and
(i) Words and Phrases Judicially Considered.

The *First Interim Supplement, 1971 to 1975* to the above *Index* was published in 1976. It covers the *Northern Ireland Law Reports* from 1971 to 1974. For 1975, it covers the *Northern Ireland Judgments Bulletin/Northern Ireland Law Reports Bulletin of Judgments* only, as the official law reports had not appeared by the date of compilation. Also covered are Northern Ireland cases in the *Criminal Appeal Reports*, *Tax Cases* and the *Taxation Reports*.

No second supplement has yet been published, but unofficial supplements are in (limited) circulation, covering cases reported up to 1985.

The *Bulletin of Northern Ireland Law* (1981 onwards) digests cases in the official law reports and in the judgments bulletins. In addition, it has digested some otherwise unreported cases. (See the figure on p. 177.)

The *Irish Digest* consists of a number of volumes published in Dublin and covering the years 1867 onwards. Coverage includes the *Northern Ireland Law Reports*.

9–10 Decisions of Tribunals

The *Reports of Decisions of the [Northern Ireland] Industrial Tribunals* were published with a limited circulation from 1966 to 1978. An example of their citation is I.T.R. 135 (N.I.). They are now distributed only to a chosen few but may be consulted by callers at the Central Office of Industrial and Fair Employment Tribunals, in Belfast. Selected decisions have been digested in the *Bulletin of Northern Ireland Law* since 1981.

The *Industrial Court (Northern Ireland) Awards* have been published since 1963. At present they are appearing at the rate of one or two per year. They are available from HMSO, Belfast, and are also digested in the *Bulletin of Northern Ireland Law*.

The Equal Opportunities Commission for Northern Ireland has produced, in a looseleaf binder, *A Casebook of Decisions on Sex Discrimination and Equal Pay*.

Selected decisions of the Fair Employment Tribunal are digested in the *Bulletin of Northern Ireland Law*.

The Lands Tribunal for Northern Ireland has produced reports in typescript since 1965. From 1981, all of these have also appeared, in digested form, in the *Bulletin of Northern Ireland Law*.

The Planning Appeals Commission, which was set up in 1973, has been producing a *Bulletin* since April 1974. It is issued monthly and distributed on an informal basis to interested persons. It rarely, if ever, includes information about public inquiries, but it provides digests of cases (which take some time to appear). However, if one is prepared to pay, it is possible to obtain a full report of a case from the Planning Appeals Commission without delay.

The *Reported Decisions of the Umpire under the Family Allowances, National Insurance and Industrial Injuries Acts (N.I.) 1948 to 1961*, published by HMSO, Belfast, in 1963, was followed in 1978 by the *Reported Decisions of the Commissioners under the Family Allowances, National Insurance and Industrial Injuries Acts (N.I.) and the Social Security Acts (N.I.) April 1961 to December 1977*. Decisions from 1978 onwards, under the Social Security (Northern Ireland) Acts 1975 onwards, are still only available unbound, as are the *Decisions of the*

Commissioner under the Supplementary Benefits (N.I.) Order 1977, which run from 1982 to 1987.

Social Security Case Law: Index to Decisions of the Commissioners in Northern Ireland covers all reported Decisions from 1948. It was published in 1986 and to date has had one Amendment published in 1989.

From 1981, all the published and selected unpublished Commissioners' Decisions are digested in the *Bulletin of Northern Ireland Law.*

ANNUAL REPORTS AND STATEMENTS OF ACCOUNTS   9–11

The various Northern Ireland government departments and agencies are obliged to publish annual reports of their activities and statements of accounts. Some reports are published by HMSO, Belfast, on behalf of the relevant department. Others are published as House of Commons Papers or Command Papers (see paras. 5–3, 5–10) by HMSO, London. *The Eighteenth Annual Report of the Standing Advisory Commission on Human Rights* is H.C. 1992–93, 739. The *Industrial Development Board for Northern Ireland: receipts and payments accounts for the year ended 31st March 1992* is Cm. 2258. Such reports can be traced through the HMSO *Daily Lists* and *Catalogues* (para. 5–14).

BOOKS AND PAMPHLETS (MONOGRAPHS)   9–12

As already stated, the student of Northern Ireland law is faced with the problem as to whether or not a statement of the law, which he/she has just read in one of the standard English textbooks is applicable to Northern Ireland.

Until 1981, practitioners, teachers and students of Northern Ireland law were nearly always obliged to use the primary materials in order to determine the law on any point. The only secondary sources available were a handful of books and pamphlets, the *Northern Ireland Legal Quarterly* (the main source), the *Gazette of the Incorporated Law Society of Northern Ireland* and various articles thinly scattered throughout United Kingdom, foreign and Commonwealth legal journals.

However, in 1980 the Council of Legal Education for Northern Ireland set up S.L.S. Legal Publications (N.I.) which produces monographs and periodical publications on various aspects of the Northern Ireland legal system. It has published books and pamphlets on areas of Northern Ireland law and practice which differ substantially from English law and practice. The books include the "Law in Action" series, primarily intended for the general public. The pamphlets include the "Recent Developments" series, designed to keep readers informed of recent changes in the law. A useful starting point for the general reader or law student is a title in the "Law in Action" series: Brice Dickson, *The Legal System of Northern Ireland* (3rd ed., 1993).

The latest S.L.S. publisher's catalogue serves as a useful bibliography on Northern Ireland law. Other bibliographies are listed in the chapter by Elizabeth Gleeson in Robert Logan (ed.), *Information Sources in Law*, Chap. 16, pp. 245–246 (para. 6–28).

In the field of welfare law, the Law Centre (N.I.) publishes training guides and regularly updated information sheets, as well as its journal *Frontline* (formerly *Welfare Rights News*). Among other pressure groups, the Belfast-based Committee on the Administration of Justice has produced a number of pamphlets, policy documents and leaflets in the human rights field—on criminal justice, police powers, etc.

Government publications can be traced through the daily *Lists* and monthly and annual catalogues published by HMSO. However, note that government departments now produce some of their material internally, by use of word processors, etc., and such material does not appear on HMSO *Lists*.

The various Northern Ireland agencies produce pamphlets as well as Annual Reports. As they are obliged to report their activities and submit their accounts annually to the government, their Annual Reports and Statements of Accounts appear in the HMSO catalogues (para. 5–14), but their miscellaneous other publications do not all appear there. The agencies include, among others: the Standing Advisory Commission on Human Rights, the Fair Employment Commission for Northern Ireland, the Equal Opportunities Commission for Northern Ireland, the Labour Relations Agency and the Northern Ireland Housing Executive.

9–13 JOURNALS

The Northern Ireland Legal Quarterly (1936–1961, 1964 onwards), published by S.L.S., is a general legal journal containing articles, notes, comments and book reviews on a wide variety of legal topics. It does not confine itself to Northern Ireland law, but contains articles of worldwide legal interest. As from 1993, articles appearing in N.I.L.Q. on European law are indexed in the *European Legal Journals Index*, and not in the *Legal Journals Index*.

The *Gazette of the Incorporated Law Society of Northern Ireland* was published irregularly between 1964 and 1982. It is succeeded by *The Writ; Journal of the Law Society of Northern Ireland* (August 1986 onwards), primarily for members of the Society, but containing items of interest to the keener student, particularly the post-graduate professional student.

The Law Centre (N.I.) publishes a social welfare law quarterly which was entitled *Welfare Rights News* (Nos. 1–21) from December 1983 to April 1991, and is now entitled *Frontline*, published from June 1991 (No. 1) onwards.

Fortnight: an Independent Review, published since 1970, is primarily concerned with local politics and current affairs but frequently contains articles or commentary relevant to the study of the Northern Ireland legal system.

Articles on Northern Ireland law appear, from time to time, in journals published outside Northern Ireland, *e.g.* "Northern Ireland's Emergency Laws and International Human Rights" by Paul Hunt and Brice Dickson, (1993) 11 N.Q.H.R. 173, N.Q.H.R. being the *Netherlands Quarterly of Human Rights*.

Indexes to Journals   9–14

A Bibliography of Periodical Literature Relating to Irish Law by Paul O'Higgins is an invaluable guide to articles published up to 1981. The original volume was published in 1966 and was followed by two supplements in 1973 and 1983. It covers articles in journals published anywhere in the world, non-legal journals, and articles on foreign law by Irish authors.

The *Legal Journals Index*, the *Index to Legal Periodicals*, the *British Humanities Index* and other current publications mentioned in Chapter 4 frequently contain references to articles on Northern Ireland law.

ENCYCLOPEDIC WORKS   9–15

The *Digest of Northern Ireland Law*, published by S.L.S. in booklet form, is designed to provide reliable, practical guidance on Northern Ireland law for all those who need access to such information on a regular basis. It is written in a style suitable for those without formal legal training (advisers in Citizens Advice Bureaux and similar agencies, businessmen, personnel officers, trade union officials, etc.) as well as for those with or in the course of legal training. The authors of the various sections have highlighted differences between English and Northern Ireland law in their particular topics. The booklets cover:

legal services;
family law;
children and the law;

general contract law;
criminal procedure;
wills and intestacy;
social security law;
legal system of the E.C.;
enforcement of E.C. law;
consumer law;
insurance law;
employment law;
company law;
judicial review;
environmental health law; and
discrimination.

The *Bulletin of Northern Ireland Law,* also published by S.L.S. and appearing 10 times a year, provides a regular, comprehensive digest of legal developments in Northern Ireland and is, therefore, an invaluable current awareness work. Included under broad subject headings are:

(a) summaries of all new legislation applicable to Northern Ireland and commencement dates;
(b) digests of written judgments and awards in the courts;
(c) selected tribunal decisions and tax cases;
(d) Practice Directions and Court Service notices; and
(e) selected recent developments in Great Britain and the Republic of Ireland and in E.C. law.

(See the figure on p. 177.)
Current Law (para. 6–8) uses "Northern Ireland" as one of its subject headings, further subdivided alphabetically by subject. (See the figure on p. 178.)

In addition there are specialised encyclopedias. The *Encyclopedia of Northern Ireland Labour Law and Practice,* published by the Labour Relations Agency, is a three-volume looseleaf work updated regularly.

scraping to her right leg, bruising to her right knee and right buttock, as well as muscular and ligamentous injuries to her left shoulder, all of which resolved satisfactorily.

Award: £4,000.

DAMAGES

22   Personal injuries - minor plaintiff - scintilla case

P. (A MINOR) v McCLEAN, Belfast Rec Ct (Judge Porter QC), 30 December 1992

The plaintiff was aged 12 when she received an injury to her foot after colliding with a car on the Ballysillan Road, Belfast. She sustained a crush injury to her left foot with some tenderness over the second and third metatarsal bones. The plaintiff had a full range of movement, a complete recovery was anticipated with no expectation of deterioration.

The plaintiff, who held a certificate in road safety, claimed to have waited some ten minutes before crossing the road. The plaintiff had got off a bus, waited, and then walked across the road. She didn't see the defendant until the defendant sounded her horn, at which point the plaintiff was at the white line in the middle of the road.

The defendant said she had been travelling at 30 mph when she saw the plaintiff run from behind a bus. The defendant braked and sounded her horn simultaneously but the plaintiff's foot struck the car. There was an independent witness to corroborate the defendant's evidence.

The Ballysillan Road has room for four lanes of traffic, although the road is not so marked. However on the day of the accident there were parked cars on both sides of the road.

HELD:

Whilst the court appreciated that the plaintiff was only 12 at the time of the accident she did hold a certificate in road safety and as such was well aware of her responsibility in crossing the road. There was no evidence of excess of speed on the part of the defendant and the case was dismissed.

(Entry prepared from Solicitor's notes).

DEFENCE

23   Armed forces - discipline

ARMY, AIR FORCE AND NAVAL DISCIPLINE ACTS (CONTINUATION) ORDER 1993 (SI 1993/1804)

The Order continues in force for a period of 12 months from 31 August 1993 the provisions of the Army Act 1955, the Air Force Act 1955 and the Naval Discipline Act 1957.

Commencement: 20 July 1993 (65p)

EDUCATION

24   Curriculum

CURRICULUM (CORE SYLLABUS FOR RELIGIOUS EDUCATION) ORDER (NI) 1993 (SR 1993/272)

The Order specifies the core syllabus for religious education.

Commencement: 1 August 1993 (£1.10)

CURRICULUM (PROGRAMMES OF STUDY AND ATTAINMENT TARGETS IN SCIENCE) ORDER (NI) 1993 (SR 1993/273)

The Order specifies programmes of study and attainment targets in science.

Commencement: 1 August 1993 (£1.10)

25   Grant-maintained integrated schools

EDUCATION (GRANT-MAINTAINED INTEGRATED SCHOOLS) (CAPITAL GRANTS) REGULATIONS (NI) 1993 (SR 1993/308)

The Regulations provide for the payment by the Dept of Education to the Trustees or Boards of Governors of grant-maintained integrated schools of grants in respect of approved expenditure of a capital nature. The 1990 Regulations (noted 90/9/27) are revoked.

Commencement: 1 September 1993 (65p)

N. IRELAND: HEALTH AND SAFETY AT WORK

the Northern Ireland Constitution Act 1973 (c.36), s.38(1)(a)(4); operative on April 1, 1993; amends the maximum amount of a candidate's election expenses.

EMPLOYMENT

565. Unfair dismissal—compensation—increase of limit

UNFAIR DISMISSAL (INCREASE OF COMPENSATION LIMIT) ORDER (NORTHERN IRELAND) 1993 (No. 254) [65p], made under S.I. 1976 No. 1043 (N.I. 16), arts. 37(2), 80(3); operative on June 22, 1993; increases the limit on the amount of compensation which can be awarded by an industrial tribunal in claims for unfair dismissal as the compensatory award or as compensation for failure to comply fully with the terms of an order for reinstatement or re-engagement; revokes the 1991 (No. 67) Order.

FAMILY

566. Family Law (Northern Ireland) Order 1993 No. 1567 (N.I. 6)

This Order contains miscellaneous amendments to family law. It abolishes the requirement for certain press notices in respect of marriages in register offices, relaxes the restrictions on marriages within prohibited degrees of relationship, makes provision as to the methods of payment under maintenance orders and establishes a new rules committee in relation to family proceedings in the High Court and county courts. The Order also transfers certain statutory functions, makes breach of a personal protection order or an exclusion order a criminal offence and disapplies the requirement for the petitioner's oral testimony in divorce cases where the petition alleges two years' separation and the respondent consents to a decree being granted or where the petition alleges five years' separation. Articles 5 to 11 and 15 come into operation on days to be appointed. The remaining provisions come into operation on August 24, 1993.

FIRE SERVICE

567. Fire Services (Amendment) (Northern Ireland) Order 1993 No. 1587 (N.I. 7)

This Order makes miscellaneous amendments to existing legislation relating to fire precautions. The Order comes into operation on August 24, 1993, except for art. 13 which comes into operation on a day to be appointed.

FOOD AND DRUGS

568. Soft drinks

SOFT DRINKS (AMENDMENT) REGULATIONS (NORTHERN IRELAND) 1993 (No. 250) [£1·10], made under S.I. 1991 No. 762 (N.I. 7), arts. 15(1), 47(2); operative on June 28, 1993 (part) and January 1, 1994 (remainder); further amend the 1976 (No. 357) Regulations.

HEALTH AND SAFETY AT WORK

569. Explosives—packaging for carriage

PACKAGING OF EXPLOSIVES FOR CARRIAGE REGULATIONS (NORTHERN IRELAND) 1993 (No. 268) [£3·20], made under S.I. 1978 No. 1039 (N.I. 9), arts.

CHAPTER 10

Republic of Ireland Law

INTRODUCTION

Having the complex historical background that Ireland does,
it is generally accepted that Irish law is difficult to find. Irish
legal history very much consists of English law in Ireland, as
with the importation of English law from the twelfth century
onwards, the existing Brehon law was effectively eradicated.
Apart from the few brief intervals of legal independence, until
1922 the Irish legal system was heavily influenced by English
authority. In 1800, after the Act of Union, the Irish Parliament
was dissolved. In 1920, the Government of Ireland Act provided
for devolved governments in both the North and South, but this
was never implemented in the South. The Anglo-Irish Treaty
of 1922 established the Irish Free State with dominion status
within the British Commonwealth. A considerable amount of
nineteenth-century English law is still in force in Ireland. It is
only within the last 20 years or so that there has been a move
away from dependence on English law and legal literature. This
divergence from English law has seen a new era of Irish legal
publishing, with the production of textbooks in all the main
subject areas. However, as with many former Commonwealth
countries, early editions of secondary materials published in the
United Kingdom are frequently of great interest. The later editions
which contain current United Kingdom legislation are now too far
removed to be of very much importance. Consequently, many
secondary sources now amended in England are still relevant to
the law in Ireland.

Parts of an Act

(1) *Number 29 of 1992*

(2) **CENSORSHIP OF FILMS (AMENDMENT) ACT, 1992**

(3) AN ACT TO ENABLE THE MINISTER FOR JUSTICE TO APPOINT PERSONS TO BE KNOWN AS ASSISTANT CENSORS TO ASSIST THE OFFICIAL CENSOR OF FILMS IN 5 THE PERFORMANCE OF HIS FUNCTIONS AND TO AMEND THE CENSORSHIP OF FILMS ACTS, 1923 TO 1970, AND THE VIDEO RECORDINGS ACT, 1989.

[*21st December,* 1992] (4)

(5) BE IT ENACTED BY THE OIREACHTAS AS FOLLOWS: 10

Definitions.   **1.**—In this Act—

"the Act of 1923" means the Censorship of Films Act, 1923;

"the Act of 1989" means the Video Recordings Act, 1989;

"the Appeal Board" means the Censorship of Films Appeal Board established by the Act of 1923;   15

"functions" includes powers and duties and references to the performance of functions include, as respects powers and duties, references to the exercise of the powers and the carrying out of the duties;

"the Minister" means the Minister for Justice;   20

"the Official Censor" means the Official Censor of Films appointed under the Act of 1923 and includes a person appointed under section 2 (3) of that Act.

(7)
Appointment of
Assistant Censors.

(6)
2.—(1) (*a*) The Minister may as occasion requires appoint such, and such number of, persons (who shall be known as 25 Assistant Censors) as he may determine to assist the Official Censor in the performance of his functions and for that purpose to perform, or to perform to such extent as the Official Censor may, subject to any directions that may be given to him by the Minister, 30 determine, the functions (or such of them as the Official Censor may, subject as aforesaid, determine) of the Official Censor.

(*b*) The references in *paragraph (a)* of this subsection to the functions of the Official Censor do not include 35

2

LEGISLATION   10-2

Bunreacht na hEireann (the Constitution)   10-3

The written Constitution of Ireland embodies the most important constitutional laws. Legislation which conflicts with the Constitution may be declared invalid by the courts. If a Bill is introduced to amend the Constitution, it can only become an Act after a public referendum.

In 1922, the Constitution of the Irish Free State, or Saorstat Eireann, was enacted and established the foundations for the machinery of government for the new State. In 1937, a new Constitution was adopted by plebiscite. This Constitution in the main provided a stabilising and reforming continuation of the 1922 Constitution, but also established a Constitution free from all elements of subservience to the British Crown.

The latest edition of the Constitution was published in bilingual format by the Stationery Office in 1980. It contains a list of amending acts up until 1979, along with the dates of their signature. Subsequent amendments appear on inserted slips. There is an alphabetical subject index at the rear.

Primary Legislation   10-4

Before a Bill can become law, it must be approved by both Houses of the Irish Parliament—Dáil and Seanad Eireann—and signed by the President. Once this has happened, the Bill becomes an Act immediately. Unless otherwise specified, the date of commencement is the date of signature by the President.

Parts of an Act   10-5
The various parts of an Act can be seen on the copy reproduced in the figure on p. 180, and are as follows:

1. official citation;
2. short title;
3. long title;
4. date of signature by the President;
5. enacting formula;
6. section and subsection;
7. marginal note.

Citation   10-6
Acts are commonly referred to by their short title and the year of publication, *e.g.* the Finance Act 1985. Acts are numbered within the year, and may also be cited in this way. Thus the Finance Act

1985 is cited officially as 10/1985. Prior to 1922, the British method
of citation in use at that time applies, so that statutes are referred to
by regnal year and by chapter number (para. 3–3).

10–7 Publication of Irish Acts
The *Acts of the Oireachtas* are the official source of Irish legislation
and are published by the Stationery Office. They are available in
two formats:

1. A4 format, which is a reprint of the Bill as passed by both
   Houses, with the addition of an Act title, number, and date
   of signature by the President;
2. Bilingual format, produced in quarto. It is this version that
   eventually appears as the official annual bound volume.

However, as there is such a delay in the production of bilingual
texts, the Stationery Office now issues annual volumes of the
A4-size Acts in English only.

More recently, Sweet & Maxwell have produced an annotated
edition of the Irish Acts, entitled *Irish Current Law Statutes
Annotated*. This is a looseleaf publication which commenced in
1984. It is issued in several parts each year, each part covering
several Acts, and is published several months after the Acts
included have been passed. From 1993 onwards, the publishers
have aimed to provide subscribers with the text of every Act
within six weeks of promulgation. Acts without notes are
published on blue paper to distinguish them from completed Acts.
These will be superseded by fully annotated or noted Acts. There
is a subject index at the rear, which is updated with each issue. The
table of contents at the front of the volume lists the Acts both
alphabetically and chronologically within each year.

10–8 Tracing an Irish Act
At the front of each volume of the *Acts of the Oireachtas* can be
found an alphabetical and a chronological List of Statutes passed
during that year. A *Consolidated Index* for the years 1922–1982 has
been produced. This contains a complete chronological Table of
the Statutes detailing:

1. year and number of the Act;
2. short title;
3. how the Act has been affected;
4. the affecting provision relating to 3 (see the figure on p. 183).

There is also a Subject Index which cites the statutes by number,

272   CHRONOLOGICAL TABLE OF THE STATUTES

Year and Number	Short Title	How Affected	Affecting Provision
1977 32—*contd.*	**Finance (Excise Duty on Tobacco Products) Act, 1977**—*contd.*	S. 10, new rate of duty. Ss. 10 (4) (5), 11 appl. with mods. S. 11 appl. with mods.	14/1980, s. 77 (4), sch. 7, pt. 4. S.I. No. 57 of 1979, par. 21 (3)–(5) S.I. No. 152 of 1979, par. 12; S.I. No. 153 of 1979, para. 3
33.	*Gaeltacht Industries (Amendment) Act, 1977.*	r.	5/1979, ss. 3,4
34.	**International Development Association (Amendment) Act, 1977.**		
35.	**Nítrigin Éireann Teoranta Act, 1977.**		
36.	*Appropriation Act, 1977.*	Spent.	
37.	**Industrial Development Act, 1977.**	S. 2 am. S. 2 am.	13/1981, s. 6. 13/1981, s. 7.
1978 1.	**Consumer Information Act, 1978.**	Ss. 9(6)(h), 18 constr.	16/1980, ss. 1(2), 57.
2.	**Agricultural Credit Act, 1978.**	S. 12 am. S. 14 am. S. 28, limitation on recovery of cert. interest.	24/1982, s. 2. 24/1982, s. 3. 6/1957, s. 42.
3.	**Shannon Free Airport Development Company Limited (Amendment) Act, 1978.**	S. 3 r., new provn.	28/1980, s. 3.
4.	**Medical Practitioners Act, 1978.**		
5.	*Social Welfare Act, 1978*	r., continuance of instrs., etc.	1/1981, ss. 310–312, sch. 6, pt. 2.
6.	*Health Contributions (Amendment) Act, 1978.*	r.	4/1979, ss. 3, 19.
7.	**Landlord and Tenant (Ground Rents) Act, 1978.**	Saving provn. S. 2(1), applic, rstrct.	21/1981, s. 16(1). 10/1980, ss. 2, 30 (3).
8.	**Road Transport Act, 1978.**		
9.	Rates on Agricultural Land (Relief) Act, 1978.	S. 1, "agricultural land" ext. S. I (2)(3) r.	20/1980, s. 4. 20/ 1980, s. 5.
10.	**Local Loans Fund (Amendment) Act, 1978.**	S.1 r., new provn.	41/1980,. 1.
11.	**Restrictive Practices (Confirmation of Order) Act, 1978**		

* *See* Interpretation Act, 1937, s. 20 (1).

year and subsection. The following chronological tables are also included:

1. lists of Irish Private Acts;
2. pre-Union Irish statutes, English statutes, pre-Union British statutes and the Local Government (Application of

Enactments) Order 1898, affected by the Acts 1922–1975, or by Regulations made under section 3 of the European Communities Act 1972;

3. provisions contained in pre-Union Irish statutes, British statutes and Saorstat Eireann statutes which have been specifically adapted or modified by orders made under the Adaptation of Enactments Act 1922 and 1931 and the Constitution (Consequential Provisions) Act 1937;

4. table of expressions used in British statutes or in Saorstat Eireann statutes which have been adapted by orders made under the Adaptation of Enactments Act 1922 or the Constitution (Consequential Provisions) Act 1937;

5. list of Regulations made under section 3 of the European Communities Act 1972.

A Supplement covering the years 1983 to 1985 can be found at the back of this *Index*, and follows the same format. Subsequent to this, a separate *Index* is issued annually.

10–9 Older Irish Acts
Prior to 1922, there are two principal sources of legislation:

A. Irish or pre-Union Statutes passed in the Parliaments held in Ireland between 1310 and 1800
These were published by Grierson in the nineteenth century in two editions:

1. folio edition of 20 volumes entitled *The Statutes at Large Passed in the Parliaments Held in Ireland;*
2. octavo edition of 12 volumes, entitled *Statutes Passed in the Parliaments Held in Ireland.*

A two-volume *Subject Index* accompanying the octavo edition contains a table showing the correspondence between the two.

These Acts were presented in a much more convenient one volume format by HMSO as the *Irish Statutes Revised 1310–1800.* This contains a chronological table which gives details of:

1. the regnal year, statute title and chapter number;
2. subject matter;
3. reason for total or partial omission (usually that it has been repealed in full or in part).

There is a Subject Index at the back of the volume.

Parts of Statutory Instrument

<u>S.I. NO. 91 of 1993</u> (2)

(1) Holidays (Employees) Act, 1973 (Public Holiday) Regulations, 1993

(4)

I, Ruairi Quinn, T.D., Minister for Enterprise and Employment, in

(3) exercise of the power conferred on me by section 14 of, and paragrapl
1(e) of the Schedule to, the Holidays (Employees) Act, 1973 (No. 25
of 1973), and the Industry and Commerce (Alteration of Name of
Department and Title of Minister) Order, 1993 (S.I. No. 19 of 1993),
hereby make the following Regulations:

1. (1)   These Regulations may be cited as the Holidays (Employees)
          Act, 1973 (Public Holiday) Regulations, 1993.

(6)   (2)   These Regulations shall come into operation on the 4th day
              of May, 1993.

2.   The first Monday in May is hereby appointed to be a public
      holiday for the purposes of the Holidays (Employees) Act, 1973
      (No. 25 of 1973).

(5) Given under my Official Seal
    this 2 day/of April, 1993.

L.S.

(PI. 9732)

RUAIRI QUINN, T.D.
Minister for Enterprise and
Employment

B. United Kingdom of Great Britain and Ireland 1801–1921

During this period Ireland, being governed directly from
Westminster , had no separate legislation. The sources of the years
1801–1921 are therefore the same as for British statutes and have
been described in Chapter 3.

Oulton's *Index to the Statutes at Present in Force in, or Affecting
Ireland, from the Year 1310 to 1835 inclusive,* with 11 annual
Supplements from 1836 to 1846, is a useful guide to early Irish
legislation.

Another source of Irish legislation which should be mentioned is the *Green Book* or Vance, *Reading made Easy of the Irish Statutes*. Published in 1862, it contains an account of the principal decisions of Irish statutes, Rules and Orders of Court from 1224 to 1860, and any amendments made to them. A Subject Index is found at the rear of the volume.

10–10 Secondary Legislation

In order to avoid the necessity of passing a huge amount of primary legislation, certain ministers or government departments are given powers under various Acts to make detailed rules and regulations. These are known as *statutory instruments*, and fulfil the same function as their British counterparts.

10–11 Parts of a Statutory Instrument
The following elements can be seen on the statutory instrument reproduced on p. 185:

1. title;
2. statutory instrument number;
3. enabling Act;
4. minister responsible;
5. date of signature;
6. date from which statutory instrument is effective.

10–12 Citation
During the year, every statutory instrument published is given its own number; for example, the Army Pensions Regulations 1985 is cited as S.I. No. 359 of 1985.

10–13 Publication
Statutory instruments are available in three formats:

1. loose typescript A4 issued by the relevant department;
2. printed quarto format—English only, published by the Stationery Office;
3. printed quarto format—bilingual (later bound in volumes and published by the Stationery Office).

Bound volumes of *Statutory Instruments* were published annually from 1948 to 1984. They are arranged numerically within each year, and there may be more than one volume for each year. From 1982 onwards, they are only available individually. Prior to 1948, statutory instruments were known as *statutory rules and orders*. These were published by the Stationery Office in 1948 as a subject collection of 39 volumes, entitled *Statutory Rules, Orders and Regulations*.

Tracing statutory instruments   10–14
The most comprehensive index to statutory instruments available at present is the *Index to Statutory Instruments* by Richard Humphreys. This three-volume work indexes all statutory instruments, rules and orders made in the period December 6, 1922 to December 31, 1986, which were numbered by the Stationery Office and published in the annual volumes of *Statutory Instruments*, or the pre-1948 set of *Statutory Rules and Orders*.

As the *Index* only covers statutory instruments until 1986, this is now considerably out of date.

Volume I indexes statutory instruments alphabetically by title, giving enabling authority and any affecting enactments. Volume II indexes enabling enactments alphabetically by title, and within this, numerically by section. Volume III is a Subject Index, covering statutory instruments in force, again at the time of publication. The headings used closely followed those used in *Halsbury's Statutory Instruments*.

Indexes produced by the Stationery Office are available up until 1986. Entitled the *Index of the Statutory Instruments*, they are published in nine volumes and cover the following years:

1922–1938
1939–1945
1946–1947
1948–1960
1961–1963
1964–1970
1971–1974
1975–1979
1980–1986

CASE LAW   10–15

Irish law reporting dates from 1615 with the publication of *Irish Equity Cases 1604–1612*, by Sir John Davies, Attorney-General. Originally in Norman French (*Le Primer Report des Cases en Ley en les Courts de Roy en Ireland*), it was reprinted in London in 1628 but was not published in English until 1762. Little else was published until the mid-eighteenth century. 1782–1800 saw a brief period of independence of the Irish courts and Parliament and an increase in the publication of reports, including Ridgeway's three-volume work on cases in the Irish House of Lords 1784–1792. From this date until the mid-nineteenth century, over 50 series of reports

Constituent Parts of a Law Report

HC   POOLE v O'SULLIVAN *(Morris J)* 55   55

---

(1) **Joseph Poole v Philip O'Sullivan:** High Court 1990 No. 9791P (Morris J) 23 October 1992 (2)

---

(3) *Limitation of Action – Computation of time – Personal injuries – Issue of summons – Court office closed on last day of limitation period – Summons issued on next available day – Whether summons issued within statutory period of three years – Whether day of accident included in three year period – Statute of Limitations 1957 (No. 6), s. 11(2)(b)*

Facts The plaintiff suffered an accident and sustained personal injuries on 8 (4) July 1987 which he claimed arose because of his employers' negligence. Following correspondence between the plaintiff's solicitors and his employers' insurance company it was agreed that proceedings should issue against a Father Philip O'Sullivan. On 4 July 1990 the plaintiff's plenary summons was transmitted to the plaintiff's solicitors' agents for issue in the High Court. The Central Office, however, was not prepared to accept the summons with the word 'Father', included in the title of the action. The summons was duly returned, the amendments were made and the summons was issued on Monday, 9 July 1990. The defendant contended that the proceedings had not been brought within the limitation period.

Held by Morris J in ruling that the plaintiff's action was not statute barred:
(5)   The three year period provided by s. 11(2)(b) of the Statute of Limitations 1957 expired on Saturday, 7 July 1990. However, since it was impossible to issue the summons on that day because the Central Office was not open, the period would be construed as ending not on that day but at the expiration of the next day upon which the Central Office was open.

(6) **Cases referred to in judgment**
Hughes v Griffiths (1862) 13 CB (ns) 324
McGuinness v Armstrong Patents Ltd [1980] IR 289
Pritam Kaur v S. Russell & Sons Ltd [1973] QB 336; [1973] 2 WLR 147; [1973] 1 All ER 617

(7) *Padraig McCartan SC and Terry O'Sullivan* **for the plaintiff**
Henry Murphy **for the defendant**

MORRIS J delivered his judgment on 23 October 1992 saying: This matter (8) comes before me by way of an application for the trial of a preliminary issue arising out of the Statute of Limitations 1957, the defendant contending that the plaintiff's proceedings have not been brought within the statutory period.

The facts and circumstances in which the application arises are as follows. The plaintiff was working as a caretaker in Scoil Assaim in Raheny on 8 July 1987 when he suffered an accident and sustained personal injuries which he were published covering case law in Ireland. In 1866 the Incorporated Council of Law Reporting in Ireland was established and in 1867 began publication of "official" reports: The Irish Common Law Series and The Irish Reports Equity Series. These two series later joined to become *The Law Reports (Ireland)* in 1878 after the Judicature (Ireland) Act 1877. In 1894, they were to become the *Irish Reports* and the volume numbers were replaced by the year of issue.

Hence the reporting of Irish case law goes back to the seventeenth century and is continued with varying levels of coverage down to the two major series of today—the *Irish Reports* and the *Irish Law Reports Monthly*, the latter providing coverage from 1976.

Citation of Law Reports   10–16

This resembles the British method of citation:

> *e.g. Gillespie*[1] v. *Attorney-General*[2] [1976][3] I.R.[4] 233[5]
> [1] plaintiff or appellant;
> [2] defendant or respondent;
> [3] year in which the case is reported;
> [4] abbreviated name of reports series;
> [5] page number at which report begins.

Format of Law Reports   10–17

The various parts of a law report (see the figure on p. 188) are:

1. names of the parties;
2. name of the court(s) in which the case was heard, and the date;
3. summary in italics;
4. headnote;
5. ruling of the court;
6. cases mentioned during the hearing;
7. names of counsel appearing for the parties;
8. judgment(s).

Often the High Court and the Supreme Court judgments will be reported together.

10–18   Recent and Unreported Judgments

Until recently, law reports in Ireland were sadly lacking in both
coverage and currency, with only a very small precentage of the
judgments delivered annually actually appearing in the reports.
Those which were published often appeared several years after
they had been decided. It must therefore be emphasised that
although the situation with regard to reporting his improved
recently, the written judgment itself is of primary importance with
regard to case law in Ireland. In 1976, following a recommendation
of the Committee on Court Practice and Procedure, the superior
courts began to distribute copies of the written judgments
delivered by the High Court, Court of Criminal Appeal and
Supreme Court, to the following:

1. the judiciary;
2. government bodies;
3. the Law Reform Commission;
4. the Garda Siochana;
5. the Attorney General;
6. the Director of Public Prosecution;
7. the legal profession;
8. universities and third level institutions.

10–19   Citation of Unreported Cases

These are cited by:

1. names of parties;
2. judge;
3. record number;
4. date.

e.g. McMillan v. *Carey*[1] McWilliam J.[2] 1978/4122p[3] 18.12.78[4]

Where the judgment is delivered in the Supreme Court,
"Supreme" appears instead of the name of the judge.

10–20   Format of Unreported Judgments

Unreported judgments are produced in typescript format on
foolscap, and more recently, on A4 paper (see p. 191).

1. plaintiff;

Format of Unreported Judgments

1992 - 262 J/R. ④

⑤
THE HIGH COURT

BETWEEN

① JOHN MEAGHER

APPLICANT

AND

② THE MINISTER FOR AGRICULTURE AND FOOD, IRELAND
AND THE ATTORNEY GENERAL

RESPONDENTS

③
Judgment of Mr. Justice Johnson delivered the 1st day of
April 1993. ⑥

     This case arises out of an application by way of
judicial review brought by the Applicant for

(1)   A declaration that the European Communities (Control
of Oestrogenic, and Andogenic and Gestagenic and
Thorstatic Substances) Regulations 1988 (Statutory
Instrument No. 218 of 1988) and "the 1988 Regulations"
and European Communities (Control of Veterinary
Medicinal Products and their Residues) (Statutory
Instrument No. 171 of 1990) and "the 1990 Regulations"
are ultra vires and void.

(2)   A declaration that the provisions of Section 3
sub-section 1 and sub-section 3 sub-section 2 of the
European Communities Act 1972 are contrary to the
Constitution and void.

(3)   An Order of Certiorari quashing a search warrant
purportedly granted by a Judge of the District Court
dated in or about the 26th day of March 1991 whereby

2. defendant;
3. judge;
4. record number;
5. court;
6. date.

10–21   Indexes and Digests

Irish Digests are available covering the period up until 1988:

O'Donnell and Brady, *Analytical Digest of all the Reported Cases in Equity* (1840);

Bunker, *Digest of All the Unreported Cases Decided in the Superior Courts of Common Law in Ireland and in Admiralty* (1865);

Gamble and Barlow, *Index to Irish Equity Cases* (2 volumes) (1838–1867);

Green and Manders, *The Law Reports Digest of Cases* (1890);

Stubbs, *Irish Law Times Digest of Cases* (1867–1893);

Murray and Dixon, *Digest of Cases* (1867–1893)

Maxwell, *Digest of Cases* (1894–1918);

Ryland, *Digest of Cases* (1919–1928);

Ryland, *Digest of Cases* (1929–1938);

Harrison, *Digest of Cases* (1939–1948);

Harrison, *Digest of Cases* (1949–1958);

Ryan, *Digest of Cases* (1959–1970);

de Blaghd, *The Irish Digest* (1971–1983);

Clancy and Ryan, *The Irish Digest* (1984–1988).

10–22   Irish Digests

These provide cases in the following ways:

1. by name of parties;
2. by subject-matter;
3. citator approach—this lists case law and legislation followed, overruled or considered by the reports so digested.

10–23   Pink Lists

Since 1976, a Subject Index to the written judgments has been published, entitled the *Index to Supreme and High Court Written Judgments,* or the *Pink Lists,* as they are commonly referred to. These are produced on average three times a year, the third part being a consolidation of Parts 1, 2 and 3. This *Index* was produced by the Incorporated Council of Law Reporting in Ireland until 1985. From 1986 onward, its production has become the joint responsibility of the General Council of the Bar of Ireland and the Incorporated Law Society of Ireland. It is issued as a Supplement to the *Gazette of the Incorporated Law Society*. This *Index* provides subject access only, in the following format:

1. main subject heading;
2. secondary subject heading;
3. summary of the case;
4. record number;
5. judge or court;
6. date;
7. parties.

Indexes to superior court judgments   10–24
These cover the years 1966–1989 in three volumes:

1. *Index to Unreported Judgments of the Irish Superior Courts 1966–1975* (*Green Index*)—published by the Irish Association of Law Teachers;
2. *Index to Irish Superior Court Written Judgments 1976–1982* (*Red Index*)—published by the Irish Association of Law Teachers;
3. *Index to Irish Superior Court Written Judgments 1983–1989* (*Blue Index*)—published by the General Council of the Bar of Ireland.

The *Red* and *Blue Indexes* each contain two sections; the first part is an Alphabetical Index by party to all the cases summarised in each volume. The Subject Index, which forms the second part, consolidates all the entries from the original *Pink Sheets*.

All written judgments from the years 1976–1989, whether reported or not, should therefore appear in these *Indexes*.

The *Green Index* differs slightly, in that it covers only unreported judgments and lacks case summaries in its Subject Index. It does, however, have a Statute Citator.

Other indexes of cases   10–25
Another very useful publication is the *Index to the Irish Law Reports Monthly*, which covers all cases reported in the I.L.R.M. from 1976–1990. A list of judges in the cases covered is given at the front of this, along with their dates.

A publication entitled *Ryans Notes of Cases* covers the period 1969–1978, but includes selected cases only.

10–26   Tracing a Judgment

If you have the title of the case, look in:

1. *Irish Digests* up to 1988;
2. *I.L.R.M. Index* 1976–1990;
3. *Green, Red* and *Blue Indexes* 1966–1989;
4. *Ryan's Notes of Cases.*

If you have an idea of the year in which the case was heard, this will save you looking through all of the *Digests.*

For judgments delivered after these dates, you will have to check individual volumes of the *Irish Reports* and the *Irish Law Reports Monthly.* However, your own library may have devised an in-house index which will help you to locate these and other unreported judgments. Ask your library staff about this.

If you do not know the name of the case in question, or you are looking for case law on a particular subject, you will use the Subject Index in the *Digests* and in the *Red Index.* For the years 1983 onwards, unbound *Pink Lists* are available and, again, individual libraries will have their own methods of making these available for consultation. Ask the library staff.

10–27   OFFICIAL PUBLICATIONS

Acts, Bills and Statutory Instruments have already been dealt with in earlier sections.

10–28   Parliamentary Debates

Debates are issued in daily parts which are unrevised. Corrections or amendments may be included in the bound volume a year later. The bound volumes are each indexed and contain a list of ministers, deputies and senators. Each volume is assigned a running number. At the start of 1986, the Dáil Debates had reached Volume 363 and the Seanad Debates Volume 113, so it should not be assumed that the volume number for the Dáil Debates would be the same in the Seanad Debates of the same date. *Consolidated Indexes* are published for the years:

Dáil Debates

1922–1927	Vols. 1–19
1927–1937	Vols. 20–68
1937–1940	Vols. 69–80

1940–1947	Vols. 81–109
1948–1954	Vols. 110–145
1954–1956	Vols. 146–160

Seanad Debates

| 1922–1936 | Vols. 1–20 |
| 1938–1948 | Vols. 21–34 |

The *Indexes* produced after 1954 are divided into sections which list alphabetically by subject and then by Member's name both the general business of the House and questions. For the previous *Indexes*, there is no division, so that general subjects, questions and members' name are all interfiled. The *Index* gives the volume and column number of the reference.

Reports of Committees   10–29

Committees are appointed by either House, usually to consider technical or specialised Bills, which may then go to report stage before the House. Certain committees appointed regularly have produced a significant number of reports.

Tracing Official Publications   10–30

This is done by way of:

1. *Iris Oifigiúil*
A weekly list of publications from the Stationery Office is listed in the Friday issue of this bi-weekly publication. Reprints are available from the Stationery Office on subscription.

2. *Catalogue of Government Publications*
These are published by the Stationery Office:

(a) quarterly—published in typescript;
(b) annual catalogue of government publications;
(c) consolidated catalogues for the years:

1922–1925
1926–1928
1929–1931
1932–1934
1935–1937
1938–1940
1941–1950

1951–1955
1956–1960

Information given is as follows:

(a) order number;
(b) title;
(c) price and postage charge;

and is grouped into the following sections:

(a) Acts;
(b) Bills;
(c) Dáil Reports;
(d) Oireachtas Reports;
(e) Stationery   Office   publications—alphabetically   by department;
(f) Statutory Instruments;
(g) general literature.

3. Maltby and McKenna, *Irish Official Publications: A Guide to Republic of Ireland Papers with a Breviate of Reports 1922–1972*
Here, the reports are grouped under broad subject headings and summarised. There are separate name and subject Indexes at the end.

10–31 JOURNALS

Journals provide the main outlet for Irish legal scholarship, and are also an important source of current developments in legislation.
There are two major professional journals:

1. the *Gazette of the Incorporated Law Society*;
2. the *Irish Law Times* (I.L.T.).

These provide articles and commentaries on legislation, relevant E.C. and English legal developments, information on legal education and the role of the lawyer in Ireland, and reviews of recent publications. The I.L.T. also provides a useful update on the progress of legislation, both primary and secondary, and of recent superior court decisions.
The other type of Irish journal available tends toward the learned journal, providing a more scholarly dimension, or concentrating on a particular aspect of the law. The titles listed below fall into this category:

1. the *Irish Criminal Law Journal*;
2. the *Dublin University Law Journal* (D.U.L.J.);
3. the *Garda Review*;
4. *Irish Jurist* (I.J.);
5. the *Irish Tax Review*;
6. the *Journal of the Irish Society for European Law* (J.I.S.E.L.);
7. the *Journal of the Irish Society for Labour Law* (J.I.S.L.L.);
8. the *Irish Student Law Review*.

Citation 10–32

The citation of journal articles follows the same format as that used in England. Abbreviations commonly used are given above.

Tracing Journal Articles 10–33

Paul O'Higgins' *A Bibliography of Periodical Literature Relating to Irish Law* (N.I.L.Q. 1966, Supplements published in 1973 and 1983) provides excellent coverage or around 5,000 articles from over 130 journals. The titles are arranged within broad subject headings with cross-references. Alphabetical subject and other Indexes are provided, along with a list of journals cited and their abbreviations.

TEXTBOOKS AND BIBLIOGRAPHIES 10–34

When searching for textbooks on a given topic, your own library catalogue will probably provide the best starting point. However, bibliographies provide an important source, and can often be more effective in narrowing down a search strategy. Most textbooks will provide comprehensive bibliographies, and many give lists of possible further reading. An excellent subject guide to Irish legal textbooks can be found in R. G. Logan's *Information Sources in Law* (Butterworths, 1986) (para. 6–28). Bibliographic information relating to Ireland and Irish law may also be found in:

Twining and Uglow, *Law Publishing and Legal Information: Small Jurisdictions of the British Isles* (1981);
Alan Eager, *Guide to Irish Bibliographic Material: Bibliography of Irish Bibliographies and Sources of Information* (2nd ed., 1980);
A. G. Donaldson, *Some Comparative Aspects of Irish Law* (1957);
A Legal Bibliography of the British Commonwealth of Nations Vol. 4, "Irish Law to 1956" (2nd ed., 1957).

CHAPTER 11

European Community Law

11–1 INTRODUCTION

European Community law is as much part of the law of this country as the laws passed by the United Kingdom Parliament. For this reason, the usual U.K. legal sources should, and often will, include references to the relevant E.C. rules. However, because this is not always so and because E.C. law is organised in a different way from English law, students also need to become familiar with E.C. sources.

Most, if not all, of the materials described in this chapter will be available in your law library, particularly if it has been designated as a European Documentation Centre. This means that the E.C. has agreed to send one copy of all publicly available documents to the library. In return, the library agrees to provide an information service on E.C. documentation. Currently, there are 44 centres based in academic libraries in the United Kingdom. The names and addresses can be obtained from your librarian or by contacting the London Office of the European Commission.

11–2 THE COMMUNITY TREATIES

The principal sources of Community law are the treaties which established the European Communities. There are three Communities:

The European Coal and Steel Community, established by the ECSC Treaty (Treaty of Paris, 1951);

The European Economic Community, established by the EEC
Treaty (Treaty of Rome, 1957);
The European Atomic Energy Community, established by the
EURATOM Treaty (Treaty of Rome, 1957);

This chapter is concerned only with the body of law made under
the Treaty establishing the European Economic Community,
which has now been renamed "the European Community" by the
Treaty on European Union (also known as the Treaty of
Maastricht).

The renaming of the European Economic Community is
potentially a source of considerable confusion. Before the
Maastricht Treaty came into force on November 1, 1993, the term
"European Community" was used in the same way as the term
"European Communities" to mean all three Communities set up
in 1951 and 1957. However, since Maastricht, the terms "European
Community Law" and "E.C. Law" refer only to the body of law
made under what used to be called the EEC Treaty. This chapter
uses the abbreviation "E.C. Law" to refer to all law made under
that Treaty, whether it was made before or after November 1993.

You may also see references to "The European Union". This is
an overall term which covers the three original Communities and
also the new areas of co-operation established by the Maastricht
Treaty.

The treaties perform two main tasks. The first is that they
represent a system of substantive rules which are binding on the
Member States, and whose aim is the establishment of a Common
Market. Secondly, and equally importantly, each treaty creates a
set of institutions and a procedural framework through which
these institutions can create secondary Community legislation and
can take other measures which have legally binding effect.

There are two further types of Community treaty: those
amending the founding treaties, such as the Single European Act
1986, and the Treaty on European Union 1992, and those
concerning the accession of new Member States. Together, these
treaties form the primary legislation of the European
Communities. The text of this primary legislation is brought
together in two single volumes. Volume 1 is entitled *Treaties
establishing the European Communities—Treaties amending these
treaties—Single European Act, Resolutions—Declarations*. Volume 2
is entitled *Documents Concerning the Accessions to the European
Communities of the Kingdom of Denmark, Ireland and the United
Kingdom of Great Britain and Northern Ireland, the Hellenic Republic,
the Kingdom of Spain and the Portuguese Republic* (1987).

A convenient, pocket-sized, shortened version of the full text volume is the *Treaties establishing the European Communities—Abridged Edition* (1987). This includes the main text of the amended treaties and amending treaties. It excludes most of the associated annexes and protocols and includes texts up to 1987.

These volumes are being replaced by a new set which will incorporate the recent significant changes to the Community Treaties made by the Treaty on European Union. This set is entitled *European Union: selected instruments taken from the Treaties*, (1993 to date). Book I (divided into two separately published volumes) contains the texts currently in force. Volume I includes those parts of the Treaty on European Union not amending the existing Treaties, plus the amended E.C. Treaty. This has already been published. The second volume will include the amended ECSC and Euratom Treaties. Book II will contain the whole collection of basic treaties in their original versions (Volume I) and the documents concerning the accessions (Volume II). OOPEC, the official publisher for the European Communities, also published a volume known as *The Treaty on European Union* in 1992.

Primary legislation which has not yet been brought together in an official set is generally published in the *Official Journal* in either the *C Series* or the *L Series* according to its official status, and can also often be found as separately published documents or even as United Kingdom Command Papers. Examples are the Austrian, Finnish, Swedish and Norwegian accession documents so far available at [1994] O.J. C241 and the Agreement on the European Economic Area. This extends the Internal Market to the above mentioned countries, plus Iceland and Liechtenstein, and is available as an OOPEC publication under that title and also at [1994] O.J. L1/1 and as Cm. 2485.

In addition to these official sources, you will find many of the important texts of primary materials have been published commercially. The two most popular student books are Foster, *Blackstone's EC Legislation* (4th ed., 1994) and Rudden and Wyatt, *Basic Community Laws* (5th ed., 1994).

You can also find the text of the Community treaties in *Halsbury's Statutes of England* (4th ed., 1989), Vol. 50, and in the *Encyclopedia of European Community Law*, Vol. B. Both have provision for keeping the information up to date and are extensively annotated. During 1995 the *Encyclopedia of European Community Law*, Vol. B, will be replaced and extended by three binders entitled *Constitutional Texts* (including the texts of the E.U. Treaties) as part of a new overall concept destined eventually to replace the whole *Encyclopedia* completely. The new work will be known as the *Encyclopedia of European Union Laws* (see para. 11–27).

SECONDARY LEGISLATION   11–3

Secondary legislation is that which is created by the institutions of
the European Communities in implementing the powers granted
to them in the Community treaties. There are different types of
legislative acts, and these are given different names depending on
whether they are made under the E.C. and EURATOM Treaties or
under the ECSC Treaty. The following table lists the different
types:

ECSC	*E.C./EURATOM*
Decisions (general)	Regulations
Recommendations	Directives
Decisions (individual)	Decisions
	Recommendations
Opinions	Opinions

Article 189 of the E.C. Treaty explains the differences between
the acts made under it, and it is with these that you will be most
concerned.

The process of making E.C. legislation is very different from that
enacting English laws. Draft legislation or proposals are put
forward by the Commission and the final versions are published
as *Commission Documents* (known as *COM Docs*) and in the *Official
Journal C Series* (para. 11–5). They are then considered by the
European Parliament and the Economic and Social Committee,
which publish *Reports* or *Opinions*. *COM Docs, European Parliament
Reports* and *Economic and Social Committee Opinions* are all available
as series and may be taken by your library, particularly if it is a
European Documentation Centre. *Economic and Social Committee
Opinions* are also published in the *Official Journal C Series*, as are the
resolutions of the European Parliament (but not the full report).
Once the various suggestions from these bodies have been
considered, and the original proposals amended if necessary (and
in some cases the European Parliament will have to consider them
again), then the Council of Ministers will adopt the directive or
regulation and it will be published in the *Official Journal L Series*.
Directives must then be implemented in the law of the Member
States.

Citation of E.C. Legislative Acts   11–4

The formal citation of a European Communities legislative act is
made up of the following elements:

1. The institutional origin of the act (Commission or Council);
2. The form of the act (Regulation, Directive, Decision, etc.);
3. An act number;
4. The year of the enactment;
5. The institutional treaty basis (E.C., ECSC, EURATOM);
6. The date the act was passed.

Regulation numbers are written with the number first and the year following. Decisions and directives are written the other way round, with the year first and the number following. All indexes will therefore always list regulations first and decisions and directives afterwards. Two examples follow:

1. Commission Regulation (EEC) No. 896/93 of 16 April 1993, setting the indicative yield for hemp seed for the 1992/93 marketing year. (This can be abbreviated to Reg. (EEC) 896/93.)
2. 93/209/EEC Commission Decision of 6 April 1993, amending Decision 93/144/EEC on certain protective measures in respect of salmon from Norway. (This can be abbreviated to Dec. 93/209/EEC.)

Between 1958 and 1967, this citation form varied. The variations are laid out in *Halsbury's Statutes* (4th ed.), Vol. 50, pp. 211–212. From 1992, directives and decisions were given separate numerical sequences, with the consequence that a directive and a decision can both be given the same number. Thus there exist both Dir. 93/12/EEC and Dec. 93/12/EEC.

A legislative act is given a date of enactment but this does not indicate the date when the act is published in the *Official Journal*: this can be up to several months later.

11–5 The Official Journal

The *Official Journal*, published by the European Communities, is the official and authoritative source of legislation. It carries the text of proposed and enacted legislation and official announcements, as well as information on the activities of Community institutions.

The *Official Journal* is published about six times a week in the following separate parts:

1. *L Series (Legislation)*: this consists of the texts of enacted legislation. This legislation is divided into two sequences.

(a) Acts whose publication is obligatory (primarily Regulations, Directives addressed to all Member States, ECSC Decisions and acts concerning the European Economic Area);

(b) Acts whose publication is not obligatory (all other legislation).

In effect, this means that all legislative acts are published in the *Official Journal*; but note that they are listed in two sequences in the *Official Journal: Index*;

2. *C Series* (*Information and Notices*): this is arranged in three parts, as follows:

  (a) Part I, *Information* from the various Community institutions:

    (i) *Commission*—the daily exchange rates for the European Currency Unit (ECU), communications and notices concerning Community policy and notifications from companies and governments applying Community law;

    (ii) *Court of Justice*—a list of new cases brought before this Court and the Court of First Instance, the operative part of the judgment of these cases and cases removed from the register;

    (iii) *European Parliament*—Minutes of the plenary sessions and written questions from members of the European Parliament;

    (iv) *Economic and Social Committee*—Opinions

  (b) Part II, *Preparatory Acts*: the texts of proposed legislation;

  (c) Part III, *Notices* of invitation to tender for commercial and research contracts and notices of staff vacancies in Community institutions;

3. *S Series* (*Supplement*): this publishes details of public contracts open to competitive tender;

4. *Official Journal: Annex*—*Debates of the European Parliament*: this contains the full text of the debates of the plenary sessions of the European Parliament and oral questions;

5. *Official Journal: Special Edition*: this gives an official English translation of the legislation enacted between 1952–1972 which was still in force at the time of the United Kingdom's accession.

The citation of references to the *Official Journal* is not standardised but the usual form is: O.J. L73 26.3.93 p. 12. An alternative form is [1993] O.J. L73/12. This refers you to the *Official Journal L Series* issue 73, dated March 26, 1993, at page 12.

11–6   The Official Journal Index

The key to any substantial source of legislative information is its index. Unfortunately, the *Official Journal Index* is less helpful than you would wish. It only indexes the adopted legislation published in the *L Series* and the cases (by subject and number only) in the *C Series*. It is issued monthly with an annual cumulation. It is divided into two parts:

> Volume 1—*Alphabetical Index;*
> Volume 2—*Methodological Table.*

The *Methodological Table* gives the *Official Journal* reference to all the legislative acts in numerical order. It also lists the cases brought before, and the judgments of, the European Court of Justice and the Court of First Instance for the period which is indexed. If, for example, you are given a reference to a legislative act, such as Reg. (EEC) 990/93 or a case, C–77/93, the *Methodological Table* will give you the reference in the *Official Journal* where you will find the text of the act or case.

The *Alphabetical Index* is used in a different way. If you have no reference, or it is incomplete or incorrect, but you know, for example, what subject you are dealing with, then you use the alphabetical subject index to find the required references.

11–7   Alternative Sources for E.C. Secondary Legislation

The most useful source is the *Encyclopedia of European Community Law*, Vol. C. This is currently divided into 11 looseleaf volumes. Some of the texts are annotated. Not all of the legislation is reproduced here: in some cases, only references to the *Offical Journal* are given. Neither is the *Encyclopedia* very up to date: the legislation included can often be a year behind. A complete *Checklist* of E.C. legislation is found at the end of the last volume. This also includes agreements, protocols, notices, etc. This is followed by an *Index* by subject to everything contained in Volume C. The references in the *Index* are to the Parts *within* the binders, *not* to the numbers on the spine of the binders. This index is much easier to use than that found in the *Official Journal*.

Graham & Trotman's *Completing the Internal Market of the European Communities: 1992 Legislation* is a reproduction of E.C. legislation for the establishment of the Internal Market by the end of 1992, and is arranged in accordance with the arrangement of the White Paper which introduced the 1992 package of proposals. It includes legislation both when it has first been proposed and later when it has been adopted. However, there is no index and you need to have some familiarity with the 1992 concepts (*e.g.* removal of technical, fiscal and physical barriers) before attempting to locate the piece of legislation you need.

There is also an important electronic source for primary and secondary legislation, called CELEX, which is the E.C.'s official legal database. It includes the full text of the treaties and the secondary legislation since 1979, and references to proposed legislation from 1973. It is available as an online database through the official host Eurobases, but it is also available through other hosts, such as JUSTIS, Profile and LEXIS. CELEX is also available on the JUSTIS CD-ROM, the Eurolaw CD-ROM, the OJCD CD-ROM and the Eurocat CD-ROM, which, if available in your library, you can search yourself.

Indexes to E.C. Legislation   **11–8**

First of all, there is the *Official Journal Index* (see para. 11–6). However, if you only want references to E.C. legislation in force, you can use the E.C.'s *Directory of Community Legislation in Force*. This is published bi-annually, in two volumes. Volume I, the *Analytical Register*, is a subject listing of all the acts in force, together with O.J. references and any amending legislation, also with their O.J. references. Volume II has a Chronological and an Alphabetical Index by subject to Volume I. The acts in the *Chronological Index* are arranged under a notation derived from CELEX, the E.C.'s own legal database. They are not immediately recognisable as a chronological listing of directives and regulations, and the *Preface* should be read first to translate them into normal numbers, or see para. 11–11.

There is also a non-official source for finding references to E.C. legislation, published by Butterworths and called *European Communities Legislation: Current Status*. This consists of two annual volumes, kept up to date by quarterly *Cumulative Supplements* published during the year, and also by a fortnightly updating sheet. It lists in chronological order references to all European Communities secondary legislation published in the *Official Journal: Special Edition, 1952–1972*, and all subsequent secondary legislation. For each year, regulations are listed first, and directives and decisions follow in a separate listing, until 1992 when, because directives and decisions were given the same numbers, *Current Status* allotted a separate sequence of numbers to directives by prefixing the real numbers with 50. There is also a *Subject Index*. This source combines the work of both the *Official Journal Indexes* and the *Directory* in one consecutive numerical listing. It also has the advantages of being more up to date and of noting amendments to legislative acts, giving the appropriate O.J. reference.

Naturally, CELEX (para. 11–7) can also be used as an index for finding E.C. legislation, and this is often the first source to try.

11–9   How to Trace the Text of an E.C. Regulation or Directive

How do you know where to find the following: Directive 92/59/EEC on general product safety? The easiest index to use is *European Communities Legislation: Current Status* generally referred to as *Current Status*. Here, E.C. legislation is arranged by year and then by type of act. "92" at the beginning of the number tells you that the act is a directive (see para. 11–4), and that it was adopted in 1992. At the relevant page you will see the entry:

92/59 [Cl Dir (EEC)]
(OJ L228 11.8.92 p24)
on general product safety

You can then find the full text of the Directive in the appropriate issue of the *Official Journal*.

Alternatively, use the *Official Journal Annual Index* for 1992. In the *Methodological Table*, there is a section entitled "Acts whose publication is not obligatory," where you will see that directives are listed, alongside decisions, in numerical order. All references will be to the *Official Journal L Series*. You will find the following entry:

92/59/EEC:
Council Directive 92/59/EEC of 29 June 1992 on general product safety.
Official Journal   No. 228   page 24   date 11.8.1992

If your reference is to the legislation made during the current year, you will need to refer to the *Official Journal: Monthly Index* and then look at the *Methodological Table* in each monthly issue until you locate your reference.

You can also use CELEX on CD-ROM by simply keying in the number of the directive.

How to Trace E.C. Legislation on a Subject Without a Reference

11–10

If you have been told, for example, that there is a directive on the copyright of computer software, but you do not have a number or even a date, you will have to use the various subject indexes to try to find the correct entry in the *Official Journal*. Using the different indexes will show you the problems associated with subject approaches to E.C. legislation, because of the differences in terminology.

The first place to look is in a comprehensive index where the fact that you do not know a date does not matter. *Current Status* provides this. At the back of the *Supplement* volume, there is nothing under "software," "computer programs" or "copyright," so you must think of wider terms to search the index. Under "intellectual property," you will find a subheading "computer programs" referring you to 91/250. When you go to the main volumes to look up this Directive number, you will find that it is called "Council Directive of 14 May 1991 on the legal protection of computer programs," and you will be given the appropriate *Official Journal* reference to find the text.

CELEX on CD-ROM will also enable you to use any subject term that is mentioned in the title or text of the directive.

If you do not have access to *Current Status* or CELEX, then use the *Official Journal's Annual Indexes* (but you will have to go through each one to find it as you do not know the year). In the 1991 *Alphabetical Index*, you will find the following entry:

Keywords/expressions	Document number	OJ reference	Legal form
international organization, legal status, market supervision, UNO	91/179	L2/89/39	D/CS
metal product, Mexico, restoration of customs duties	2250/91	L1/204/36	R/COM
copyright			
approximation of laws, computer piracy, data-processing law,' software	91/250	L2/122/42	L/CS
broadcasting, information medium, television	70/89 76/89	C1/201/13 C1/201/14	2/T 2/T
monopoly, public prosecutor's department, tax	270/86	C1/12/4	2/CJ

The document number heading tells you the Directive number: 91/250, and the O.J. reference tells you that it will be found in the 1991 *Official Journal*, L122, at page 42.

If you still cannot find your piece of legislation, then it may be that it is too recent to be in any of these indexes (including their updates, such as the *Supplements* and fortnightly updating sheets of *Current Status* or the *Official Journal: Monthly Indexes*). If so, you may find the *Common Market Reporter*, Vol. 4, "Current Developments" useful (there is a "Topical Index to Current Developments" which is very up to date), or *Butterworths EC Brief*, which is a weekly index sheet of new proposals, legislation, and cases from the E.C. arranged in broad subject groupings. An annual cumulation of this is produced.

Other sources you can use are the *Encyclopedia of European Community Law*, Vol. C; *Halsbury's Laws of England*, Vol. 51 and 52 (or its equivalent, Vaughan, *Law of the European Communities Service*), or the E.C.'s *General Report on the Activities of the European Communities* and the *Bulletin of the European Communities*, since 1994 retitled the *Bulletin of the European Union*. These last are particularly useful for finding what legislation there has been on a broad topic such as company law, because they are arranged by subject, not chronologically.

In the *General Report on the Activities of the European Communities*, turn to the contents pages and look for the heading that covers "Company law." In the 1991 *Report*, this heading comes under section 2, "Completing the internal market." However, this entry could be different in earlier *Reports*. You may have to go carefully through the contents pages to locate the particular subject you want. The section on "Company law" is short but it gives you references to other sources where you can find further information. By reading a succession of *General Reports*, you can build up a history of the subject.

To find more up-to-date information than is contained in the *General Reports*, turn to the *Bulletin of the European Union*, which is a monthly review of the Union's work. It is arranged in a standard format in each issue. Here company law will be dealt with in Part One, under the heading "Internal Market" and then under the sub-heading "Company law." Both the *General Reports* and the *Bulletin* give references to the *Official Journal*. From 1992, Butterworths also publish a review of the year which is part of the annual cumulation of the *EC Brief*, entitled *Butterworths Annual European Review*.

Alternatively, you can use *Halsbury's Laws of England* (para. 6–3) to find out what the law is on a subject. At the back of Volume 52 of the fourth edition of *Halsbury's Laws of England*, you will find an Index to Volumes 51 and 52. Under the heading "company," there are various sub-headings including "EEC Law. See EC company law." Under that heading, you will find a large number of sub-headings, such as "Draft directive—Fifth directive, 11.62." By turning to paragraph 11.62, in Volume 51 you will find the history of that Directive. To bring the information up to date, refer to the *Cumulative Supplement* and looseleaf *Current Service* volumes.

You may also use Vaughan, *Law of the European Communities Service* which can be used as a noter-up to Volumes 51 and 52 of *Halsbury's Laws*. Company law is dealt with in section 11 of Volume 2, labelled "Undertakings," the E.C. term for companies.

How to Trace if E.C. Legislation is Still in Force 11–11

How do you discover if Directive 79/7/EEC, dealing with equal treatment for men and women in matters concerning social security, is still in force? You can find the directive most easily by its number. The simplest source to use is *Current Status*. Here you should go straight to the chronological/numerical listing and find Directive 79/7/EEC listed under the year 1977. As the act is still in force, it will be printed in normal type (not in italics). The reference to the appropriate issue of the *Official Journal* is given and any amendments are listed. If you want to check that the directive has remained in force since the annual volumes were published, then check in the *Supplement*, again under the chronological/numerical listing and in the fortnightly updating sheets.

However, if you do not have access to *Current Status*, you can use the official source, the *Directory of Community Legislation in Force*. Look in Volume II of the latest edition of the *Directory* and use the *Chronological Index*. The acts there are arranged by year and type of act but in a notation which is not instantly recognisable. The notation is that given by CELEX, the official legal database, and is explained in the *Preface*. A document number is split into components derived from the sector number of the database (whether it is dealing with adopted or proposed legislation, or cases), the year of the act (the last two digits), the type of act (*e.g.* Directive, Decision or Regulation) and the number of the act (in four digits). Thus Directive 79/7/EEC is written as 379L0007: 3 is the sector number for adopted legislation, *79* is the year of the act, *L* signifies that the act is a directive and *0007* is the seventh directive of 1979.

Once you have worked out how to convert your directive number into a CELEX document number, you can find it in the *Chronological Index*, where you will be referred to a page in Volume I of the *Directory*. There you will find a list of all E.C. legislation on social security that is in force. It also gives you the reference to the

Official Journal where you can see the full text. Amendments to the legislation are also listed. If the legislation was not in force, it simply would not be printed in that edition of the *Directory*.

11–12   How to Know if a Proposal Has Become Law

In the United Kingdom, draft legislation is introduced into Parliament and becomes law during the same parliamentary session. This is not the case with E.C. legislation, which may take years to become law or ultimately after a considerable time fail to become law. How, for example, would you know if the Commission's proposal for a Directive on unfair terms in consumer contracts has become law? Finding a proposal and what stage it has reached in the legislative process can only be done by subject, as no official numbers are given until the legislation has been passed.

The Commission introduced a proposal on this subject in 1990, published as COM(90)322/final and in O.J. C243 28.9.90 p. 2. An amended proposal was introduced in 1992, COM(92)66/final and O.J. C73 24.3.92 p. 7.

One way of tracing its progress is to look in the *General Report on the Activities of the European Communities*. If you do not know the date when the proposal was introduced, go to the latest *General Report* and work backwards. If you know the date of the proposal, then begin with the *General Report* for that year and work forwards. To bring your information up to date, look at the most recent issues of the monthly *Bulletin of the European Union*.

The *General Report* for 1993 gives the complete legislative history and sources for all stages of the legislative process. If neither the *General Report* nor the latest issues of the *Bulletin* give the final date of adoption by the Council then you must either search the contents list of all issues of the *Official Journal L Series* up to the present date to see if the proposal has both been adopted *and* published, or you can use one or more of the alternative sources suggested below.

These sources include those which we have already discussed under para. 11–10. Volumes 51 and 52 of *Halsbury's Laws* is a good place to start. Once *Halsbury's* has mentioned the proposal, you can check the *Cumulative Supplement* and the *Service* volume at the same paragraph number to see if the proposal has progressed. You can use Vaughan, *Law of the European Communities Service* in the same way, with the additional advantage that, under each subject, there is a list of adopted and proposed legislation, to enable you to find the correct reference to a *Commission Document* (see para. 11–3) and the *O.J. C Series*. The *Common Market Reporter*, Vol. 4, "Current Developments" section is another source. *Butterworths EC Brief* will also enable you to find references to proposals, the various texts of the legislative process and final adoption by the Council. All these sources inform us that the Directive was published in O.J. L95 21.4.93 p. 29, although it had been adopted in March.

How to Trace Whether a Directive Has Been Implemented in the United Kingdom

11–13

Directives, once adopted by the Council of the European Union, must be implemented by Member States by the most appropriate method for each country. In the United Kingdom, this is generally done by passing an Act of Parliament or issuing a statutory instrument. Member States are given a set period of time in which to do this.

There are two main hard copy sources which enable you to find out how a Directive has been implemented in the United Kingdom. The first is *Butterworths EC Legislation Implementator*. This lists all directives in chronological order and gives an O.J. reference for each, the target date by which it must be implemented and the Act or statutory instrument which implements it. The *Implementator* is issued twice yearly and is kept up to date by the fortnightly updating sheets which come with its sister publication, *Current Status* (para. 11–8).

The second source is known as *National Implementing Measures*, issued every six months, and is taken from the E.C.'s database Info92. This deals only with those measures creating the Internal Market by the end of December 1992. The first initiative to do this was a White Paper called *Completing the Internal Market*, issued in 1985, which arranged the areas of law to be dealt with under special subject areas. *National Implementing Measures* is also arranged by these subject areas and because of this, and the fact that it has no index, it can be difficult to use. However once you have located your Directive (*e.g.* the Toy Safety Directive is found under Part II, "The Removal of Technical Barriers," and then under the sub-heading "The New Approach in Harmonization") you can not only find the *Official Journal* reference, etc., and the United Kingdom implementation, but also the implementing legislation of other Member States.

You can also find the implementing legislation of all Member States by using CELEX (para. 11–7).

11–14 CASE LAW

There are two courts which interpret and enforce E.C. law. The first, the European Court of Justice, has been in existence since the Communities were founded. The second, the Court of First Instance, gave its first judgments in 1990. The ECJ hears all types of cases, including appeals from the CFI, but the CFI only hears competition, anti-dumping and staff cases. The latter are where officials of the E.C. have complaints against their employers. The case law of both courts has assumed a position of great importance.

The *C Series* of the *Official Journal* carries notices of cases pending before the courts. Brief details only of the nature of the proceedings and the judgment are provided.

11–15 European Court Reports

The official source of European Court judgments is the *Reports of Cases before the Court*. These are more commonly known as the *European Court Reports* (abbreviated to E.C.R.). In this series, the opinion of the Advocate General is given alongside the judgment. This is an important stage in the proceedings before the European Court of Justice. The Advocate General's opinion is not binding on the court, but it is of great use to students of Community law in that it will include a thorough analysis of the facts and legal arguments in the case. There is an English language set of the *Reports* covering the judgments of the courts since 1954. Since 1990, the *Reports* have been spilt into two parts in each issue. Part I contains ECJ cases and Part II contains CFI cases. Since 1994 staff cases are being published in a separate series known as *Reports of European Community Staff Cases* (ECR-SC), and are not all translated into other languages.

Although the E.C.R. is the official series, it suffers from major delays in publication. Precise and accurate translation into the various Community languages results in delays of up to two years which makes it impossible to use it for recent cases. However for the 1994 *Reports* onwards, English translations are appearing much earlier although there is still a delay in translating cases into English before this date. The indexing for this series is also poor and late. Older indexes (before 1985) allow you to trace the case by the names of the parties, by subject and by case number. Since 1985, only indexes by subject and by date are available for each year. From 1990 onwards, these are again divided by court.

Citation of European Court of Justice and Court of First   11–16
Instance Cases

The case citation is made up as follows:

1. case number;
2. year;
3. names of parties;
4. citation: indicating where the case can be found in the
   European Court Reports (E.C.R.):
   e.g. Case C–59/89 *Commission* v. *Germany* [1991] E.C.R. I–2607
   Case T–12/90 *Bayer* v. *Commission* [1991] E.C.R. II–219.
   Alternatively the citations for the European Court Reports
   can be written as follows: [1991] I E.C.R. 2607 and [1991] II
   E.C.R. 219.

Note that each case after 1990 is preceded by the letter C
(European Court of Justice) or the letter T (Court of First Instance).
Also note that a case with a reference . . . /89, for example, means
that the application or reference to the court was made in 1989. The
judgment was not necessarily given in that year. This means that
you cannot automatically go to the E.C.R. for the year 1989 to find
the judgment.

Other Sources of E.C. Case Law   11–17

Some libraries subscribe to *Judgments or Orders of the Court and
Opinions of the Advocates General*. These are printed in a typescript
format, and are sent out in regular batches. They are issued on the
day of judgment in French and in the language of the case, which
means that generally the only judgments available immediately in
English are those including English or Irish parties. Translations
are available about 18 months later, except for 1994 onwards
where they are usually available within two or three weeks. They
are not indexed and are not considered authoritative.

The *Proceedings of the Court of Justice* is a weekly bulletin giving a
summary of the judgments and opinions of the court during the
week in question. It is not an authoritative source, but primarily a
current awareness service. At the end of the year, the *Synopis of the
Judgments Delivered by the Court of Justice for the year* . . . is issued,
which is an index to the contents of that year's issues. This
arranges the judgments, but not the opinions, under 19 headings
such as "social policy" and "free movement of goods."

The *Times* and *The Financial Times* report the significant
European Court judgments in their law reports section.

The *Common Market Law Reports* (C.M.L.R.) is the main alternative source to the *European Court Reports*. It is published weekly by Sweet & Maxwell and also covers cases with an E.C. dimension in national courts. It scores over the E.C.R. because it appears sooner with a full, if not official, report. Whilst it does not report all cases, it does report all cases of significance. It has a similar range of indexes to the E.C.R.

European Community Cases (C.E.C.) is another source of E.C. case law which comes as part of the subscription to C.C.H.'s *Common Market Reporter* (see para. 11–10) or may be purchased separately. Only very important cases are covered. It includes various indexes. The most recent cases are filed in a separate volume entitled *European Community Cases*. For very up-to-date information, with a summary, but not a full report, of the case, you should turn to the section entitled "Current Developments" in volume 4 of the *Common Market Reporter*. There are indexes to this section by subject and by case number, just before the section begins.

The Court of Justice's own *Digest of Case-Law relating to the European Communities* has so far only been published as *A Series* (most ECJ cases) and *D Series* (cases relating to the Brussels Convention). Only a digest of the cases is published and it is not up to date.

Finally, the case law file of CELEX (para. 11–7) contains all the judgments and opinions delivered by the European Court of Justice since 1970. Cases are only included in CELEX when they are published in the *European Court Reports* and as the English version of these still has a two year delay in publication, CELEX is not up to date either (except for 1994 onwards where the *European Court Reports* are being published more promptly). However the French version of the *European Court Reports* is available much more quickly, both in printed form and on CELEX. All the following paragraphs which describe ways of searching for case law will also apply to searching on CELEX.

11–18   Tracing Cases With an E.C. Dimension

As mentioned above, the published sets of law reports produce their own indexes. The *Current Law Case Citators* (para. 2–12) index some cases, as does its sister publication, *European Current Law*. In addition, there are two cumulative indexes to European Communities case law.

The first is *Butterworths EC Case Citator and Service*. This covers most European Community case law from 1954 (some less important cases are omitted). There are indexes by case number, first party name, subject keywords, legislation covered and nicknames or "names in common usage". The *Citator* is updated twice a year but in the meantime fortnightly updating sheets are issued, where you can trace very recent cases by subject, name of parties and case number. Sources given are the *European Court Reports* and the *Common Market Law Reports*, but where a case has not yet been published in either of these an O.J. reference or transcript date is given. The transcript is a reference to the *Judgments or Orders of the Court* (see para. 11–17).

The second is the *Gazetteer of European Community Law* (1983), with two *Annual Supplements*. This is an index to the whole of the E.C. case law for the years covered, plus much national case law with an E.C. dimension. It covers the years 1953–1983 and, in the two *Annual Supplement* volumes, 1989 and 1990. The *Gazetteer* allows you to trace cases through the names of the parties, case numbers or by subject. There is also a "Case Search/Tracker" in the original volumes and a "Law Tracker" for 1989 and 1990 (see paras. 11–21 and 11–22).

How to Find a Court of Justice Judgment if You Have the Reference   11–19

Suppose you are given the following case reference: Case C–196/89 *Nespoli* v. *Crippa*. How do you find it?

The first index you should turn to is the *Butterworths EC Case Citator*, as this covers every year. A judgment for a case with the number 290/83 may have been given in any year subsequent to 1983, and therefore it is best to use the *Butterworths EC Case Citator* to find a case where you do not know the year of judgment. When you have a case number, *e.g.* Case C–196/89, go to the numerical list of cases. By the side of number C–196/89 there are two citations: one for the official *European Court Reports* and the other for the *Common Market Law Reports*. If you do not have a full reference for your case but were only given the names of the parties "Nespoli" and "Crippa," look up the first name in the alphabetical list of names. You will not find the case under the second name. The full citation will be given in all cases.

Alternatively, particularly for older cases, you should use the *Gazetteer of European Law*. You can use it in much the same way as the *Butterworths EC Case Citator*.

If these reference works are not available, there are alphabetical and numerical indexes to the more important cases registered up to 1985 at the front of Volume 52 of *Halsbury's Laws* (4th ed.). More recent cases can be traced in the (separate) index contained in the Table of Cases, first in the *Cumulative Supplement* and then in the *Current Service* binder (para. 6–4). The *European Legal Journals Index* (para. 11–26) may enable you to trace full references to recent developments in various journals. Some journals, *e.g.* the *European Law Review* have alphabetical and numerical indexes to cases.

CELEX can also be used to trace judgments by name, number and subject, but references will only be given to the official reports, the *European Court Reports*.

11–20   How to Find a Judgment of the Court of Justice on a Subject

What can you do if you want to find cases on, for instance, the Common Customs Tariff? You will find a long list of these cases under that heading in *Butterworths EC Case Citator* but there is no such heading in the *Gazetteer*. You will find them there, however, under the main heading "Customs", sub-headed "Classification". It is best to be aware of the different ways in which each index will list cases by subject. Also note that *Butterworths EC Case Citator* does not aim to index all its cases by subject.

The Digest (para. 6–10) summarises cases on European Community law under appropriate subject headings. Volume 21 contains the main collection of cases on E.C. law, with alphabetical and case number indexes. You can then find more recent cases by using the *Cumulative Supplement* and the *Continuation Volumes*.

11–21   How to Trace Cases Which Refer to the Leading Case

You may want to know if a European Court case, such as Case 139/79, has been referred to in a later judgment. Turn to the *Gazetteer of European Law*. The answer is in Volume II, in the section called "Case Search", Part IV. This lists cases in numerical order. Under 139/79, there are nine cases listed. The next two volumes for 1989 and 1990 (under the part heading of "Case Tracker") list seven more cases. Those in **bold** type are considered to be the most important.

Current Law also indexes cases which have been considered in English courts in its usual way (see para. 2–12).

11–22   How to Trace Cases on E.C. Primary or Secondary Legislation

What do you do if you want to find cases which are concerned with specific provisions of Community law? For example, how do you find out what cases have been heard in the European Court of Justice on Directive 90/366/EEC on the right of residence for students? First of all, turn to *Butterworths EC Case Citator*. This lists cases by treaty provision, regulations, directives, and decisions. In the section on directives, under the number 90/366, you will find

Case C–295/90 *European Parliament* v. *Commission*. The *Gazetteer*, for the 1989 and 1990 volumes only, has a section called "Law Tracker" which has the same purpose of tracking cases by legal provision. However, it has no mention of any cases under Directive 90/366, but does list cases under Directive 90/364 which *Butterworths EC Case Citator* does not. So bear in mind that neither index is comprehensive.

How to Trace Recent Judgments   11–23

Because of publication delays, this can be a difficult task. Let's look at Joined Cases C–63–64/91 *Jackson and Cresswell* v. *Chief Adjudication Officer*. The judgment in this case was announced on July 16, 1992. With an important case such as this one, look for a law report in the newspapers. *The Financial Times* carried the case in its "European law" section on August 4, 1992. *The Times* did not report the case until October 22, 1992. To find the newspaper references, you can use their respective indexes but these are published three months in arrears. Alternatively, your library may take the *Daily Law Reports Index*, which indexes the newspaper law reports and is published fortnightly and cumulated quarterly and annually (para. 2–15).

The transcript of the judgment was available in English libraries around August 7, 1992. The essence of the judgment was published in the *Official Journal* C201 8.8.92 p. 15 (use the *Methodological Index* to the *Official Journal*).

Butterworths EC Case Citator gave both the transcript and the O.J. references in its updating sheet for August 26, 1992. A substantial summary of the case was included in issue 22, 1992 of the *Proceedings of the Court of Justice of the European Communities*, which was issued at the end of August 1992. (Use the Index to the 1992 *Proceedings of the Court of Justice of the European Communities*.) The *Current Law Case Citator* (para. 2–12) gives a reference to *The Times* law report and a digest of the case in the *Current Law Year Book* 1992 (para. 6–9).

The first substantial published report of the *Jackson and Cresswell* case appeared in *European Community Cases*: [1992] 2 C.E.C. 313, issued in October 1992. It later appeared in *Common Market Law Reports*: [1992] 3 C.M.L.R. 389, which was not published until December 1992. In April 1993, it was also published in the *Weekly Law Reports*: [1992] 2 W.L.R. 658. Some of these reports were cited in the April 21, 1993 updating sheet of *Butterworths EC Case Citator*. Publication of the authoritative report in the *European Court Reports* will probably be delayed for over two years on the current publishing schedule but already appears on CELEX in French.

This pattern of publication is broadly similar for other cases, but non-English cases will take longer to appear in English and the less important ones will not appear in newspapers and *Current Law*.

11–24 BOOKS

The E.C. publishes a wealth of material which provides introductions, overviews and summaries of topics. All these will be available at your local European Documentation Centre (see para. 11–1) and you should consult the library catalogue there. The *General Report on the Activities of the European Communities* and the *Bulletin of the European Union* have already been mentioned (see para. 11–10) as source materials for tracing E.C. legislation. Other important annual reviews on legal topics include the *Report on Competition Policy* and the *Report on Social Developments*. The former covers Community competition policy and its enforcement and the latter will include employment law developments. The Court of Justice issues an annual report, which is an account of the important cases of the year, plus a description of the organisation of the court.

The main E.C. official monographs on the E.C. legal system include *The Community Legal Order* (2nd ed., 1990); *The Court of Justice of the European Communities* (European Documentation No. 5, 1986); *The ABC of Community Law* (European Documentation No. 2, 1994) and *Thirty Years of Community Law* (1982).

There are now a number of textbooks explaining both the E.C. institutions and their part in the legislative process, and the substantive law of the E.C. You must also remember that E.C. law becomes part of English law either with direct effect (regulations and decisions) or after being implemented as Acts or statutory instruments (directives). This means that many English textbooks (particularly the looseleaf encyclopedic works) will include a chapter or section on Community law.

United Kingdom government publications which apply particularly to E.C. law include the Reports of the House of Lords Select Committee on the European Communities. These very often discuss proposed E.C. legislation in great detail. In addition, every six months the government issues a publication entitled *Developments in the European Community*, which describes European Communities policy over the previous six months.

The Department of Trade and Industry issues a number of publications, mainly aimed at businesses and their advisers (including legal advisers), explaining E.C. policy and legislation. It is probable that your library's Official Publications Department will hold these.

JOURNALS 11–25

Many legal journals cover E.C. topics in a selective manner. The major English language titles that specialise in the subject include the *Common Market Law Review;* the *European Business Law Review,* the *European Competition Law Review;* the *European Law Review; The International and Comparative Law Quarterly* and the *Yearbook of European Law.*

How to Find Articles on E.C. Law 11–26

If you want to look for recent articles on the E.C. Directive on unfair contract terms, the best source of information is the *Legal Journals Index* (para. 4–3) until the end of 1992. From 1993, the *European Legal Journals Index* is the best source to use, although the *Legal Journals Index* still covers E.C. law in exclusively English journals. In both these publications, entries are arranged both by subject and by the name of the legislation. In the *Subject Index*, you can look under such terms as "Unfair Contract Terms" and "Consumer Protection". In the *Legislation Index*, you can look under "Council Directive on Unfair Terms in Consumer Contracts (draft)" or, after the Directive has been adopted, under "Council Directive 93/13 on Unfair Terms in Consumer Contracts."

Alternatively, you can use the *Index to Legal Periodicals* (para. 4–5), which also has entries arranged by subject. The *Current Law Year Book* has a subject index to articles written during the year. The issues of the *Current Law Monthly Digest* contain details of more recent articles, also by subject (para. 4–4).

European Access (University of Wales, Cardiff 1982–1988; 1989 to date) is also a good source for finding material on E.C. issues. Legislative proposals and adopted legislation are listed under appropriate subject headings, together with other E.C. publications and journal and newspaper articles about them. There is a detailed contents listing and a *Subject Index* in each issue. It is published six times a year and also includes other E.C. information, including a bibliographic review or "snapshot" on various subjects. Topics covered include each of the E.C. institutions, "The Environment and Europe" and "The Enlargement of the Community."

LEGAL ENCYCLOPEDIAS 11–27

Volumes 51 and 52 of *Halsbury's Laws of England* (4th ed.), cover the E.C. They are a comprehensive account of E.C. institutional and policy developments up to the middle of the 1980s. The information in these volumes is kept up to date by the *Cumulative Supplement* and looseleaf *Service* binders (para. 6–4). The *Current Service* contains E.C. developments at the back of each *Monthly Review*, including a separate index to E.C. matters. The *Annual Abridgement* to *Halsbury's Laws* also contains a substantial account of major E.C. developments during the year in question, including new secondary legislation and judgments.

Halsbury's Laws, Vols. 51 and 52 have been republished as two stand-alone volumes edited by David Vaughan, and entitled *Law of the European Communities Service*. These, in turn, are being replaced by a four-volume looseleaf work, containing updating material, of the same name. The arrangement conforms with that of *Halsbury's Laws*, Vols. 51 and 52, and so the *Noter-up* in the looseleaf by Vaughan can also be used to note up Volumes 51 and 52.

The *Common Market Reporter* and Smit and Herzog, *Law of the European Communities* are two other encyclopedic works which comment upon E.C. legislation. Because they are looseleaf, they are kept reasonably up to date.

The Encyclopedia of European Community Law is another encyclopedia devoted exclusively to Community law. It is divided into three sections: Volume A consists of United Kingdom sources. This comprises the European Communities Act 1972 and the statutes and statutory instruments which implement E.C. directives. Volume B contains the official English texts of all the European Community Treaties plus other agreements concluded between the Member States and with non-Member States (para. 11–2). Volume C contains the E.C. secondary legislation. Each set of volumes has its own index at the back of the last binder in the volume. All three volumes will eventually be replaced by a new work entitled *Encyclopedia of European Union Laws*. Volume A has already been discontinued (in 1993) and will be replaced by a finding guide to United Kingdom implementing legislation, rather than a reproduction of the texts of this legislation.

CHAPTER 12

Public International Law

INTRODUCTION

Early definitions of international law described it as "a body of rules governing the relations between states." In modern times, this definition has been expanded so that the concept now includes regulation of the relationships not only between states, but also between international organisations and individuals.

This chapter helps you find the international law materials in the library. Remember that public international law should be distinguished from private international law, or conflict of laws, which deals with the interrelationship of domestic municipal law of different states, rather than regulating the international relations between different states.

International law has no legislature, and no system of binding precedent in its judicial forums. Its observance therefore depends on the adherence by nations to its principles, which are mainly embodied in international treaties and international custom. The rules of international law only have binding effect from their inclusion in a treaty or convention or because they have been recognised as an international custom. States which do not ratify a particular treaty are not bound by its provisions. With the growth of international organisations, another body of international law is being created by them and it is therefore necessary for you to know how to find the legal publications of the major international organisations. You should also be aware of the way in which international law is constantly developing and expanding into new subject areas, such as the law of the sea, which means that there is a constant flow of new publications.

As a student of international law, you will need to look well beyond the confines of the traditional law library to locate the various materials you will need, as they will also be found in international relations and official publications collections. To help you in your researches, this chapter describes the various generally accepted sources of international law and tells you about the materials comprising each source.

12–2 SOURCES

The most frequently accepted definition of the sources of international law can be found in Article 38(1) of the Statute of the International Court of Justice which states that disputes submitted to it will be decided according to the principles of international conventions, international custom, general principles of law, judicial decisions and the writings of leading commentators.

12–3 TREATIES

As defined in the Vienna Convention on the Law of Treaties, a treaty is a written agreement concluded between two or more states or international organisations and governed by international law. Treaties come in many different disguises, such as protocols, conventions, charters, statutes, accords, etc. In this modern technological age, with its vastly improved communications, the huge growth of international trade and the growth of international interdependence, the volume of treaty publishing has become enormous and it is often difficult to trace particular treaties.

12–4 General Collections

The first major category of treaty publishing is the general collection, of which there are three major series. The *Consolidated Treaty Series* (1969–1986) edited by Clive Parry, and published in 231 volumes by Oceana, covers the years 1648 to 1920. It attempts to reprint the original text and official translations (if any) of all treaties published during that period. The treaties are arranged chronologically, with French or English translations where available. There is a multi-volume *Index-Guide* which contains a general chronological list of treaties, plus a party/country Index.

How to use the Consolidated Treaty Series   12–5
Start with the *Index-Guide* volumes, which can be distinguished by
the colour binding on the spine. They are divided into three
sections. The *Party Index* is black. This lists countries
alphabetically, and within each country gives a chronological list
of the treaties concluded by that country, the names of the parties
and the volume and page number within *C.T.S.* where the treaty is
published. The *General Chronological List* is red. This lists all treaties
from 1648 to 1920 by date. It is a useful listing of all the treaties
traced by the editors of *C.T.S.* It not only gives the *C.T.S.* reference,
but also references to the publication of treaties in other
collections. The *Special Chronology* is green. This deals with
colonial and other less important treaties and you will probably
not need to use it.

Let's suppose that you are looking for a bilateral treaty between
Great Britain and Belgium, setting the boundary between Uganda
and the Congo. You know that the date of the Treaty was 1910; you
can therefore go straight to the *Chronological List* and under 1910
you will find the following entry:

> 1910: 14 May Agreement between Belgium and Great Britain
> settling the boundary dispute between the Congo and
> Uganda, Signed at Brussels.
> 211 CTS 103
> CVII B.S.P. 348 (Eng)

You will therefore be able to find the Treaty in the *Consolidated
Treaty Series*, Vol. 211, at page 103. The reference to *B.S.P.* is to
British and Foreign State Papers (see para. 12–9).

If you do not know the date of the treaty, go to the *Party Index*
and in the entries under Belgium you will find:

> 1910 May 14
> Belgium Great Britain
> 211 CTS 103

The *Consolidated Treaty Series* ends in 1920, because this is the
first year covered by the *League of Nations Treaty Series*. This series
continues until 1946 and contains over 4,000 treaties in 205
volumes. There are *Subject* and *Chronological Index* volumes
interspersed between the texts.

How to use the United Nations Treaty Series   12–6
The third important series is the *United Nations Treaty Series* which
started publication in 1946 when the U.N. took over the functions
of the dissolved League of Nations. The U.N. publishes the text of

every treaty entered into by any of its members, as all treaties have to be registered with the Secretariat. They are published in order of registration, and not by date of conclusion, which can make them extremely difficult to locate. So far, over 1,300 volumes have been published and they appear at the rate of over 40 a year. The series is very late in publication; volumes published in 1993 related mainly to 1986, so it is not useful for obtaining recent treaties. The figure on p. 225 shows the title page of a typical volume from *United Nations Treaty Series*

To locate a treaty, start with the *Index* volumes, which are published for every 50 volumes of treaties. Each *Index* contains a *Chronological Index* listing treaties in order of the date on which they were signed, plus an *Alphabetical Index*. If you need to find the Convention of Paris on the protection of industrial property as revised in Stockholm in 1967, check in the *Chronological Index* for that period. The entry is shown in the figure on p. 226.

The number in the first column is the volume number and that in the second column is the page in the *U.N. Treaty Series*. The *Index* also tells you whether the treaty is bilateral or multilateral, and which states have acceded to it (*i.e.* become parties to it after it was originally signed) or ratified it.

If you are unsure of the date, check in the subject section of the *Alphabetical Index* under "Industrial Property" (see the figure on p. 227).

The symbol I denotes a treaty or international agreement *registered* with the U.N. Secretariat. Occasionally, the symbol II appears, which means that the treaty is *filed and recorded* with the Secretariat. The other number following the I is the serial number of the treaty, and the other numbers are the volume and page numbers.

12–7   National Collections

The second method of publication of texts of treaties is by country, many countries publishing separate collections of treaties. The *United Kingdom Treaty Series* is the official series published by the Foreign and Commonwealth Office. Treaties are published in this series only after ratifiction. They may have appeared earlier as *Command Papers* (see para. 5–3). The *Treaty Series* forms a sub-series to the Command Paper series and every treaty has both a Command Paper number and a Treaty Series number followed by the year of issue.

The figure on p. 229 shows the first publication in the Command Paper series of an Extradition Treaty with Italy which had not been ratified.

Treaties and international agreements registered or filed and recorded with the Secretariat of the United Nations

VOLUME 1087	1978	I. Nos. 16634-16656

TABLE OF CONTENTS

I

Treaties and international agreements registered on 27 April 1978

1967 (*continued*)

14 Jul (*continued*)	Multil. (*continued*)	Berne Conv. for the protection . . . (*continued*) notif. under art.38(2) (*continued*)		
		Norway 1970,22 Jul	828	227
		Portugal 1970,25 Aug	828	227
		South Africa 1970,17 Sep	828	227
		Tunisia 1970,18 Sep	828	227
		Turkey 1970,17 Sep	828	227
		Yugoslavia 1970,20 Jul	828	227

objections to access. by German Dem. Rep.:
Argentina, Belgium, Canada, Denmark, France, Gabon, Germany, Fed. Rep. of, Greece, Haiti, Holy See, Iceland, Iran, Ireland, Israel, Japan, Luxembourg, Madagascar, Niger, Portugal, South Africa, Spain, UK, USA   828   225
sign.:
Austria, Belgium, Bulgaria (with decl. and reserv.), Cameroon, Congo, Denmark, Finland, France, Gabon, Germany, Fed. Rep. of, Greece, Holy See, Hungary, Iceland, India, Ireland, Israel, Italy, Ivory Coast, Japan, Liechtenstein, Luxembourg, Madagascar, Mexico, Monaco, Morocco, Niger, Norway, Philippines, Poland (with decl. and reserv.), Portugal, Romania, Senegal, South Africa, Spain, Sweden, Switzerland, Tunisia, Yugoslavia
See also: 1883,20 Mar v.LXXIV:289
            1908,13 Nov v.1:217
            1914,20 Mar v.1:243
            1928,2 Jun v.CXXIII:233
            1948,26 Jun v.331:217
            1967,14 Jul v.828:3

14 Jul   Multil.   Paris Conv. for the protection of industrial property of   F   1:11851   828   305
Stockholm   Mar 20, 1883, as rev. at Brussels on Dec 14, 1900, at Washington on Jun 2, 1911, at The Hague on Nov 6, 1925, at London on Jun 2, 1934, at Lisbon on Oct 31, 1958, at Stockholm on Jul 14, 1967
access.(*a*), notif. of deposit of instrument of access.(*na*) and of ratif.(*nr*) and ratif.:

			828	
Australia (with decl.) 1972,25 May(*na*)			828	309
Bulgaria (with decl. and reserv.) 1970,27 Feb(*nr*)			828	309
Canada (with decl.) 1970,7 Apr(*na*)			828	309
Chad 1970,26 Jun(*nr*)			828	309
Czechoslovakia (with decl.) 1970,29 Sep(*na*)			828	309
Denmark (with notif. of applic. to Faeroe Islands) 1970,26 Jan			828	307
Finland (with decl.) 1970,15 Jun(*nr*)			828	311
German Dem. Rep. 1968,20 Jun(*a*)			828	307
Germany, Fed. Rep. of (with decl. of applic. to *Land Berlin*) 1970,19 Jun(*nr*)			828	309
Hungary (with decl. and reserv.) 1969,18 Dec			828	307
Ireland 1968,27 Mar			828	307
Israel 1969,30 Jul			828	307
Jordan 1972,17 Apr(*na*)			828	311
Kenya 1971,26 Jul(*nr*)			828	311
Liechtenstein 1972,25 Feb(*nr*)			828	311
Madagascar 1972,10 Jan(*nr*)			828	311
Malawi 1970,25 Mar(*na*)			828	311
Morocco 1971,6 May(*nr*)			828	311
Romania (with decl.) 1969,28 Feb			828	307
Senegal 1968,19 Sep			828	307
Spain 1972,14 Jan(*nr*)			828	311

Indonesia (*continued*)

USA:agric. commodities (*continued*)
I:10453 Suppl. Agr. (17 Nov 1969):amend. 1971,30 Dec v.836:345
I:10813 Suppl. Agr. (10 Apr 1970):amend. 1971,30 Dec v.836:347
I:11013 (2 Oct 1970):amend. 1971,18 Nov v.822:410
I:11259 Suppl. Agr., 13th (17 Mar 1971):
amend. 1971,10 Nov v.822:428
amend. 1971,21 Dec v.837:324
amend. 1972,5 Jan v.823:435
I:11504 1971,7 Aug v.807:9
amend. 1971,23 Dec v.837:348

Industrial co-operation: *See* Economic co-operation; Industry; Technical co-operation

Industrial designs: *See* Patents

Industrial development: *See* Industry

Industrial property:

multil.:
commercial and industrial trademarks:int. registration:[Agr. of Madrid] (2 Jun 1934):access. LoN 4833 v.828:530
industrial designs:int. classification:[Locarno Agr.] I:11853 1968,8 Oct v.828:435
access. v.828:437
notif. of deposit of instrument of ratif. v.828:437
objections to access. by German Dem. Rep. v.828:437
ratif. v.828:437
sign. v.828:435
industrial property:protection:[Conv. of Paris] I:11847 1958, 31 Oct v.828:107
denunc. v.828:113
notif. of deposit of instrument of access. v.828:111,113
notif. of deposit of instrument of ratif. v.828:111,113
objections to access. by German Dem. Rep. v.828:113
objections to decl. by Fed. Rep. of Germany v.828:111
sign. v.828:107
success. v.828:113
industrial property:protection:[Paris Conv.] I:11851 1967, 14 Jul v.828:305
access. v.828:307
notif. of deposit of instrument of access. v.828:309,311
notif. of deposit of instrument of ratif. v.828:309,311
notif. under art. 30 (2) v.828:311
objections to access. by German Dem. Rep. v.828:309
objection to decl. by Fed. Rep. of Germany v.828:311
ratif. v.828:307
sign. v.828:305
industrial property:protection:[Union Conv. of Paris] (6 Nov 1925) LoN 1743
access. v.828:526
territorial applic. by USA v.828:526
industrial property:protection:[Union Conv. of Paris] (2 Jun 1934) LoN 4459
access. v.828:528
territorial applic. by USA v.828:528

Industry:

See also Economic and social development; Labour

Brazil:IBRD:Guarantee Agr.:
COSIPA Steel Expansion Project I:12091 1972,14 Jun v.845:143
MBR Iron Ore Project I:12082 1971,25 Aug v.845:29
Denmark:Poland: economic and industrial co-operation I:11911 1970,3 Dec v.833:9
Ethiopia:IDA:Development Credit Agr.:*Agric. and Industrial Development Bank Project* I:12156 1972,10 May v.849:113
Finland:
USSR:economic, technical and industrial co-operation: development I:11595 1971,20 Apr v.814:237
Yugoslavia:economic, industrial and technical co-operation I:12055 1971,4 Jun v.843:3
France:USSR:economic, technical and industrial co-operation:development I:12048 1971,27 Oct v.842:127
IBRD:
Brazil:Guarantee Agr.:
COSIPA Steel Expansion Project I:12091 1972,14 Jun v.845:143
MBR Iron Ore Project I:12082 1971,25 Aug v.845:29
India:Guarantee Agr.:*Industrial Credit and Investment Project, 9th* I:12085 1971,27 Oct v.845:59
Mexico:Guarantee Agr.:*Industrial Equipment Fund (FONEI) Project* I:12158 1972,2 Jun v.849:169
Turkey:
Guarantee Agr.:*Ammonia-Urea Manufacturing Project* I:12093 1972,30 Jun v.845:175
Loan Agr.:*Steel Plant Expansion Project* I:11992 1972, 28 Apr v.838:191
IDA:
Ethiopia:Development Credit Agr.:*Agric. and Industrial Development Bank Project* I:12156 1972,10 May v.849:113
India:Development Credit Agr.:*Industrial Imports Project, 7th* I:12163 1972,26 Sep v.849:253
Pakistan:Development Credit Agr.:*East Pakistan Small Industries Project* I:11615 1970,10 Jun v.815:277
India:
IBRD:Guarantee Agr.:*Industrial Credit and Investment Project, 9th* I:12085 1971,27 Oct v.845:59
IDA:Development Credit Agr.:*Industrial Imports Project, 7th* I:12163 1972,26 Sep v.849:253
Mexico:IBRD:Guarantee Agr.:*Industrial Equipment Fund (FONEI) Project* I:12158 1972,2 Jun v.849:169
Pakistan:IDA:Development Credit Agr.:*East Pakistan Small Industries Project* I:11615 1970,10 Jun v.815:277
Poland:Denmark:economic and industrial co-operation I:11911 1970,3 Dec v.833:9
Turkey:IBRD:
Guarantee Agr.:*Ammonia-Urea Manufacturing Project* I:12093 1972,30 Jun v.845:175
Loan Agr.:*Steel Plant Expansion Project* I:11992 1972, 28 Apr v.838:191
USSR:
Finland:economic, technical and industrial co-operation: development I:11595 1971,20 Apr v.814:237

The figure on p. 230 shows an agreement with China, published in the *Treaty Series*, which has been ratified. The heading on the top right-hand corner gives the name of the country as it is a bilateral treaty (if it was a multilateral treaty, then the subject matter would be printed here). The number on the top left hand corner refers to the original, pre-ratification, Command Paper number.

12–8   How to use the United Kingdom Treaty Series
Start with the *Indexes to Treaty Series* which appear under three titles:

(a) the *General Index to Treaty Series*, of which the latest issue to appear was for 1977–79;
(b) the *Annual Index to Treaty Series*; and
(c) the *Supplementary List of Ratifications, Accessions, Withdrawals etc.*, which appears about four times a year.

Each *Index* is divided into numerical and subject sequences. The subject headings chosen are wide and slightly idiosyncratic, but once mastered are useful.

If you need to trace the Convention relating to a Uniform Law on the International Sale of Goods of 1964 and to find out if the United Kingdom is a signatory, then it can be found in the *Index to Treaty Series* under "Private International Law" as illustrated on p. 231. The entry gives details of the signatories to the Convention, its Treaty Series number and its Command Paper number.

12–9   British and foreign State Papers
This series was produced by the Foreign Office Library between 1812 and 1968. It contains the text of important treaties and conventions, not only between Great Britain and other countries, but also a selection of those made between other countries. Treaties are sometimes presented as part of a collection of all existing treaties on a particular topic, and the years indicated on the volume do not necessarily mean that the volume only contains material for those years. For example, Volume 1 has the years 1812–1814 on the spine but among its contents are "the treaties of alliance and commerce between Great Britain and Portugal subsisting in … 1814" The earliest of these treaties is dated 1373.

The best way of finding material in *British and Foreign State Papers* is by using the cumulative general *Indexes*, which are numbered volumes in the series. The index volumes are numbers 64, 93, 115, 138, 165 and 170. They contain both a chronological and an alphabetical subject index.

One other national series of note which you may be referred to is

$$\left[\begin{array}{c} \text{Royal Crest} \\ \text{omitted} \end{array} \right]$$

Italy No. 1 (1986)

Extradition Treaty

between the
United Kingdom of Great Britain and Northern Ireland and the Italian Republic

Florence, 12 March 1986

[Instruments of ratification have not been exchanged]

Presented to Parliament
by the Secretary of State for Foreign and Commonwealth Affairs
by Command of Her Majesty
June 1986

LONDON
HER MAJESTY'S STATIONERY OFFICE
£1·90 net

Cmnd. 9807

The Agreement was
previously published as
China No. 1 (1984),
Cmnd. 9247

CHINA

[Royal Crest omitted]

Treaty Series No. 14 (1985)

Agreement

between the Government of the
United Kingdom of Great Britain and Northern Ireland
and the Government of the People's Republic of China

on the Establishment of a British Consulate-General at Shanghai and a Chinese Consulate-General at Manchester

Peking (Beijing), 17 April 1984

[The Agreement entered into force on 14 January 1985]

*Presented to Parliament
by the Secretary of State for Foreign and Commonwealth Affairs
by Command of Her Majesty
April 1985*

LONDON
HER MAJESTY'S STATIONERY OFFICE
£1·75 net

Cmnd. 9472

	Date	Treaty Series No.	Command No.
PRIVATE INTERNATIONAL LAW (continued)—			
Convention relating to a Uniform Law on the International Sale of Goods	The Hague, 1 July, 1964– 31 Dec., 1965	74/1972	Cmnd. 5029
Signatures—			
Belgium	6 Oct., 1965		
France	31 Dec., 1965		
Germany, Federal Republic of*	1 July, 1964		
Greece (*ad referendum*)	3 Aug., 1964		
Holy See*	2 Mar., 1965		
Hungary	31 Dec., 1965	74/1972	Cmnd. 5029
Israel*	28 Dec., 1965		
Italy	23 Dec., 1964		
Luxembourg	7 Dec., 1965		
Netherlands	12 Aug., 1964		
San Marino	24 Aug., 1964		
United Kingdom	21 Aug., 1964		

* With reservation in respect of ratification.

	Date	Treaty Series No.	Command No.
Ratifications—			
Belgium (with reservations)	12 Dec., 1968	74/1972	Cmnd. 5029
Germany, Federal Republic of (also applies to Berlin (West)) (with declaration) ...	16 Oct., 1973	121/1973	Cmnd. 5586
Israel	3 Dec., 1971		
Italy (with declaration)	22 Feb., 1972		
Netherlands (for Kingdom in Europe) (with declaration)	17 Feb., 1972	74/1972	Cmnd. 5029
San Marino (with declarations)	24 May, 1968		
United Kingdom (with declarations) ...	31 Aug., 1967		

	Date	Treaty Series No.	Command No.
Convention relating to a Uniform Law on the Formation of Contracts for the International Sale of Goods	The Hague, 1 July, 1964– 31 Dec., 1965	75/1972	Cmnd. 5030
Signatures—			
Belgium	6 Oct., 1965		
France	31 Dec., 1965		
Germany, Federal Republic of*	1 July, 1964		
Greece (*ad referendum*)	3 Aug., 1964		
Holy See*	2 Mar., 1965		
Hungary	31 Dec., 1965	75/1972	Cmnd. 5030
Israel*	28 Dec., 1965		
Italy	23 Dec., 1964		
Luxembourg	7 Dec., 1965		
Netherlands	12 Aug., 1964		
San Marino	24 Aug., 1964		
United Kingdom	8 June, 1965		

* With reservation in respect of ratification.

	Date	Treaty Series No.	Command No.
Ratifications—			
Belgium	1 Dec., 1970	75/1972	Cmnd. 5030
Germany, Federal Republic of (also applies to Berlin (West)) (with declaration) ...	16 Oct., 1973	121/1973	Cmnd. 5586
Italy	22 Feb., 1972		
Netherlands (for Kingdom in Europe) (with declaration)	17 Feb., 1972	75/1972	Cmnd. 5030
San Marino (with declaration)	24 May, 1968		
United Kingdom	31 Aug., 1967		
Convention on the Service Abroad of Judicial and Extrajudicial Documents in Civil or Commercial Matters	The Hague, 15 Nov., 1965	50/1969	Cmnd. 3986

the *United States Treaties and Other International Agreements*
(U.S.T.), published by the Department of State since 1950. There is
a long delay in publication, the first part of volume 35 covering
1982–83 being published in 1992. In a similar way to the *U.N.
Treaty Series*, each treaty also has a running "T.I.A.S." (Treaties and
other International Acts Series) number, which is assigned when it
is first issued as a separate document. U.S. treaties before 1950 are
published in C. Bevans, *Treaties and other International Agreements
of the U.S.A. 1776–1949*, in 12 volumes plus an *Index*.

The *European Treaty Series* contains the texts of treaties
concluded between the Member States of the Council of Europe.
This series is produced as a number of separate booklets and each
treaty is numbered according to the date of its signature. These
treaties are also published in the *European Yearbook (Annuaire
Européen)*.

12–10   Hague Conventions

You may sometimes be referred to "The Hague Convention on..."
While there are numerous treaties which happen to have been
signed at The Hague, this very often refers to those drafted at
sessions of The Hague Conference on Private International Law.
The drafts are published as part of the set of documents for each
conference, but they are also collected in a small paperback
Collection of Conventions, of which the latest edition covers the 32
Conventions published between 1951 and 1988. Between editions,
a list of current signatures and ratifications is published in the
International and Comparative Law Quarterly. These conventions do
not appear in the *U.N. Treaty Series*.

12–11   Subject Collections

In recent years, several collections of treaties covering particular
subject areas have been published, frequently in looseleaf form.
They can be a useful place to start a search when you know the
subject matter of the treaty you are trying to track down. For
example, the treaty establishing the Swiss Inter-Cantonal
Arbitration Tribunal can be found in Clive Schmitthoff's
International Commercial Arbitration. Tax treaties are amongst the
easiest to find, as there are several specialist publications devoted
purely to them, for example Diamond and Diamond, *International
Tax Treaties of all Nations*, and the looseleaf sections of *European
Taxation*, published by the International Bureau of Fiscal
Documentation.

Finding Treaties   12–12

If you cannot trace a treaty in the Indexes to the various collections described above, then there are other Indexes, both national and international, which can provide some extra help.

National Indexes   12–13

United Kingdom   12–14

For treaties concluded by the United Kingdom, there are two main sources. Parry and Hopkins, *Index of British Treaties* was first published in three volumes in 1970, and covered treaties concluded by the United Kingdom between 1101 and 1968. Volumes 2 and 3 contain a *Chronological List of Treaties*, giving details of the place and date of signature, entry into force and termination (where applicable). The references given in brackets at the end of the entry show where the treaty can be found. This Index covers both bilateral and multilateral treaties to which the United Kingdom is a party. Volume 1 is an *Index*, divided into separate indexes to bilateral and multilateral treaties. A fourth volume covering 1969 to 1988 appeared in 1991.

The *Index to Treaty Series*, which forms part of the Treaty Series, has already been mentioned (para 12–8).

United States   12–15

The best known American index is *Treaties in Force*, published annually by the Department of State. It lists all treaties and ageeements which are in force in the United States on January 1 of each year. Part 1 lists bilateral treaties by country and by subject; Part 2 lists multilateral treaties in an alphabetical subject arrangement. Igor Kavass has recently completed a revised *United States Treaty Index: 1990 Consolidation*, in 12 volumes. This is updated with *Current Treaty Index* pamphlets. The *Index* is also issued on CD-ROM.

International Indexes   12–16

A most welcome addition to treaty indexes was *Multilateral Treaties: Index and Current Status*, edited by Bowman and Harris and published in 1984. A product of the Treaty Research Centre at the University of Nottingham, it offers status information on over 800 major treaties. Cumulative supplements appear each year.

How to use Bowman and Harris   12–17

A helpful feature of this index is the word index within the Subject Index. If you need to find the Convention relating to a Uniform Law on the Formation of Contracts for the International Sale of

Goods, check in the word index and under "Goods, Sale" you will find references by number to the relevant entries.

The figure below shows the entry for this treaty. The entry gives the full title, the date and place of conclusion, the date of entry into force, the duration, the language of the authentic text and a most useful "Notes" section, which gives the purpose of the treaty and, in this instance, tells you that it is due to be replaced by a new U.N. Convention (which has in fact been in force since 1988). This section also gives details of any periodical articles about the treaty.

TREATY 462	CONVENTION RELATING TO A UNIFORM LAW ON THE FORMATION OF CONTRACTS FOR THE INTERNATIONAL SALE OF GOODS
CONCLUDED	**1 Jul 64,** The Hague
LOCATION	834 UNTS 169; UKTS 75(1972), Cmnd 5030; 45 Vert A 615; 3 ILM 864; 13 AJCL 453
ENTRY INTO FORCE	23 Aug 72. Later acceptances effective 6 months after deposit: Art 8
DURATION	Unspecified. Denunciation permitted on 1 year's notice: Art 10
RESERVATIONS	Certain declarations and derogations permitted under Arts 2-4. Withdrawal of same effective 3 months after notification: Art 5
AUTHENTIC TEXTS	E F
DEPOSITARY	Netherlands
OPEN TO	As for treaty 463: Arts 6, 7
PARTIES (9)	BELGIUM 1 Dec 70; GAMBIA 5 Mar 74; GFR* 16 Oct 73; ISRAEL 30 May 80; ITALY 22 Feb 72; LUXEMBOURG* 6 Feb 79; NETHERLANDS* 17 Feb 72; SAN MARINO* 24 May 68; UK 31 Aug 67
TERRITORIAL SCOPE	See Art 11. Declared applicable: GFR - Berlin (West); NETHERLANDS - Kingdom in Europe
SIGNATORIES	FRANCE 31 Dec 65; GREECE 3 Aug 64; HUNGARY 31 Dec 65; VATICAN CITY 2 Mar 65
NOTES	This Convention, to which the Uniform Law is annexed, will be replaced by the 1980 UN Convention on the Sale of Goods (treaty 775) for the parties to both.

To check whether the information in the original entry is still correct, look in the *Cumulative Supplement*. Using the same example, you will see that Germany, Italy and the Netherlands have withdrawn from the treaty.

If you need to find a bilateral or multilateral treaty agreed between two obscure parties, probably the best source is the *World Treaty Index*, the second edition of which was published in 1983 to 1984. It is a massive computer-generated index, covering the years from 1920 to 1984 and lists the treaties by subject, by parties and chronologically, but it is quite difficult to use and not widely available as it is expensive.

An easier source, though now very out of date, is the *Harvard Law School Library Index to Multilateral Treaties*, which is a chronological listing of international treaties to which three or more countries were parties, from 1596 to 1963.

Other Sources of Treaty Information   12–18

Finding treaties can be difficult, especially as some of the official series take so long to print a document, and there are some other helpful sources apart from the collections noted above.

International Legal Materials, published by the American Society of International Law, is very useful. It is a bi-monthly periodical which provides up-to-date information on legal aspects of public and private international relations. It frequently reproduces the texts of treaties and other agreements before they are published elsewhere. Issues also include such items as decisions of international arbitral tribunals and important U.N. Security Council Resolutions. It has annual Indexes, as well as two *Cumulative Indexes* which together cover Volumes 1–18 (1962–1979).

Government bulletins, press releases and circulars often contain the texts of treaties shortly after they are signed. The *U.S. Department of State Bulletin* is published weekly and has a special section entitled "Treaty Information".

National official gazettes also sometimes contain the texts of treaties by that country and some gazettes have special sections devoted to such texts, for example, the German *Bundesgesetzblatt*, Pt. II. Other countries like the United Kingdom have separate treaty series, *e.g.* the Netherlands *Tractatenblad*. The British Library Official Publications Library in London has the best collection of such gazettes in the United Kingdom.

LAW REPORTS   12–19

Court Reports   12–20

As stated above, international law does not have a system of binding precedent, although international tribunals are reluctant to change principles which they have laid down in earlier decisions. Because it is a permanent institution operating independently under its own statute, the International Court of Justice has developed a considerable body of case law and has thus been instrumental in the development of international law. The official reports of the Court are entitled *Reports of Judgments, Advisory Opinions and Orders*; this is published in parts, which are cumulated into an annual volume. Each volume has a subject index. A second series is entitled *Pleadings, Oral Arguments and Documents*. It contains the documents filed in each case heard by the Court, and appears on an irregular basis, usually several years after the corresponding decision. The ICJ also publishes the *Yearbook of the International Court of Justice* which contains useful information on cases that the Court has heard during the year under review.

You may also sometimes be referred to the reports of the ICJ's predecessor, the Permanent Court of International Justice which was set up by the League of Nations and operated between 1922 and 1940. Its publications had a complicated numbering system; the main series to mention being series A: *Judgments* and series B: *Advisory opinions*, which were amalgamated in 1931 into series A/B containing both types of document. The *Pleadings* appear in series C.

12–21 General Reports

Because it is difficult to isolate cases relating to international law from the mass of domestic cases published each year, various series of specialized international law reports are published, the most important one being the *International Law Reports*. This covers reports from several countries, and includes the decisions of international tribunals as well as of international courts. Cases are published in full in their original form and where necessary translations of foreign judgments are provided. There are summaries following each report. The series is arranged according to a comprehensive classification scheme. Some volumes cover one topic, others cover several. Four volumes a year are published and a two-volume set of consolidated tables and indexes to volumes 1–80 was published in 1990–1991. You will see that I.L.R. was originally published as the *Annual Digest of Public International Law Cases*, as it was then just a digest (summary) of the cases. As the reports grew longer, this was reflected in 1950 in a change of title.

12–22 National Series

Some countries produce national series of international law reports. In this country *British International Law Cases* covers cases from 1607 to 1970. This series is designed to complement I.L.R. Cases are published in full, but no headnotes are added. Each volume gives a cumulative list of the cases published giving full references to the original reports. There is an index in each volume, plus a cumulative index for the last eight volumes. Unfortunately it is doubtful whether any further volumes are ever likely to be published. Another useful source of information on law reports is the *British Yearbook of International Law* which every year contains a section entitled "Decisions of British Courts ... involving questions of Public or Private International Law". You should also remember that many of the leading textbooks contain comprehensive lists of cases.

In America the major series is *American International Law Cases*, which contains full reprints of both federal and state cases involving international law.

Reports of Arbitrations   12–23

The awards of international arbitral tribunals have always been of importance as a source of international law. The most important series is the *Reports of International Arbitral Awards* published by the United Nations Office of Legal Affairs. There are also various series of reports covering arbitrations before specific tribunals, for example the Iran–U.S. Claims Tribunal. A.M. Stuyt's *Survey of International Arbitrations 1794–1989* (1990) is a useful source of information. The figure on page 238 shows a sample page.

The arbitrations are listed by parties and by subject matter. Details of the award are also given including the date, the party in whose favour the award was made, whether it was accepted and where the text may be found. There are also references to the *Encyclopedia of Public International Law* and to another important collection edited by Professors Coussirat-Coustère and Eisemann, the *Repertory of International Arbitral Jurisprudence 1794–1988*, published in four volumes in 1989–1990. This consists of extracts from awards in a classified arrangement. The source for each extract is given by a coded reference, and using this you can look up the full details in the chronological Table of Awards.

Digests of Case Law   12–24

During the early years of its existence, it was often difficult to obtain copies of the ICJ's decisions and this prompted some commentators to produce digests of its reports. One of the most important of these is *Hambro's Case Law of the International Court*, which appears in several volumes and which you may find useful it you cannot obtain full reports. It contains extracts from the decisions arranged by subject matter.

Example page from A. M. Stuyt's Survey of International Arbitrations 1794–1989

No. 428

1. FRANCE – UNITED STATES OF AMERICA.

2. Interpretation of air transport services agreement of March 27, 1946 (UNTS 139-114).

3. Arbitral Tribunal: P. Reuter (F.), H.P. de Vries (USA); R. Ago (Pres.).

4. Compromis, Paris.
   a. January 22, 1963.
   b.
   c. RIAA XVI-7; UNTS 473-3; TIAS 5280.

5. I. Award, Geneva.
   a. December 22, 1963.
   b.
   c.
   d. RIAA XVI-11; ed. Geneva; AJIL 1964-1016; ILR 38(1969)-182; RGDIP 1965-189; ILM 1963-668.

   II. Decision interpreting the Award, Geneva.
   a. June 28, 1964.
   b.
   c.
   d. RIAA XVI-73; RGDIP 1965-259.
   e. AFDI 1964-352, 1965-389; Journal of air law and commerce 1964-231; RBDI 1966-1; RGDIP 1965-189; Revue française de droit aérien 1964-448; ENC 2-101/2; Rep. 3016, 3052, 3070, 3086, 3092, 3096/8, 3506/7.
   See No. 439.

12–25   STATE PRACTICE/CUSTOMARY INTERNATIONAL LAW

Custom is regarded as the second source of international law. This term is generally defined as state practice. State practice comprises a wealth of sources of law and is the body of materials which together illustrate the type of action taken by a state in an international situation. These materials include national legislation, diplomatic correspondence, legal opinions, evidence given before courts and tribunals, parliamentary proceedings, etc.

12–26   Digests

Several states produce digests of these materials to make them more readily accessible. In the United Kingdom, the *British Digest of International Law* began publication in the 1960s but it is still incomplete and unlikely to be finished in the foreseeable future.

A historical source of state practice is Clive Parry, *Law Officers' Opinions to the Foreign Office 1793–1860*, published by Oceana in 95 volumes, with Volumes 96 and 97 containing *Indexes*. It is a collection of opinions, principally of the Advocate General (a forerunner of the Legal Adviser to the Foreign Office) on policy matters relating to the foreign and colonial affairs of this country during that period. Opinions delivered between 1861 and 1939 were issued by the same publisher on microfilm.

The *British Yearbook of International Law* contains a section entitled "U.K. materials on international law," which is an excellent survey of items published during the year under review relating to international law. It includes extracts from parliamentary debates, answers given to parliamentary questions, evidence given to committees, and speeches given by U.K. representatives at international meetings. It also gives details of any U.K. legislation involving international law.

British and Foreign State Papers contain a wealth of international material. From 1812 to 1968, there are selections from diplomatic papers and circulars. These provide valuable background material to international events that is not easily obtainable elsewhere.

Collections of Documents   12–27

Other useful starting places for retrieving information relating to state practice are the commercially published multi-volume series on particular areas of international law. They are rather like vastly overgrown "cases and materials" books, but each series only covers one area of international law. They contain extracts from treaties, law reports, proceedings, background papers and documents from international organisations. Good examples are Durante and Rodino, *Western Europe and the Law of the Sea*, Ruster and Bruno, *International Protection of the Environment; Treaties and Related Documents*, and *New Directions in the Law of the Sea*. The advantage of these series is that you can find in one place extracts from all the different materials on a particular subject, plus information on where the original documents can be found.

TREATISES   12–28

Textbooks   12–29

The writings of leading commentators, or jurists, are accepted as another source of international law. There is a very distinguished history of academic scholarship in international law. Famous writers include Grotius, Gentili, Pufendorf and Savigny. The Carnegie Endowment for International Peace has collected many of these works together and reprinted them in a series entitled

Classics of International Law. Among later writers in this country, Oppenheim, *International Law* has been described as being "as nearly official as anything of the kind can be." A ninth edition of Volume 1: "Peace" appeared in 1992 in two parts. Volume 2: "Disputes, War and Neutrality" was last published in 1952.

12–30   Students' Textbooks

There are many good students' textbooks, including Akehurst, *Modern Introduction to International Law* (6th ed., 1987) and Starke, *Introduction to International Law* (10th ed., 1989). The leading casebook is that by D. J. Harris, *Cases and Materials on International Law* (4th ed., 1991).

12–31   SECONDARY SOURCES

12–32   Journals

The first international law journal was the *Revue de Droit International et de Législation Comparée*, which initially appeared in 1869, almost 40 years before the American Society of International Law started publication of the *American Journal of International Law* (1907). There are now large numbers of journals worldwide, devoted to international law in general and to particular topics. Some of the better known titles, which may be available in your law library, are the *Virginia Journal of International Law*, the *Georgetown Journal of International Law* and the *Harvard Journal of International Law*. Many other American unversities have begun to publish international law journals as well as a general law review. Journals devoted to particular subject areas include the *Journal of International Law and Economics*, the *Journal of World Trade* and the *Journal of Air Law and Commerce*. Some of these journals occasionally contain extensive research guides and bibliographies, which can be a most useful source of information.

12–33   Newsletters and Bulletins

To trace very recent information on international law, newsletters and bulletins can be useful. The *Bulletin of Legal Developments* is published fortnightly by the British Institute of International and Comparative Law and contains a wealth of useful information on legal developments and forthcoming legislation in both this country and abroad.

Yearbooks 12–34

Yearbooks, which normally contain a collection of articles and documents relating to international law, are another useful source of information and several countries publish them, including Australia, Canada, France, Germany, Italy, Japan and Switzerland. The *British Yearbook of International Law* is an excellent example of the genre. It contains not only the various items mentioned earlier in this chapter but also summaries of the decisions of leading international tribunals, such as the European Court of Human Rights, together with a comprehensive book review section, and digests of national cases relating to international law.

Yearbooks are also published in particular subject areas, for example, the *Yearbook Commercial Arbitration*.

Proceedings 12–35

Other useful sources of articles on international law are proceedings of courses, conferences and other international meetings. The most notable of these are the *Recueil des Cours* (collected courses) of The Hague Academy of International Law, which contains the texts of lectures given each year by leading international law scholars from all over the world. There are regularly published indexes, and a useful biography and bibliography for each person delivering the lectures. The proceedings of the conferences of the International Law Association are also important.

FINDING BOOKS AND JOURNALS 12–36

Bibliographies 12–37

There are several bibliographies of international law on both general and specific subjects. John Merrill, *A Current Bibliography of International Law* (1978) and Ingrid Delupis *Bibliography of International Law* (1975) are useful for books and articles, though the lists at the beginning of each chapter in the new edition of Oppenheim are more up to date. Elizabeth Beyerly *Public International Law; A Guide to Information Sources* (1991) is a well-annotated guide, which includes primary as well as secondary sources.

There are several specialist institutes within universities devoted to research into particular areas of international law and they frequently produce excellent bibliographical tools. The Centre for the Study of the Law of the Sea at Dalhousie University in Halifax, Nova Scotia, produces a *Marine Affairs Bibliography*. The Centre for Air and Space Law at McGill has published Kuo Lee Li, *Worldwide Space Law Bibliography* (1978) and the Centre for the Study of Human Rights at Columbia has published *Human Rights; A Topical Bibliography*.

12–38   Library Catalogues

The catalogues of the larger law libraries frequently contain useful information about international law. Some of them are published in book form and may well be available in the main reference section of your library. The Harvard Law School Library, *Catalog of International Law and Relations* first appeared in 1965, and was re-issued in microfiche as part of the complete library catalogue in 1984, when a supplement to 1981 was added.

12–39   Indexes of Journal Articles

A most useful index is that published semi-annually since 1975 by the Max Planck Institute for Comparative Public Law and International Law in Heidelberg. It is entitled *Public International Law: A Current Bibliography of Books and Articles*. It is a comprehensive bibliography covering over 1,000 journals and should be the starting place for research projects on international law. Many international law journals are indexed in the general legal journal indexes including the *Current Law Index* (U.S.A.), the *Index to Legal Periodicals* (para. 4–5) and the *Index to Foreign Legal Periodicals* (para. 4–6). English journals covering international law are indexed in the *Legal Journals Index* (para. 4–3).

12–40   Online Sources

There is not yet much international law available on databases in this country. LEXIS (para. 7–9) has little pure international law online, other than treaty information from *International Legal Materials* and the *U.S. Department of State Bulletin*. Other countries are a litle more advanced. In Belgium, the ORBI database has been created. It consists of the documentation system of the Belgian Ministry of Foreign Affairs and is available here through EURONET. There is some international relations material available on DIALOG. Your librarian can tell you whether it is possible to get access to these databases.

INTERNATIONAL ORGANISATIONS 12–41

There is no agreed scientific classification of international organisations. The term "international intergovernmental organisation" is usually used to describe an organisation set up by agreement between two or more states, as distinct from "non-governmental" organisations set up by individuals.

There are currently over 4,000 international organisations in existence, of which one alone, the United Nations, produces over 180,000 items of documentation a year. The total number of publications produced by international organisations each year is therefore massive.

It is extremely difficult to trace the publications of international organisations, not only because there are so many of them, but also because the organisations themselves frequently do not produce comprehensive catalogues or lists of their publications. These publications can be most conveniently divided into two main groups: sales publications and documents. You are most likely to need material in the first group, which includes all those publications issued in printed form and generally available. The second group comprises documents which are mainly produced for internal use by the organisation concerned and are not normally of wide outside interest. Obviously, sales publications cover a vast subject area and legal documents form only a small part of the total output of international orgnisations.

United Nations 12–42

The largest and most important of international organisations is of course the United Nations. Its central institutions include the General Assembly, the Security Council, the Secretariat, the Economic and Social Council and the International Court of Justice, which has already been mentioned. The U.N. also operates through a large number of specialised agencies with wide-ranging interests, some of which you may not realise are part of the United Nations system. They include the International Civil Aviation Organization, the World Health Organization, the International Labour Organization, the International Monetary Fund, and the GATT (General Agreement on Tariffs and Trade). Two bodies particularly concerned with international law are the International Law Commission, charged with the development and codification of international law, and the U.N. Commission on International Trade Law (UNCITRAL), which works on the harmonisation and unification of the law of international trade.

All these bodies produce an overwhelming number of

documents and sales publications. Individual documents are usually only to be found in larger libraries, particularly depository libraries which receive them automatically and reasonably quickly. Luckily most of the more important U.N. agencies publish a *Yearbook*, which contains not only an annual report on activities, but reprinted working documents, drafts of treaties, summaries of meetings and special reports. There is for example an *UNCITRAL Yearbook* and an *International Law Commission Yearbook*. The U.N. Secretariat publishes the *United Nations Juridical Yearbook*. Unfortunately, it can be two or three years before the material is collected and published in this form.

The U.N. frequently convenes conferences on legal topics and then publishes the proceedings. Such proceedings often contain the texts of conventions or other agreements reached at the conference, usually as part of the "Final Act". The United Nations Conferences on the law of the sea are a good example. There is also a *United Nations Legislative Series*, which contains materials on legal matters. These are normally compiled following a resolution from the General Assembly asking for further information on a particular topic.

U.N. documents are often cited by their official document number, which may not always be used in your library catalogue to identify them. A useful aid, though published in 1970, is the *List of United Nations Document Series Symbols*, which will help you identify "A/CN4/219" as an International Law Commission document.

12–43 **Bibliographies to U.N. materials**
In order to help find such publications, organisations like the U.N. do produce some bibliographies. The U.N. libraries in both Geneva and New York publish monthly bibliographies of books, articles and journals, soon to be issued on CD-ROM. These are library accessions lists and so contain not only material published by the U.N. itself, but anything relevant to U.N. activities which has been acquired by the library. The *United Nations Documents Index*, now known as *UNDOC*, is a product of UNBIS, the U.N.'s online bibliographical information system. It is published in hard copy four times a year, with annual cumulations which have been issued on microfiche since 1984. It attempts to provide a key to recent U.N. documents, proceedings and publications. Each issue follows a standard arrangement by issuing body, and there is a subject index. There are plans to issue the UNBIS databases on CD-ROM during 1994. An interesting introductory guide is Peter Hajnal, *Directory of United Nations Documentary and Archival Sources*, published in 1991. Your library may subscribe to the *International Bibliography: Publications of Intergovernmental*

Organisations, which is a quarterly listing of publications of the major intergovernmental organisations received by Kraus/ UNIPUB, an American publishing house.

Council of Europe   12–44

The Statute of the Council of Europe was signed in 1949 by 10 European states. By August 1993, there were 31 Member States, with others such as Russia and Ukraine having "guest" status. Its objectives are, broadly, European co-operation in the fields of human rights, social, cultural, legal and administrative matters. Its main organs are the Committee of Ministers, formed from the foreign ministers of Member States, and the Parliamentary Assembly. The Secretariat in Strasbourg is divided into Directorates in a similar way to the E.C. Commission. Subjects include political affairs, social and economic affairs, human rights, legal affairs and environment and local authorities.

Treaties   12–45
A major part of the work of the Council is the preparation of Conventions, some signed by all Member States and others, so-called "partial agreements," by smaller groups of Member States. They are published individually in the *European Treaty Series*, which now contains over 150 treaties. A looseleaf binder contains a current *Chart of Signatures and Ratifications*. A collected edition of the treaties is published under the title *European Conventions and Agreements*, of which four volumes covering 1949–1982 (E.T.S. Nos. 2–108) have so far appeared. Several of the conventions are the subject of *Explanatory Reports*, issued as separate pamphlets.

Documents   12–46
The Committee of Ministers issues its *Recommendations to Member States* as individual documents. For example, number R (92) 15 was on teaching and research in the field of law and information technology. Subject compilations are produced from time to time. Volume V (1989–1992) of a series relating to crime problems was published in 1993.

The Parliamentary Assembly issues three series: The *Official Reports of Debates* are in three volumes a year, with a brief annual Subject Index. *Texts adopted* comprise the equivalent of legislation, namely opinions, recommendations, resolutions and orders, each in their own continuous numbered sequence. The *Documents (Working Papers)* include written questions, reports from subject committees, and reports from the Committee of Ministers to the Assembly. Again, a single numbered sequence is carried over from session to session.

Also published on a regular basis are the records of proceedings of the Standing Conference of Local and Regional Authorities of Europe. There are two series: the *Official Report of Debates* and *Texts Adopted*.

12–47   Reports
A general overview of the year's work of the Council of Europe can be found in the *Annual Report on the Activities of the Council of Europe*, published by the Secretariat. It contains useful lists of texts adopted by each organ during the year, including judgments of the European Court of Human Rights. Also listed are the reports of conferences such as the Standing Conference of European Ministers of Education and the proceedings of the Colloquy on European Law. Individual reports on specific subjects are issued by the respective Directorates with colour-coded covers, *e.g.* mauve for human rights, red for social affairs, blue for legal affairs, green for nature and environment. These are best traced using the *List of Publications* issued by each Directorate, usually annually. A number of information sources have unfortunately been discontinued as a result of cutbacks in funding, but may be useful for background research. These include the *Exchange of Information on Research in European Law*, of which the last is No. 20 (1991) and the *Information Bulletin on Legal Activities*, which ends with No. 31 (January 1991). Informal public information is provided by the bi-monthly *Forum* and by *Press Releases* issued by the Directorate of Press and Information.

12–48   European Convention on Human Rights
The most well-known work of the Council of Europe is in the field of human rights. The Convention for the Protection of Human Rights and Fundamental Freedoms (otherwise known as the European Convention on Human Rights) was drawn up in 1950 and came into force in 1953. The European Commission on Human Rights was formed in 1953 to investigate complaints against states said to be in breach of the Convention. The European Court of Human Rights (ECHR), which hears cases referred to it by the Commission, was set up in 1959.

12–49   *Text*
The text of the Convention itself can be found in several sources. The main official source is the volume of *European Convention on Human Rights Collected Texts*, published for the C.E. in 1986 by Nijhoff. As well as the Convention itself and its eight Protocols, the Rules of Procedure of the Commission, the ECHR and the Committee of Ministers (under Articles 32 and 54) are included.
The *Collected Edition of the Travaux Préparatoires* (preparatory

documents) leading up to the promulgation of the Convention was published in eight volumes between 1975 and 1985.

Reports   12–50
The decisions (on admissibility) and reports of the Commission in cases not transmitted to the Court (under Articles 30 and 31 of the Convention) are issued individually for each case, and eventually appear in the series *Decisions and Reports*, issued quarterly but with a long delay (October 1989 issue published in 1993). Commission reports in cases which they have referred to the Court are published in the publications, Series B, mentioned below. Similarly, the decisions of the Court appear first in pamphlet form, and then in its Series A: "Judgments and Decisions". Documents submitted by the parties appear in Series B: "Pleadings, Oral Arguments, Documents". The *European Human Rights Reports* are a commercially published series containing all judgments of the Court, selected reports and decisions of the Commission and resolutions of the Committee of Ministers relating to human rights.

Indexes   12–51
If you do not have a reference to the published reports, it is not easy to trace recent human rights decisions. The *Digest of Strasbourg Case-law Relating to the European Convention on Human Rights* covers the period 1955–1982, the main body of it arranged in order of Articles of the Convention. Volume 6 of the set contains Indexes. Looseleaf supplements to the first two volumes first appeared in 1988. Vincent Berger, *Case Law of the European Court of Human Rights*, Vol. 1: 1960–1987; Vol. 2: 1988–1990, gives two- to three-page summaries of all the decisions of the Court in chronological order, and includes an index by Convention Article and a bibliography. The Commission's *Decisions and Reports* series has cumulative indexes every 10 volumes, the last one covering 1985–1989.

The Commission has its own online database (Système d'Information sur les Droits de l'Homme—Human Rights Information System), which contains the texts of Court judgments, and Commission decisions, as well as an up-to-date list of signatures and ratifications of the European Convention on Human Rights. The Human Rights Information Centre at the British Institute of International and Comparative Law in London is able to search this database for a fee.

Yearbook   12–52
The *Yearbook of the European Convention on Human Rights* summarises the year's activity of the Commission, the Court and

the Committee of Ministers in the human rights area. Summaries of the main decisions of each are given, together with lists of other relevant documents (*e.g.* working papers of the Parliamentary Assembly) and a bibliography. There is the usual delay in publication; Volume 32 for 1989 appeared in 1993.

APPENDIX I

Abbreviations of Reports, Series and Journals

This alphabetical list contains a selection of the more commonly **A1–1** used abbreviations in the United Kingdom, the E.C. and the Commonwealth. It is not exhaustive and further information can be found in D. Raistrick, *Index to Legal Citations and Abbreviations* and in the I.A.L.S. *Manual of Legal Citations*, Vols. I and II, the *Index to Legal Periodicals*, the *Legal Journals Index*, *The Digest (Cumulative Supplement)* and the *Current Law Citators* also contain lists of abbreviations, at the front.

A.C.—Law Reports Appeal Cases 1891–
A.J.—Acta Juridica
A.J.I.L.—American Journal of International Law
A.L.J.—Australian Law Journal
A.L.R.—American Law Reports Annotated
A.L.R.—Australian Law Reports, formerly Argus Law Reports
All E.R.—All England Law Reports 1936–
All E.R. Rep.—All England Law Reports Reprint 1558–1935
Am. J. Comp. L.—American Journal of Comparative Law
Anglo-Am. L.R.—Anglo-American Law Review
Ann. Dig.—Annual Digest of Public International Law Cases (1919–1949). (From 1950 this series has been published as the International Law Reports—I.L.R.)
App. Cas.—Law Reports Appeal Cases 1875–1890

B.C.L.C.—Butterworths Company Law Cases
B.D.I.L.—British Digest of International Law
B.F.S.P.—British and Foreign State Papers
B.I.L.C.—British International Law Cases
B.J.A.L.—British Journal of Administrative Law
B.J. Crim.—British Journal of Criminology
B.J.L.S.—British Journal of Law and Society
B.L.R.—Building Law Reports
B.L.R.—Business Law Review
B.N.I.L.—Bulletin of Northern Ireland Law
B.T.R.—British Tax Review
B.Y.I.L.—British Yearbook of International Law
Bull. E.C.—Bulletin of the European Communities
Business L.R.—Business Law Review

C.A.R.—Criminal Appeal Reports
C.A.T.—Court of Appeal Transcript (unpublished)
C.B.R.—Canadian Bar Review
C.D.E.—Cahiers de Droit Européen
C.J.Q.—Civil Justice Quarterly
C.L.—Current Law
C.L.J.—Cambridge Law Journal
C.L.P.—Current Legal Problems
C.L.R.—Commonwealth Law Reports (Australia)
C.M.L.R.—Common Market Law Reports
C.M.L. Rev.—Common Market Law Review
C.P.D.—Law Reports Common Pleas Division 1875–1880
C.T.S.—Consolidated Treaty Series
Calif. L. Rev.—California Law Review
Camb. L.J.—Cambridge Law Journal
Can. B.R.—Canadian Bar Review
Ch.—Law Reports Chancery Division 1891–
Ch.D.—Law Reports Chancery Division 1875–1890
Co. Law.—Company Lawyer
Colum. L. Rev.—Columbia Law Review
Com. Cas.—Commercial Cases 1895–1941
Constr. L.J.—Construction Law Journal
Conv.; Conv.—N.S.—Conveyancer and Property Lawyer
Cox C.C.—Cox's Criminal Law Cases
Cr. App. R.; Cr. App. Rep.—Criminal Appeal Reports
Cr.App.R.(S.)—Criminal Appeal Reports (Sentencing)
Crim. L.R.—Criminal Law Review

D.L.R.—Dominion Law Reports (Canada)
D.U.L.J.—Dublin University Law Journal

E.C.R.—European Court Reports
E.G.—Estates Gazette
E.G.L.R.—Estates Gazette Law Reports
E.H.R.R.—European Human Rights Reports
E.I.P.R.—European Intellectual Property Review
E.L. Rev.—European Law Review
E.R.—English Reports
Eng. Rep.—English Reports
Eur. Comm. H.R. D.R.—European Commission for Human Rights
  Decisions and Reports
Eur. Court H.R. Series A/Series B—European Court of Human
  Rights Series A & B
Euro C.L.—European Current Law
Ex.D.—Law Reports Exchequer Division 1875–1880

F.L.R.—Family Law Reports
F.L.R.—Federal Law Reports
F.S.R.—Fleet Street Reports
F.T.—Financial Times
Fam.—Law Reports Family Division 1972–
Fam. Law—Family Law

Grotius Trans.—Transactions of the Grotius Society

H.L.R.—Housing Law Reports
Harv. L. Rev.—Harvard Law Review

I.C.J. Rep.—International Court of Justice Reports
I.C.J.Y.B.—International Court of Justice Yearbook
I.C.L.Q.—International and Comparative Law Quarterly
I.C.R.—Industrial Cases Reports 1975–
I.C.R.—Industrial Court Reports 1972–1974
I.J.; Ir. Jur.—Irish Jurist
I.L.J.—Industrial Law Journal
I.L.M.—International Legal Materials
I.L.Q.—International Law Quarterly
I.L.R.—International Law Reports
I.L.R.M.—Irish Law Reports Monthly
I.L.T.; Ir.L.T.—Irish Law Times
I.R.—Irish Reports
I.R.L.R.—Industrial Relations Law Reports
I.R.R.R.—Industrial Relations Review & Reports
Imm.A.R.—Immigration Appeal Reports
Ir. Jur.—Irish Jurist
I.T.R.—Industrial Tribunal Reports

J.B.L.—Journal of Business Law
J.C.—Session Cases: Justiciary Cases (Scotland)
J.C.L.—Journal of Criminal Law
J.C.M.S.—Journal of Common Market Studies
J.I.S.E.L.—Journal of the Irish Society for European Law
J.I.S.L.L.—Journal of the Irish Society for Labour Law
J.L.S.—Journal of Law and Society
J.L.S.—Journal of the Law Society of Scotland
J. Legal Ed.—Journal of Legal Education
J.O.—Journal Officiel des Communautés Européennes
J.P.—Justice of the Peace Reports (*also* Justice of the Peace (journal))
J.P.I.L.—Journal of Personal Injury Litigation
J.P.L.—Journal of Planning and Environment Law
J.R.—Juridical Review
J.S.P.T.L.—Journal of the Society of Public Teachers of Law
J.S.W.L.—Journal of Social Welfare Law

K.B.—Law Reports: King's Bench Division 1901–1952
K.I.R.—Knight's Industrial Reports

L.A.G. Bul.—Legal Action Group Bulletin
L.G.C.—Local Government Chronicle
L.G.R.—Knight's Local Government Reports
L.J.—Law Journal 1866–1965 (newspaper)
L.J. Adm.—Law Journal: Admiralty N.S. 1865–1875
L.J. Bcy.—Law Journal: Bankruptcy N.S. 1832–1880
L.J.C.C.R.—Law Journal: County Courts Reports 1912–1933
L.J.C.P.—Law Journal: Common Pleas N.S. 1831–1875
L.J. Ch.—Law Journal: Chancery N.S. 1831–1946
L.J. Eccl.—Law Journal: Ecclesiastical Cases N.S. 1866–1875
L.J. Eq.—Law Journal: Chancery N.S. 1831–1946
L.J. Ex.—Law Journal: Exchequer N.S. 1831–1875
L.J. Ex. Eq.—Law Journal: Exchequer in Equity 1835–1841
L.J.K.B. (or Q.B.)—Law Journal: King's (or Queen's) Bench N.S. 1831–1946
L.J.M.C.—Law Journal: Magistrates' Cases N.S. 1831–1896
L.J.N.C.—Law Journal: Notes of Cases 1866–1892
L.J.N.C.C.R.—Law Journal Newspaper: County Court Reports 1934–1947
L.J.O.S.—Law Journal (Old Series) 1822–1831
L.J.P.—Law Journal: Probate, Divorce and Admiralty N.S. 1875–1946
L.J.P.D. & A.—Law Journal: Probate, Divorce and Admiralty N.S. 1875–1946

L.J.P. & M.—Law Journal: Probate and Matrimonial Cases N.S. 1858–1859, 1866–1875
L.J.P.C.—Law Journal: Privy Council N.S. 1865–1946
L.J.P.M. & A.—Law Journal: Probate, Matrimonial and Admiralty N.S. 1860–1865
L.J.R.—Law Journal Reports 1947–1949
L. Lib.J.—Law Library Journal
L.M.C.L.Q.—Lloyd's Maritime and Commercial Law Quarterly
L.N.T.S.—League of Nations Treaty Series
L.Q.R.—Law Quarterly Review
L.R.A. & E.—Law Reports: Admiralty and Ecclesiastical Cases 1865–1875
L.R.C.C.R.—Law Reports: Crown Cases Reserved 1865–1875
L.R. C.P.—Law Reports: Common Pleas Cases 1865–1875
L.R. Ch. App.—Law Reports: Chancery Appeal Cases 1865–1875
L.R. Eq.—Law Reports: Equity Cases 1866–1875
L.R. Ex.—Law Reports: Exchequer Cases 1865–1875
L.R.H.L.—Law Reports: English and Irish Appeals 1866–1875
L.R. P. & D.—Law Reports: Probate and Divorce Cases 1865–1875
L.R.P.C.—Law Reports: Privy Council Appeals 1865–1875
L.R.Q.B.—Law Reports: Queens' Bench 1865–1875
L.R.R.P.; L.R. R.P.C.—Law Reports: Restrictive Practices Cases 1957–1973
L.S.—Legal Studies
L.S. Gaz.—Law Society Gazette
L.T.—Law Times
L.T.R.; L.T. Rep.—Law Times Reports (New Series) 1859–1947
L.T.Jo.—Law Times (newspaper) 1843–1965
L.T.O.S.—Law Times Reports (Old Series) 1843–1860
L. Teach.—Law Teacher
Law & Contemp. Prob.—Law and Contemporary Problems
Lit.—Litigation
Liverpool L.R.—Liverpool Law Review
Ll. L.L.R.; Ll.L.R.; LL.L. Rep.—Lloyd's List Law Reports *later* Lloyd's Law Reports
Lloyd's L.R.; Lloyd's Rep.—Lloyd's List Law Reports *later* Lloyd's Law Reports

M.L.J.—Malayan Law Journal
M.L.R.—Modern Law Review
Man. Law—Managerial Law
Med. Sci. & Law—Medicine, Science & the Law
Mich. L. Rev.—Michigan Law Review

N.I.—Northern Ireland Law Reports

N.I.J.B.—Northern Ireland Law Reports Bulletin of Judgments
N.I.L.Q.—Northern Ireland Legal Quarterly
N.I.L.R.—Northern Ireland Law Reports
N.L.J.—New Law Journal
N.Y.U.L. Rev.—New York University Law Review
N.Z.L.R.—New Zealand Law Reports
New L.J.—New Law Journal

O.J.—Official Journal of the European Communities
O.J.C.—Official Journal of the European Communities: Information and Notices
O.J.L.—Official Journal of the European Communities: Legislation, *e.g.* 1972, L139/28
O.J.L.S.—Oxford Journal of Legal Studies

P.—Law Reports: Probate, Divorce and Admiralty 1891–1971
P. & C.R.—Planning (Property from 1968) and Compensation Reports
P.C.I.J.—Permanent Court of International Justice Reports of Judgments
P.D.—Law Reports: Probate Division 1875–1890
P.L.—Public Law
P.N.—Professional Negligence

Q.B.—Law Reports: Queen's Bench Division 1891–1901, 1952–
Q.B.D.—Law Reports: Queen's Bench Division 1875–1890

R.D.E.—Rivista di Diritto Europeo
R.G.D.I.P.—Revue Générale de Droit International Public
R.M.C.—Revue du Marché Commun
R.P.C.—Reports of Patent, Design & Trade Mark Cases
R.R.—Revised Reports
R.R.C.—Ryde's Rating Cases
R.T.R.—Road Traffic Reports
R.V.R.—Rating & Valuation Reporter
Rec.—Recueil des Cours
Rec.—Recueil de la Jurisprudence de la Cour (Court of Justice of the European Communities)

S.A.—South African Law Reports
S.C.—Session Cases (Scotland)
S.C. (H.L.)—Session Cases: House of Lords (Scotland)
S.C.(J.)—Session Cases: Justiciary Cases (Scotland)
S.C.C.R.—Scottish Criminal Case Reports
S.I.—Statutory Instruments

S.J.—Solicitors' Journal
S.L.R.—Law Reporter/Scottish Law Review
S.L.T.—Scots Law Times
S.R.—Statutory Rules (Northern Ireland)
S.R. & O.—Statutory Rules and Orders
S.T.C.—Simon's Tax Cases
Scolag.—Bulletin of the Scottish Legal Action Group
Sol. Jo.—Solicitors' Journal
St. Tr.; State Tr.—State Trials 1163–1820
Stat.L.R.—Statute Law Review
State Tr. N.S.—State Trials (New Series) 1820–1858

T.C.—Reports of Tax Cases
T.L.R.—Times Law Reports
Tax Cas.—Reports of Tax Cases
Tul. L. Rev.—Tulane Law Review

U. Chi. L. Rev.—University of Chicago Law Review
U.K.T.S.—United Kingdom Treaty Series
U.N.T.S.—United Nations Treaty Series
U.N.J.Y.—United Nations Juridical Yearbook
U.N.Y.B.—Yearbook of the United Nations
U. Pa. L. Rev.—University of Pennsylvania Law Review
U.S.—United States Supreme Court Reports
U.S.T.S.—United States Treaty Series

V.A.T.T.R.—Value Added Tax Tribunal Reports
V.L.R.—Victorian Law Reports (Australia)

W.I.R.—West Indian Reports
W.L.R.—Weekly Law Reports
W.N.—Weekly Notes
W.W.R.—Western Weekly Reporter

Y.B.—Yearbook (old law report), *e.g.* (1466) Y.B.Mich. (the term) 6
    Edw. 4, pl. 18, fol.7. (plea, folio)
Y.B.W.A.—Yearbook of World Affairs
Yale L.J.—Yale Law Journal
Yearbook E.C.H.R.—Yearbook of the European Convention on
    Human Rights

More detailed information on legal and law-related materials
can be found in the following publications.

D. Butcher, *Official Publications in Britain* (2nd ed., London: Library Association, 1991);

R. G. Logan, (ed.) *Information Sources in Law* (London: Butterworths, 1986);

E. M. Moys, (ed.) *Manual of Law Librarianship: The Use and Organization of Legal Literature* (2nd ed., London: Gower, 1987);

J. E. Pemberton, *British Official Publications* (2nd ed., Oxford: Pergamon, 1973);

Glanville Williams, *Learning the Law* (11th ed., London: Stevens, 1982);

D. D. Mackey, *How To Use a Scottish Law Library* (Edinburgh: W. Green, 1992).

APPENDIX II

Words and Abbreviations in English and Latin

This alphabetical list contains some of the more commonly used **A2–1** words and abbreviations (in English and Latin) which you may encounter in textbooks and law reports. There is a separate list of abbreviations for the names of law reports in Appendix I.

A.G. or Att. Gen.—Attorney-General
A.G.—German incorporated company
Ab initio—from the beginning
Abstracts—summary of journal articles, books, etc. Usually arranged in subject order
Ad valorem—according to the duty. A duty levied
Aliter—otherwise
Amicus curiae—a friend of the court (a bystander who informs the judge on points of law or fact)
Annotations—notes
Anon.—anonymous
Applied (apld.)—the principle in a previous case has been applied to a new set of facts in another case
Approved—the case has been considered good law
Art.—Article (in an international Treaty or Convention)
Article—an essay published in a journal
Autrefois acquit—previously acquitted
Autrefois attaint—previously attained
Autrefois convict—previously convicted

B.—Baron (Exchequer)

B.C.—Borough Council

Bibliography—a list of books

Bills—draft versions of proposed legislation, laid before Parliament for its approval

Blue Book—a government publication, issued with blue covers to protect it because of its length

c.—chapter (Act)

C.—Command Paper 1836–1899

C.A.—Court of Appeal

C.A.T.—Court of Appeal Transcript (unreported)

C.A.V. (*curia advisari vult*)—the court deliberated before pronouncing judgment

C.B.—Chief Baron

C.C.—County Council

C.C.A.—Court of Criminal Appeal

C.C.R.—County Court Rules

c.i.f. (cost, insurance, freight)—a contract for the sale of goods in which the price quoted includes everything up to delivery

C.J.—Chief Justice

Cd.—Command Papers 1900–1918

CD-ROM—Compact Disc—Read Only Memory

cf. (confer)—to compare or refer to

Chronological—arranged in order of date

Cie.—French abbreviation for company (compagnie)

Citation—(1) a reference to where a case or statute is to be found; (2) the quotation of decided cases in legal arguments

Citator—a volume containing a list of cases or statutes with sufficient details to enable them to be traced in the volumes of law reports or statutes

Cl.—clause (in Bills)

Classification number (classmark)—a system of numbers, or letters and numbers, used to indicate the subject matter of the book. In many libraries the books are arranged on the shelves in the order indicated by this number

Cm.—Command Papers 1986–

Cmd.—Command Papers 1919–1956

Cmnd.—Command Papers 1956–1986

Command Paper—a form of parliamentary paper, issued "by Command of Her Majesty." Every Command Paper has its own individual number

Comrs.—Commissioners

Considered—the case was considered but no comment was made

Cumulative; Cumulation—combining the information in a number of previous publications into one sequence

Cur. adv. vult.—the court deliberated before pronouncing judgment

D.C.—Divisional Court

D.P.P.—Director of Public Prosecutions (whose name appears in criminal appeals to the House of Lords, and certain other circumstances)

De facto—in fact

De jure—by right

De novo—anew

Deb.—Debates

Dec.—Decision (E.C.), *e.g.* Dec. 82/112/EEC

Decd.—deceased

Delegated legislation—rules created by subordinate bodies under specific powers delegated by Parliament

Digest—a summary

Digested—summarised

Dir.—Directive (E.C.), *e.g.* Dir. 82/262/EEC

Distinguished—some essential difference between past cases and the present case has been pointed out

Doubted—the court's remarks tend to show case was inaccurate

E.A.T.—Employment Appeal Tribunal

ECHR—European Convention on Human Rights

ECJ—Court of Justice of the European Community

E.C.—European Community

ECSC—European Coal & Steel Community

Et seq. (*et sequentes*)—and those following

Ex cathedra (from the chair)—with official authority

Ex officio—by virtue of an office

Ex p. (*ex parte*)—the person on whose application the case is heard

Ex post facto—by a subsequent act; retrospectively

Ex rel. (*ex relatione*)—report not at first hand

Explained—previous decision is not doubted, but the present decision is justified by calling attention to some fact not clear in the report

ff.—and what follows

f.o.b. (free on board)—cost of shipping to be paid by vendor

Folio—technically this refers to the way in which a book is made up; usually used to denote a large book, often shelved in a separate sequence

Followed—same principle of law applied

GmbH.—German incorporated private company

Green Book—a term sometimes used to refer to *The County Court Practice*

Green Paper—a government publication setting out government proposals, so that public discussion may follow before a definite policy is formulated

H.C. Deb.—House of Commons Debate

H.L.—House of Lords

HMSO—Her Majesty's Stationery Office

Hale P.C.—Hale, *Historia Placitorum Coronae* (Pleas of the Crown)

Hansard—Parliamentary Debates

Headnote—a brief summary of a case found at the beginning of the law report

ICJ—International Court of Justice

I.R.C.—Inland Revenue Commissioners

Ibid. (ibidem)—in the same place

Id. (idem)—the same

In b. (in bonis)—in the goods of

In camera—hearing in private

In curia—in open court

In re—in the matter of

Infra—below

Inter alia—amongst other things

Inter vivos—during life: between living persons

Ipso facto—by the mere fact

J. (plural JJ.)—judge

JANET—Joint Academic Network

J.P.—Justice of the Peace

K.C.—King's Counsel

L.C.—Lord Chancellor

L.C.B.—Lord Chief Baron

L.C.J.—Lord Chief Justice

L.J. (plural L.JJ.)—Lord Justice

L.V.App.Ct.—Lands Valuation Appeal Court (Scotland)

Legislation—the making of law: any set of statutes

Loc. cit. (loco citato)—at the passage quoted

LPC—Legal Practice Course

M.R.—Master of the Rolls

M.V.—motor vessel

Microfiche; Microfilm—a photographic reduction of an original onto a sheet of film (microfiche) or a reel of film (microfilm). A reading machine (which enlarges the image) is needed to consult microfilm or fiche

N.V.—Dutch incorporated company
Nisi prius—unless before
Nolle prosequi—unwilling to prosecute
Non-parliamentary papers—government publications which are not required to be laid before Parliament for their approval. They are usually entered in the library catalogue under the name of the government department which publishes them

O.H.—Outer House of the Court of Session (Scotland)
Obiter dictum—a judicial observation on a point not directly relevant to the case (not binding as precedent)
Op. cit.—the book or reference previously cited
Ord.—Order (Rules of the Supreme Court)
Orse—otherwise
Overruled—a higher court holds the decision to be wrong

P.C.—Privy Council
PCIJ—Permanent Court of International Justice
Pace—by permission of
Pamphlet—a small booklet usually less than 50 pages in length. It may be shelved in a separate sequence
Parl. Deb.—Parliamentary Debates
Pari passu—on equal footing; proportionately
Parliamentary papers—papers required by Parliament in the course of their work. These include: House of Lords and House of Commons Papers and Bills, Debates, Command Papers and Acts
Per—as stated by
Per curiam—a decision arrived at by the court
Per incuriam—through want of care (a mistaken court decision)
Periodical—a publication with a distinctive title which appears regularly
Periodicals index—(1) an index to the contents of a particular journal; (2) a subject index to articles in a number of journals
Per pro. (per procurationem)—as an agent; on behalf of another
Per se (by itself)—taken alone
Post—after (a later line or page)

Q.C.—Queen's Counsel
Q.S.—Quarter Sessions

q.v. (quod vide)—which see
Quantum meruit—as much as he had earned/deserved

r.—rule
R( )—Decision of administrative tribunal—letter in brackets indicates the appropriate tribunal, *e.g.* R(SB) 15/84
R v.—Rex, Regina (the King, Queen) against
R.S.C., Ord.—Rules of the Supreme Court, Order
Ratio decidendi—the ground of a decision
Re—in the matter of
Rec.—Recueil
Reg.—Regina (the Queen)
Reg.—Regulation (E.C.), *e.g.* Reg. 467/82/EEC
Regnal year—the year of the monarch's reign

s. (plural ss.)—section of Act
S.A.—French company (société anonyme)/South Africa
s.c.—same case
S.G.—Solicitor-General
S.I.—Statutory Instrument
S.R. & O.—Statutory Rules and Orders
S.S.—steamship
Sched.—schedule (to an Act)
Scienter—knowingly
Semble—it appears
Sessional papers—a collection of all parliamentary papers published during a particular session of Parliament
Sessional set—a collection of all parliamentary papers issued during a particular session of Parliament, bound up into volumes
Statutes—Acts of Parliament
Sub judice—in course of trial
Sub nom. (sub nomine)—under the name
Sub voce—under the title
Supra—above

T.S.—Treaty series
Table of cases/statutes—a list of cases or statutes in alphabetical order
Treaty—(1) negotiations prior to an agreement; (2) an agreement between nations

Ultra vires—beyond the powers granted
Union catalogue/union list—a catalogue of the contents of a number of libraries

v.—versus
V.C.—Vice-Chancellor
Venire de novo—motion for a new trial
Viz. (*videlicet*)—namely; that is to say

White Book—a term sometimes used to refer to *The Supreme Court Practice*
White Paper—a parliamentary paper, usually containing a statement of government policy

APPENDIX III

How Do I Find? A Summary of Sources for English Law

A3–1 ABBREVIATIONS (2–4)

D. Raistrick, *Index to Legal Citations and Abbreviations*.
Sweet & Maxwell's Guide to Law Reports and Statutes.
University of London Institute of Advanced Legal Studies, *Manual of Legal Citations*.
The front pages of: *Current Law Case Citator; The Digest*, Vol. 1 and the *Cumulative Supplement; Index to Legal Periodicals; Halsbury's Laws of England*, Vol. 1; *Legal Journals Index*.
Price and Bitner, *Effective Legal Research* (for American abbreviations).

A3–2 BOOKS

Tracing Books on a Subject

Consult the subject index in the library catalogue (6–25).
Consult bibliographies (see below).

Tracing Books by an Author

Consult the author (or name) index in the library catalogue (1–5).
Consult bibliographies (see below).

Tracing Books if you Know the Title

If your library's catalogue does not contain entries under titles, consult bibliographies (see below) to find the author's name, then consult the author index in the library catalogue.

BIBLIOGRAPHIES   A3–3

D. Raistrick, *Lawyers' Law Books* (entries under subjects) (6–27).
Law Books Published (entries under authors, titles and subjects) (6–31).
Current Publications in Legal and Related Fields (authors, titles and subjects) (6–33).
Legal Bibliography of the British Commonwealth (useful for older books) (6–36).
Bibliography on Foreign and Comparative Law (6–36).
International Legal Books in Print (authors, titles, subjects) (6–29)
British National Bibliography (British books, on all subjects, published since 1950. Entries under authors, titles, subjects) (6–38).
Whitakers Books in Print (entries under authors and titles: the CD-ROM "Bookbank" allows searching by other methods) (6–38).
Books in Print (American books in print—authors, titles and separate *Subject Guide to Books in Print*) (6–38).
R. G. Logan (ed.), *Information Sources in Law* (6–28).
Bibliographical Guide to the Law (useful for foreign language books) (6–35).
Law Books 1876–1981 (6–34).
Specialist legal bibliographies (6–36)—ask the library staff for advice.
The catalogues of large specialist and national libraries, *e.g. British Library's General Catalogue of Printed Books; Library of Congress Catalog*, etc. (6–36, 6–38).

CASES   A3–4

If You Know the Name of the Case (summary: 2–15)

Current Law Case Citators (2–12).
The Digest (for English, Scottish, Irish and Commonwealth cases of any date). Consult the *Consolidated Table of Cases* and the *Cumulative Supplement* (for more recent cases) (2–13).
Law Reports: Consolidated Index (2–14).
English Reports, Vols. 177–178 (for English cases *before* 1865) (2–9).

All England Law Reports Consolidated Tables and Index 1936– and *All English Law Reports Reprint Index*, 1558–1935 (2–14, 2–10).

For Very Recent Cases

Latest issue of *Current Law Monthly Digest*—the cumulative Case Citator (2–15).
Latest *Pink Index* to the *Law Reports* and the List of Cases *inside* the latest issue of the *Weekly Law Reports* (2–15).
Current Tables and Index to the *All England Law Reports* (2–15).
Cases in recent copies of *The Times* and other newspapers.
Daily Law Reports Index (2–15).
Electronic sources (*e.g.* LEXIS (7–9); Lawtel (7–10)).
Summaries of cases in weekly journals, *e.g. Solicitors' Journal; New Law Journal* and in *Legal Journals Index* (2–15).

Scottish Cases

Scots Digest (8–4).
Faculty Digest (8–4).
Scottish Current Law Case Citators (2–12).
The Digest (2–13).

Irish Cases

Greer and Childs, *Index to Cases Decided in the Courts of Northern Ireland 1921–1970* and Supplement (9–9).
Irish Digests (10–22).
The Digest (2–13).
Index to Supreme and High Court Written Judgments (*Pink Lists*) (10–23).
Index to Irish Superior Court Written Judgments 1976–1982 (10–24).

Commonwealth Cases

The Digest (2–13).

Tracing Cases On A Subject (6–7)

The Digest (6–10, 6–11).
Current Law Year Books (6–8, 6–9).
Halsbury's Laws of England (6–4).
Law Reports: Consolidated Index (6–13).
LEXIS (7–9).

Tracing the Subsequent Judicial History of A Case (6–14)

Current Law Case Citators and latest issue of *Current Law Monthly Digest* (for cases judicially considered after 1947) (6–14).
The Digest (6–11).
Law Reports Index (table of cases judicially considered) (6–14).
All England Law Reports: Consolidated Tables and Index (cases reported and considered) (6–14).
LEXIS (7–9).

Are there any Journal Articles on this Case? (2–16)

Legal Journals Index (2–16, 4–3).
Current Law Case Citators (entries enclosed in square brackets are journal articles) (2–12, 2–16).
Latest issue of *Current Law Monthly Digest* (entries in lower case in the Cumulative Table of Cases indicate cases judicially considered or where the case appears in the title of the article) (2–16).
Index to Legal Periodicals (table of cases commented upon, at the back of the volume) (2–16).
Indexes to individual journals, *e.g. Modern Law Review; Law Quarterly Review.*

DIRECTORIES (1–13)   A3–5

Solicitors and Barristers' Directory and Diary (1–13).
Butterworths Law Directory and Diary (1–13).
Havers' Companion to the Bar.
Hazell's Guide to the Judiciary and the Courts (1–13).
Legal Aid Handbook (1–13).

GENERAL STATEMENTS OF THE LAW   A3–6

Textbooks. Consult the library catalogues and bibliographies (A3–2) to trace relevant publications.
Halsbury's Laws of England (6–3).
Specialised legal encyclopedias (6–5).

GOVERNMENT PUBLICATIONS   A3–7

Tracing Publications on a Subject (5–18)

Consult the subject index to the library's government publications collection, if one exists.

Consult HMSO's Daily *Lists* and Monthly, Annual and Five-yearly
Catalogues (5–14).
*Subject Catalogue of the House of Commons Parliamentary Papers
1801–1900* (5–18).
General Index 1900–1949, 1950–1959, etc. (5–14).
Catalogue of British Official Publications not Published by HMSO
(5–18).
Keyword Index to British Official Publications Not Published by HMSO
(5–18).
Current Law Monthly Digests and *Current Law Year Books* (6–8, 6–9).
Lawyers' Law Books includes the main government reports on each
subject (6–27).

Index to Government Publications

HMSO *Daily List* (5–14).
HMSO Monthly and Annual *Catalogues* (5–14).
General Index . . . 1900–1949 (5–14).
Keyword Index to British Official Publications not Published by HMSO
(5–18).
Catalogue of British Official Publications not Published by HMSO
(5–12).
HMSO in Print (on microfiche) (5–14).
POLIS (5–18).
UKOP CD-ROM (5–18).

If you know the Name of the Chairman of a Report

S. Richard, *British Government Publications; an Index to Chairmen and
Authors* (several volumes, covering 1800 onwards) (5–16).
Committee Reports Published by HMSO Indexed by Chairman (5–16).
Monthly, annual and five-yearly *HMSO Catalogues* (5–14).

Law Commission Reports And Working Papers (5–20)

The Law Commission's *Annual Reports* (issued as House of
Commons Papers) include a complete list of all the Law
Commission reports and working papers, showing whether the
recommendations of each report have been implemented (5–20).
HMSO Daily List, and the monthly and annual *HMSO Catalogues*
include new Law Commission reports as they are published
(5–14).

JOURNAL ARTICLES

Articles on a Subject

Legal Journals Index (4–3).
Index to Legal Periodicals (4–5).
Index to Foreign Legal Periodicals (4–6).
Current Law Monthly Digests (under appropriate subject heading) (4–4) and *Current Law Year Books* (at the back of the volumes) (4–4, 6–9).
Annual Abridgement to *Halsbury's Laws of England* (under appropriate subject heading) and the *Monthly Reviews* (in the looseleaf *Service* volume) (4–8).
Index to Periodical Articles Related to Law (4–10).
British Humanities Index (4–12).
Other non-legal journal indexes (4–11 *et seq.*)

Articles on a Case

Legal Journals Index (4–3).
Current Law Case Citators (entries enclosed in square brackets are journal articles) (2–12, 2–16).
Latest *Current Law Monthly Digest* (entries in lower case type in the cumulative table of cases) (2–16).
Index to Legal Periodicals (table of cases commented upon) (2–16).
For recent cases, look in the weekly journals, *e.g. Solicitors' Journal, New Law Journal, Justice of the Peace,* and specialist journals, *e.g. Criminal Law Review.*

Articles on an Act

Legal Journals Index (4–3).
Current Law Statute Citators (3–13).
Indexes to journals (under the appropriate subject heading).

Tracing Journals

Consult the library's periodicals catalogue (1–9).
If the journal is not available in your library, consult the *Union List of Legal Periodicals* (4–22) to find out where a copy is available.
Union lists of the journals available in your own area or region may be available—ask the library staff for advice.

A3–9   STATUTES

Collections of the Statutes

Older statutes
Statutes of the Realm (3–16).
Statutes at Large (various editions) (3–17).
C. H. Firth and R. S. Rait, *Acts and Ordinances of the Interregnum* (3–18).
Statutes in Force (3–7).

Modern statutes
Public General Acts and Measures (3–6).
Law Reports: Statutes (3–8).
Current Law Statutes Annotated (3–9).
Statutes in Force (3–7, 6–17).
Butterworth's Annotated Legislation Service (3–10).
Halsbury's Statutes (3–11, 6–19).

Collections of Acts by subject
Statutes in Force (6–17).
Halsbury's Statutes (6–19).

Annotated editions of the statutes
Current Law Statutes Annotated (3–9).
Butterworth's Annotated Legislation Service (3–10).
Halsbury's Statutes (3–11, 6–19).

Statutes in force
Statutes in Force (3–7, 6–17).
Index to the Statutes (6–18).
Halsbury's Statutes (3–11, 6–19).
Chronological Table of the Statutes (3–14).
Current Law Statute Citators (3–13).
Is it in force? (3–12).
LEXIS (7–9).

Tracing Statutes on a Subject

Statutes in Force (6–17).
Halsbury's Statutes (6–19).
Index to the Statutes (6–18).
Halsbury's Laws (6–3).
Current Law Monthly Digests and *Current Law Year Books* (6–20).
LEXIS (7–9).

Indexes to the Statutes

Chronological Table of the Statutes (shows whether Acts of any date are still in force) (3–14).
Is it in force? (3–12).
Index to the Statutes (alphabetically arranged by subject, and lists all the Acts dealing with that subject) (6–18).
Halsbury's Statutes (alphabetically arranged by subject. Consult alphabetical list of statutes, then look in the *Cumulative Supplement* and *Noter-up* service to check if an Act is still in force) (6–19).
Public General Acts: Tables and Index (annual—brings the information in the *Chronological Table of Statutes* up to date) (3–14).

Local and Personal Acts—Indexes
Index to Local and Personal Acts 1801–1947 (3–19).
Supplementary Index to the Local and Personal Acts 1948–1966 (3–19).
Local and Personal Acts; Tables and Index (annual) (3–19).

Is this Act Still in Force? Has it been Amended?

Is it in force? (shows whether Acts passed since 1961 are still in force) (3–12).
Chronological Table of the Statutes (indicates if an Act of any date is in force) (3–14).
Current Law Statute Citators (3–13).
Public General Acts: Tables and Index (annual—brings the information in the *Chronological Table* up to date—see the table "Effects of Legislation") (3–14).
Halsbury's Statutes (consult the main volumes, the *Cumulative Supplement and* the looseleaf *Service* volume) (3–11).
Lawtel (7–10).

What Cases have there Been on the Interpretation of this Act?

Current Law Statute Citators (3–13).
Halsbury's Statutes (6–19).

What Statutory Instruments have been Made Under this Act?

Current Law Statute Citators (3–13).
Index to Government Orders (3–25).
Halsbury's Statutes (3–11).

Have Any Journal Articles been Written About this Act?

Current Law Statute Citators (3–13).
Legal Journals Index in the legislation index (4–3).
Other Indexes to journal articles (see heading "Journal Articles," above), under appropriate subject heading.

Has this Act been Brought into Force by a Statutory Instrument?

Halsbury's Statutes (3–12).
Current Law Statute Citators (3–13).

A3–10   STATUTORY INSTRUMENTS

Collections of Statutory Instruments

Statutory Rules and Orders and Statutory Instruments Revised (all statutory instruments in force in 1948) (3–22).
Statutory Instruments (annual volumes—subject index in last volume of each year) (3–22).
Halsbury's Statutory Instruments (selective—arranged by subject) (3–23).
SI-CD (3–22).

Is this Statutory Instrument in Force? Has it been Amended?

Halsbury's Statutory Instruments (3–23).
Table of Government Orders (indicates for every statutory instrument whether it is still in force) (3–24).

What Statutory Instruments Have Been Made Under This Act?

Current Law Statute Citators (3–13).
Index to Government Orders (3–25).
Halsbury's Statutes (3–11).
Lawtel (7–10).

Has this Act been Brought into Force by a Statutory Instrument?

Halsbury's Statutes—Is It in Force? volume (3–12).
Current Law Statute Citators (3–13).

Indexes to Statutory Instruments

Table of Government Orders (chronological, showing whether each
Instrument is still in force) (3–24).
Index to Government Orders (arranged by subject) (6–23).
Halsbury's Statutory Instruments (chronological, alphabetical and
by subject) (3–23, 6–22).
Lists of Statutory Instruments (monthly and annually—entries by
subject, and under the numbers of the Instruments) (3–22).
HMSO Daily Lists (includes all new Instruments as they are
published) (6–24).
LEXIS (7–9).
Lawtel (7–10).

THESES   A3–11

University of London Institute of Advanced Legal Studies, *Legal
Research in the United Kingdom 1905–1984* (6–39).
University of London Institute of Advanced Legal Studies, *List of
Current Legal Research Topics* (6–39).
Index to Theses (6–39).
Dissertation Abstracts (6–39).

WORDS AND PHRASES   A3–12

For the meaning of words and phrases, use legal dictionaries
(1–12).
For Latin phrases, use legal dictionaries and Broom's *Legal Maxims*
(1–12).

Judicial and Statutory Definitions of Words and Phrases

Words and Phrases Legally Defined (6–15).
Stroud's Judicial Dictionary (6–15).
The entry "Words and Phrases" in: *Law Reports: Consolidated Index;
Current Law Monthly Digests* and *Current Law Year Books*; and
indexes to the *All England Law Reports, Halsbury's Laws,* and *The
Digest.*

APPENDIX IV

Creating a Search Strategy for Online Information Retrieval

The Example of LEXIS

A4–1   Planning a search strategy

In order to make the most economical use of online databases, you should plan, in advance, what you are going to do when connected to the computer. This is known as planning the *search strategy*.

LEXIS allows you to search quickly through thousands of cases, statutes and statutory instruments. It can rapidly trace cases in which a particular case or Act has been mentioned and find, within seconds, *all* cases or statutes which mention a particular word, or words. Let us suppose, for example, that you want *all* cases on terrorism. Because the database contains the full text of each case, you need to think how judges, in talking about terrorism, would phrase their judgments. They might talk about "terrorist" and about "terrorism," and cases using either of these words would probably be of interest to you. You can instruct the computer to look for:

TERRORIST or TERRORISM

What if you have a more complicated problem? Suppose you wish to find out what cases there are dealing with the negligence of surveyors. Prepare your search strategy by deciding what words judges use for this issue. The words "surveyor" or "valuer" might be used in the judgment, so you must tell the computer to search for both terms:

274

SURVEYOR or VALUER

By typing in these terms, LEXIS will discover all cases which mention *either* of these words. But this information is far too general for your problem. You want to know about negligence of surveyors. Here the judges might use words such as:

NEGLIGENCE or NEGLIGENT or NEGLIGENTLY

So you can type in these words as alternatives for LEXIS to work on. You can see that they have a common stem "Negligen...." As a short cut, you can instruct the computer to search for any words which begin Negligen. ... This is done by using the "truncation mark". The truncation mark in LEXIS is ! (an exclamation mark). If you type in NEGLIGEN! the computer searches for *any* word beginning with "negligen ..." You must be careful with this method or you may end up with many words that you do not want, or simply had not thought about. For instance, if you put in TERROR! in the search for terrorism/terrorist it would also retrieve cases mentioning "terrorstricken", "terrorise" and, of course, "terror".

In LEXIS, unlike most other databases, you do not need to add a truncation mark to a singular word in order to include the plural (as long as the plural is regular). For instance, if you search for SURVEYOR, LEXIS will also search for the words "SURVEYORS", "SURVEYOR'S" and "SURVEYORS' ".

You can instruct the computer to link the two parts of the search by telling it to search for cases in which surveyor or valuer *and* negligence (or the alternative words) are mentioned in the same case. You can do this by typing in:

(SURVEYOR or VALUER) and NEGLIGEN!

The computer will respond by informing you of the number of cases which mention surveyor or valuer *and* negligen ... in the same case. This technique helps you to narrow down the number of cases that you might want to read.

You can refine this strategy further by looking for words which appear close together in the law report. For instance, let's suppose that you want to find all cases which mention *Laker Airways* v. *Department of Trade*. If you type in:

LAKER W/5 TRADE

you are asking the computer to find every mention of Laker within five words of Trade. So W/ ... followed by a number instructs the computer to search for words which occur within so many words of each other.

You can use this technique to link negligence more closely with surveyor. This will make sure that there is a relevant connection between the two words "negligence" and "surveyor." Otherwise, both the words may appear somewhere in the same case but be unassociated with the issue of the negligence of surveyors. If you specify that the two words should appear fairly close to each other, say within 20 words, then you are likely to find that there is a relevant connection for your purposes.

SURVEYOR W/20 NEGLIGEN!

Of course, this short cut also runs the danger of missing relevant cases where the key words do not occur within the stated 20-word proximity. Practice will help you to develop a search strategy which will retrieve all the relevant cases and avoid picking up too many irrelevant cases.

A4–2   *SUMMARY: SEARCH STRATEGY*

Although different command languages use different words and symbols, all languages have the same features to enable words to be linked by an "and" or "or" connection and allow words to be truncated. In LEXIS, the four most useful words and symbols that you are likely to need when planning your search strategy are:

(a) **OR**: This tells LEXIS to look for alternative words. Doctor OR Surgeon; Surveyor OR Valuer; Negligence OR Negligently OR Negligent. It has the effect of *widening* the search and increasing the number of possible cases which may be relevant.

(b) **AND**: This tells LEXIS to link together two (or more) words and to refer you only to the cases which contain *both* words. Surveyor AND Negligence; Elephant AND Circus. Both words must appear in the same case. LEXIS will not report on cases which deal only with an elephant or only with a circus. "And" has the effect of *narrowing down* (or limiting) your research. "And" retrieves fewer cases than the word "or".

(c) **W/5**: W/ … means "Within so many words of." This example instructs LEXIS to find two words when they are located in the case within five words of each other. You can choose any number between 1 and 100. Do not bring the words too close together or you will miss relevant cases. The effect of using "W/ …." is again to *narrow down* (or limit) your search.

(d) !: In LEXIS this is the "truncation mark". It instructs the computer to search for words which have the same beginning (stem) but different endings, *e.g.* negligen! will retrieve negligent, negligence, etc. Its effect is to *widen* the search.

There are other commands which you may need to use from time to time. For instance, each law report and statute is divided up into parts (or *segments*). Law reports can be searched looking for all cases heard in a particular court, or all judgments by a particular judge. The most common segment search is to ask the computer to retrieve a specific case. Let's suppose you want to see the case of *Gillick v. West Norfolk and Wisbech Area Health Authority*. A search for *Gillick W/4 West Norfolk* will retrieve the *Gillick* case itself, and also other cases in which the *Gillick* case has been referred to. If you only want to retrieve the *Gillick* case itself, the best way to do this is with a segment search. Our search would be: NAME (*Gillick W/4 West Norfolk*). This would retrieve *only* the *Gillick* case. Full details of segment searches are found in the *LEXIS User Guide*.

Accessing LEXIS   A4–3
Once you have formulated your search, you are ready to log on to LEXIS. If you are using a standard keyboard, there should be a LEXIS overlay above the function keys, showing you which keys on the standard keyboard you should use for LEXIS functions.

You will first need to switch on the computer and gain access to LEXIS. This will vary between institutions. Once you have made contact, the LEXIS computer will welcome you and ask you to identify yourself. Each user, when he or she has been trained, is given a password which must be typed in at this point. The password prevents unauthorised use. Training in the use of LEXIS is required, so the explanations here do not go into detail. Contact your librarian, law teacher or Butterworth's Telepublishing Ltd., 4–5 Bell Yard, London WC2 for details of the training programme. Once you have been trained, you will receive the *LEXIS User Guide* which explains the procedures for searching.

After you have entered your password, the computer displays a list of all the different *libraries* (see para. 7–9) on the screen and invites you to select one. Probably the most useful library for law students is the English general library (*ENGGEN*). This contains cases and statutory material on all subjects. If you are going to use this library, type in ENGGEN on the keyboard and press the Enter key which sends the message to the computer.

Next, the screen shows a list of different "*files*" and asks you to choose between them. Do you want cases, statutes, statutory instruments or a combination of both statutes and statutory instruments? Let's suppose you want cases. You type in CASES, and press the Enter key. The computer informs you that it is ready for you to begin your search.

Let's return to the search for information on terrorism. You will have decided before operating the terminal that you are searching for all cases which mention terrorism or terrorist. So you type in

TERRORISM or TERRORIST

and press the Enter key. The computer searches through *all* the cases in its files looking for any mention of *either* of these two words. It will also pick up references to "terrorists" as the plural, is formed by adding "s," is automatically retrieved. After a few seconds, the computer informs you that it has found a certain number of cases which mention the stated words. You can look at these cases (to see if they are relevant) by pressing the KWIC key (Key Word in Context). This shows you the search word (terrorism/terrorist) together with the surrounding sentences in the law report. This gives you the context in which the word is found. Normally, this is enough to let you decide whether the case is relevant. If you then want a list of the cases, press the CITE key and a complete list of the citations of all the cases which the computer has retrieved will be displayed on the screen. You can also print this list. Ask your librarian or tutor for details. You can then go to the actual reports in the library to read the cases.

If the printed report is not available in your law library, then LEXIS can be used to print the full report. This is especially useful for transcripts which are not reported in any law reports.

A4–4   Modifying your search strategy

It could be that, at your first attempt, you are unsuccessful with your search strategy and fail to find the information you need. If, for example, you key in a command which produces 500 cases which refer to the word you are searching for, then obviously you must rethink your strategy. You have defined the search far too widely. You must limit the search by adding another word or words to your command. For example if you put in NEGLIGEN! on its own then you would be informed of thousands of cases which are concerned with various aspects of negligence. So you must narrow the search by asking for negligence *and* surveyors. This command will reduce the number of cases significantly.

To modify your search, press M (for modify) and then the Enter button. You can now type in a new search word or words. Your modified search would begin with the word "and". For instance, if you have retrieved too many cases using the search word "negligence", you can modify the search by transmitting "M", followed by: "and (surveyor or valuer)". The computer will search through all the negligence cases and retrieve only those which mention surveyors or valuers. If you are still having difficulty in retrieving helpful material, you must reconsider your search strategy. This is best done by "signing off" from LEXIS, as time thinking (as opposed to researching) still costs money. Press the "sign off" key, answer LEXIS' question as to whether you intend to return to the search later and then rethink your commands to the computer. If you have instructed the computer that you will return, when you rejoin the computer your original material reappears. You can then modify your search, or you can erase the search by pressing the New Search key, which allows you to start again. You can always obtain advice on search strategy by telephoning the Customer Service Department at Butterworth's Telepublishing.

This section only provides a brief outline of the types of searches that LEXIS can undertake. Further details are found in the *LEXIS User Guide*, which you should consult before starting a search. The *Guide* will tell you, for example, how to find all cases discussing the interpretation of a particular section of an Act and what statutory instruments brought sections of an Act into force; it will also enable you to discover in which cases named barristers, solicitors or judges were involved. If a statute has been amended by subsequent legislation LEXIS will display the amended, up-to-date version of the Act. It will retrieve all references to statutes or statutory instruments on a subject, and provide you with the full text of the Act or statutory instrument. If you remember the facts of a case but not its name; or if you know only the name of one of the parties in the dispute, LEXIS can find the case. Sometimes such a search would be impossible with conventional printed sources. Almost always LEXIS is faster than conventional methods.

Remember that LEXIS does not contain information about what books, journal articles and theses have been written about the law in this country (although it does have the text of some American journals). It contains mainly *primary* sources. Other databases exist which contain background material relevant to lawyers. Your librarian can tell you which of these are available and can, where relevant, get access to the information on your behalf.

INDEX

Titles of publications are shown below in italics.

281